# A Council by Another Name?

## The Synod on Synodality and What Comes Next

*Christoph Theobald, SJ*

LP
A

LITURGICAL PRESS
ACADEMIC

Collegeville, Minnesota
litpress.org

Previously published as *Un nouveau concile qui ne dit pas son nom ? Le synode sur la synodalité, voie de pacification et de créativité* © Editions Salvator, Paris, 2023.*

* See page ix.



**Library of Congress Cataloging-in-Publication Data**

Names: Theobald, Christoph, author.
Title: A council by another name? : the synod on synodality and what comes next / Christoph Theobald.
Other titles: Nouveau concile qui ne dit pas son nom. English
Description: [First English edition.] | Collegeville, Minnesota : Liturgical Press Academic, [2025] | "Previously published as Un nouveau concile qui ne dit pas son nom ? Le synode sur la synodalité, voie de pacification et de créativité © Editions Salvator, Paris, 2023." | Includes bibliographical references and index. | Summary: "In A Council by Another Name? Christoph Theobald explains why synodality is a constitutive dimension of the church. Theobald cites Pope Francis's call for cooperation and creativity as an essential element for confronting the current difficulties effectively and welcoming a new and decisive vision of the church within human history and society"—Provided by publisher.
Identifiers: LCCN 2025014150 (print) | LCCN 2025014151 (ebook) | ISBN 9780814689714 (trade paperback) | ISBN 9780814689721 (epub) | ISBN 9798400801983 (pdf)
Subjects: LCSH: Councils and synods. | Councils and synods (Canon law) | Catholic Church—Government. | Catholic Church—Doctrines. | BISAC: RELIGION / Christian Theology / Ecclesiology | RELIGION / Christianity / Catholic
Classification: LCC BX823 .T4313 2025 (print) | LCC BX823 (ebook)
LC record available at https://lccn.loc.gov/2025014150
LC ebook record available at https://lccn.loc.gov/2025014151

*To my St. Francis Xavier community,*
*who accompanied this work with many fraternal exchanges*

"Having participated in the synod as an expert, eminent French Jesuit theologian Christoph Theobald is uniquely positioned for this book. He weaves together a commentary of the synod documents, expert knowledge of Vatican II, and a real familiarity with what is going on in the church. According to the author, the Synod on Synodality (which brings us close to a Third Vatican Council) requires a profound conversion of all the faithful, and not only institutional reform. His courageous and wise voice deserves to be heard on this side of the ocean, too."

— Jos Moons, SJ, co-author of *The Future of Synodality: How We Move Forward from Here*

"What a gift this book is—an assessment of the Synod on Synodality by one of the preeminent interpreters of Vatican II, who has been closely involved in the synod process over several years. As a Synod peritus, Christoph Theobald's insider view leads him to see this 'synodalization' of the Catholic Church as the basis of a new vision of the church for the twenty-first century—new, but a vision that is thoroughly grounded in the vision of Vatican II. As an eyewitness account and as an astute theological interpretation, this book will be a highly valued resource for synodal formation in local churches, as they seek to embed the synodal vision more deeply into all aspects of their ecclesial life and mission."

— Ormond Rush, Australian Catholic University

"Those seeking to understand more deeply the synodal process 'For a Synodal Church: Communion, Participation, Mission' (2021–2024) will be richly rewarded in reading this reliable and accessible firsthand account of learning from the experience of journeying together by the respected theological advisor to the General Synod, Christoph Theobald, SJ. At every turn he holds together the challenge and creative force of listening to God in the Word and in others, and of personal conversion and institutional reform. He helpfully points to the roots of synodality in the themes of the Second Vatican Council as he describes the ways the synod calls us to carry them forward to meet the challenges of a new era. He invites us to set out on the synodal path, led by the Holy Spirit into a new Pentecost, the first fruits of which can be discerned in the experience of the synodal assembly."

— Catherine E. Clifford, Saint Paul University, Ottawa

# Contents

# Preface to the Third Edition[1]

On October 27, 2024, the second phase of the world Synod on Synodality of the church came to an end. A new phase, the third, then began. Its challenge now is the reception of the synodal path by all the local churches on the planet, each in its specific context. After the vote on the Final Document by the assembly gathered in Rome, Pope Francis declared that he would not publish the traditional post-synodal exhortation, deeming the adopted text, which reflects what was experienced, sufficient, because it "already contains very substantial indications which can guide the mission of the Churches, on different continents."[2]

Should this third edition of the book have been rewritten from the perspective of the end of the universal phase of the synod and the beginning of its reception? For various reasons, I did not take this option but instead retained my original account of the whole journey, while adding a new chapter on the second session (chap. 6), substantially modifying the last chapter on the vision of the church that emerged during the synod (chap. 7), and expanding the conclusion to include some major benchmarks for its implementation.

My aim is not only to involve the reader in the synodal journey, which has been gradually proceeding since 2021, and in the experience of mutual listening that this process has made possible, but also to recognize the limitations of my own point of view, which, dependent on many other perspectives, has evolved throughout the process. Only at the end did the conviction that this synod is the first of the

[1] Though the present edition is the first publication of this book in English, two previous editions (of 2023 and 2024) were published in its original French during the course of the synod.—Trans.

[2] Pope Francis, "Final Greeting of His Holiness Pope Francis," October 26, 2024, https://www.vatican.va/content/francesco/en/speeches/2024/october/documents/20241026-sinodo-vescovi.html.

Latin Church on the Holy Spirit become clear to me. Let us be clear: the synod's intention was not to discuss the Holy Spirit but rather to ask how we can listen together to what the Holy Spirit is saying here and now to the churches (see Rev 2:7, etc.). The novelty of the synod consists precisely in having posed this "constitutional" question for the first time and having responded to it *by practicing and proposing* to the whole church a synodal way of discerning what has been heard and of making decisions accordingly in a fraternal climate of transparency and responsibility.

Understanding the synod's challenge in this way means saying that it is not over, because many concrete questions, raised during its first phase and summarized during the first session, will have to find solutions, no doubt differing according to the contexts, thanks to this new "framework" that offers us spiritual and institutional beacons to move forward together. What this procedural framework will become and how it will change in contact with the various contexts of the world is unpredictable at this time. But it doesn't matter. By abandoning certain ways of proceeding and living in the church of the second millennium, those ways that were practiced and codified by the synod have laid the foundations for a new Catholic culture that is both global and respectful of cultural differences. Only by progressing along this path of reception, difficult because it is unprecedented, will the synod be able to show—or not—its fruitfulness, while at the same time answering the question posed by the title given to this work from the very first edition: *An incognito council?*

As in the introduction to the first and second editions, I would like to conclude by expressing my hope that this work—a *work in progress*—will help readers engage in a peaceful and creative reception of the Final Document and encourage them to follow, wherever they are, the synodal path inaugurated by Pope Francis.

Paris
January 6, 2025
Feast of the Epiphany of the Lord

❖ ❖ ❖

Since this preface was written, two important events have taken place, which enrich the expectations raised by the new subtitle of this third edition: *and What Comes Next . . .*

On March 15, 2025, the General Secretariat of the Synod published the Letter on the Accompaniment Process of the Implementation Phase of the Synod, addressed at the express request of Pope Francis to local churches and church groups (text available on the synod website, synod.va). This letter first announces, "For now, therefore, a new Synod will not be convened" in October 2028, but rather that it will ultimately culminate in the celebration of an ecclesial assembly. The purpose of this assembly will be to evaluate the state of the reception of the Synod on Synodality and to consolidate "the path taken so far."

The preparation for this assembly should follow the same synodal procedures and rhythm that marked the first phase of the synod, starting from the local churches, passing through their national and continental groupings, and culminating in the Roman assembly. I have no hesitation in interpreting this decision as confirmation of the "turning point" introduced by the world Synod on Synodality in the post-conciliar history of Catholicism, a "turning point" anticipated from the outset by the title of this book.

However, on April 21, 2025 (Easter Monday), Pope Francis died, and on May 8, his successor, Cardinal Robert Francis Prevost, was elected by the College of Cardinals and took the name Leo XIV. Upon his presentation on the balcony of St. Peter's Basilica, he spoke of the synodal church: "To all of you, brothers and sisters in Rome, in Italy, throughout the world: we want to be a synodal Church, a Church that moves forward, a Church that always seeks peace, that always seeks charity, that always seeks to be close above all to those who are suffering."[3]

His pontificate will show how he receives this legacy from his predecessor and envisages the "now" of a synodal church on our planet, tested by violence and anxiety in the face of uncertainty about its future.

Paris<br>
May 18, 2025<br>
Fifth Sunday of Easter

[3] "Pope Leo XIV: 'Peace Be with All of You,'" Vatican News, https://www.vaticannews.va/en/pope/news/2025-05/pope-leo-xvi-peace-be-with-you-first-words.html.

# Introduction

On October 7, 1999, at the European synod of bishops, Cardinal Carlo Maria Martini made headlines by expressing his desire for a new council. The archbishop of Milan was, of course, too wise to use this word. What he asked for was nonetheless clear for all to see, as he called for "an experience of universal confrontation between bishops at the dawning of the new century." Martini was aware that the church needed to address a growing number of unresolved questions. He didn't hesitate to list them before the synodal assembly: "the dramatic lack of ordained ministers, the position of women in society and in the Church, the participation of the laity in certain 'ministerial responsibilities,' sexuality, the discipline of marriage, ecumenical hope." "Disciplinary and doctrinal knots, little mentioned these days," he added, "but which reappear periodically as sore points on the path of the European churches."

In the years since, the problems, far from diminishing, have only increased. Indeed, the range of problematic points has actually become denser and more complex: the list of issues addressed by the Synodal Way of German dioceses, which emerged from the study on "Sexual Abuse of Minors by Priests, Deacons and Male Members of Religious Orders" (MHG Study), and the recommendations of the report of the Independent Commission on Sexual Abuse in the Church (CIASE) in France clearly proves it. Moreover, the prevailing feeling is that of having to deal with a complex web, without knowing which thread to pull to unravel it. This gives rise to a feeling of powerlessness and discouragement shared by many, and reveals, even more so than in the past, divisions within the church, or even its "archipellization," to use the expression coined by Jérôme Fourquet, a French political scientist. At the same time, we have heard the voicing of expectations, from the most basic, such as the desire for a church of more authentic brother- and sisterhood, to the most demanding: an in-depth reform of our ecclesial structures.

In 2021, Pope Francis caused surprise, not by convening a new gathering of the synod of bishops (since Paul VI, it has met regularly) but by giving its next gathering an unexpected theme: the "synodality of the church." Our astonishment (and, for some, dismay) increased when we learned that the usual consultations would take place *in a synodal form*, to be implemented at the level of the smallest units of the church, before the results would be taken up by the dioceses and made the subject of national syntheses, which would then be deliberated on a continental level and, finally, on a worldwide level, in order to nourish new synodal exchanges within our local communities.

Could this be *a council under another name*, fulfilling the wish expressed by Cardinal Martini so many years ago? For anyone who remembers Pope Francis's first interview in Jesuit publications, in which he confessed to being "a little cunning" or "clever" (*un po' furbo*), this hypothesis is plausible. Indeed, we share the perplexity of many observers who fail to see how a council could be convened today; it would require the participation of all the world's bishops, but since Vatican II, their number has doubled to almost 5,400! Pope Francis's proposal would seem to make a virtue of necessity: it not only inaugurates a *new synodal form* in the Roman Catholic Church, but it also extends the council's synodal way of proceeding to *the whole people of God* and thus—as a cunning work of the Holy Spirit—it finds a way to *progressively unravel the web of problems* in the Catholic Church.

Let us be clear: it's a daring bet, and there's no guarantee it will be won—as has always been the case during the many crises the church has faced in its two-thousand-year history.

To test our hypothesis, we must first take note of what Pope Francis has said about synodality, starting in 2013 in his apostolic exhortation *Evangelii Gaudium*, and especially in his speech on October 17, 2015, on the fiftieth anniversary of the institution of the Synod of Bishops by Paul VI.

His main intuition is very simple: he recalls that the word *synod* (= *syn-hodos* in Greek) means "to journey together." He invites the whole church to do this. To help the church find its way, he appeals to its deepest "spiritual being" and to everyone's ability "to hear what the Spirit says to the churches" (Rev 2:7), while at the same time undertaking a reform of its institutional structure, whose ultimate aim is to make possible the experience of individual and collective listening.

To understand the simplicity and depth of this invitation, nothing is more appropriate than to begin by "effectively journeying together," by reading the Scriptures together and thus entering an experience of listening. This challenge is described in the first chapter.

Tasting the benefits of such a reading on a common journey will then lead us to *reflect on* what we are experiencing and to appropriate the *double affirmation*—the *new*, not to say "revolutionary"—affirmation of Francis's October 2015 speech. There, he makes "synodality"—let's translate it right away: "journeying together"—"a constitutive element of the Church," which, he adds, offers us at the same time "the most appropriate interpretive framework for understanding the hierarchical ministry itself." It's clear that the stakes are high: this is unquestionably an unprecedented reading of the event and the work of the Second Vatican Council (1962–65). The second chapter therefore attempts to understand Pope Francis's intuition by confronting it with the council's vision of the church and testing its relevance in the current crisis context of our democratic societies.

The next step is to *implement* this intuition, which is already well underway. Existing institutions (such as the secretariat of the Synod of Bishops) have been transformed, new groups and organizations established, and interaction between the different levels of ecclesial life stimulated. The churches are "navigating by sight," gradually learning to benefit from experiences lived and interpreted together. We can call this way of moving forward "enlightened pragmatism," a term that will become progressively more precise as this book unfolds. It's hardly surprising that this new way of situating ourselves on the shifting boundary between our institutional rules of the game and our human and ecclesial encounters involves a lot of trial and error, and it doesn't immediately succeed in getting everyone involved. Resistance and discouragement in the wake of so many aborted reforms run deep. However, Pope Francis wanted to set a synodal process in motion, rather than organize an "event" that might well remain without a future. We can already see that the complex web of relevant questions is becoming more organized. I demonstrate this in the third chapter, the longest in this book, without forgetting that the very nature of this "process" is to remain unfinished. Indeed, we always live within history.

This brings me to the main issue at stake in the synodal process, namely the *experience* of *conversion and reform*, the latter being, since the beginning of the second millennium of the Latin Church, the ceaselessly reiterated attempt to respond collectively to the singular invitation of *metanoia* (= conversion), addressed by Jesus Christ to one and all (see Mark 1:14-15). But when we move on to the ecclesial level, an entire gestalt is evoked and called into question; think, for example, of the sacralized image of the priest, seen as the centerpiece of the church as it has been understood since the reforms of the sixteenth century. Changing the way we look at ecclesial reality and shifting the spotlight to its synodality is by no means self-evident, and the more we try to do it, the more resistance we encounter. Converting our mentalities is a difficult and slow process. Pope Francis's intuition was to start by establishing new approaches in small areas of experimentation, gathering successful experiences and learning to think differently at the same time, so that a new vision can emerge. The conversion experience has a personal side and an institutional side, both of which are intimately intertwined. The theological character of the synodal process, its rootedness in the Holy Spirit, demands that we articulate these two sides; opposing them, or advancing on one side without considering the other, would necessarily lead to the distortion of synodality. The fourth chapter develops this idea further.

Finally, we will take a step back and ask ourselves why, at this point in the history of the church and our societies, synodality is arousing such interest, to the point of becoming the "path . . . which God expects of the Church of the third millennium," as Pope Francis characterized it in his address of October 17, 2015. Of course, there are many reasons for this, and I will list them when the time comes. But one, and perhaps the most decisive, is worth mentioning at the outset. Today, we are discovering even more clearly that it is impossible to listen to God speaking to us without at the same time listening to others—including to those who have been forced to remain mute and to the silent cries of our earth. This kind of listening—I like to call it stereophonic—makes it possible for us to speak to one another in truth and decide our future together, and it is waiting for new community spaces to be implemented.

In this respect, the crisis in the church and in our democracies reveals the same spiritual ills and institutional deficiencies, requiring similar solutions. Pacifying our churches by listening to all voices, and informally and institutionally seeking a true understanding of all, is the only antidote to the recurring and increasingly ideological divisions. This pacification, which needs to be constantly put back on the drawing board, proves to be the *sine qua non* condition for the awakening of a common creativity, enabling us, amid the accumulation of problems that characterizes the church's current crisis, to imagine a different future. As we recall Pentecost and ponder the constantly evolving shapes of humanity and the church, we may well ask whether the "messianic people" (Dogmatic Constitution on the Church, *Lumen Gentium*, chap. 2) that we form with so many other Christians and Jews is entering a new phase in its spiritual history. This is the question I address in my final chapter.

This whole journey, which necessarily includes some repetition at different levels of depth, is to some extent contained in the first chapter, which invites us to "journey together," Scriptures in hand, letting them inspire the interpretation of what happens to us along the way.[1]

It is my wish that this book will help my readers to engage with greater confidence and knowledge in the current synodal process.

Dun-le-Palestel (Creuse), France
July 31, 2023
Feast of St. Ignatius of Loyola

❖ ❖ ❖

The first session of the 16th Ordinary General Assembly of the Synod of Bishops was held in Rome from October 4 to October 29, 2023. The first edition of this work was published on October 11, 2023—the feast of Pope St. John XXIII. After the second session, which

[1] I deliberately refrain from referring here to other studies on synodality. Readers wishing to delve deeper into certain questions will find an excellent bibliography in Jos Moons, "Synodality and the Roman-Catholic Church: An Academic Bibliography (2013–2024)," *Cahiers Internationaux de Théologie Pratique*, série 'Documents' n. 17, www.pastoralis.org.

took place from October 2 to October 27, 2024, we needed to take a new step forward.

It would have been possible to rewrite some chapters of this book based on the results of the first session, as they appear in the Assembly's Letter to the People of God (October 25, 2023) and in the Synthesis Report, *A Synodal Church in Mission* (October 28, 2023).[2] But after a careful reading of the first edition, I noticed that most of my reflection on and analysis of resistance to the synodal process were confirmed in those documents. So I asked myself where and how I could insert the milestone that would introduce us to the second session of the synod. Because the first four chapters of the book analyze the issues at stake in the first phase, including its *Instrumentum Laboris*, and how to embark upon a path of spiritual and institutional conversion, it seemed appropriate to set the milestone in a new chapter 5. The next chapter broadens the angle of view, anticipates the issues at stake, and deals with the new vision of the church within human history and society.

The title of the book also found confirmation during the synod's second phase, although I still include the question mark that indicates the tension between the canonical status of the synod and its ambition. To the arguments put forward in the conclusion, we can add the simple observation that the Synthesis Report covers virtually all the themes addressed by the Second Vatican Council.

As I did when I published the first edition, today I want to help even more readers, especially our church leaders, to trust in the synodal process and commit themselves to it.

Paris
January 25, 2024
Feast of the Conversion of St. Paul, Apostle

[2] These texts can be found at https://www.synod.va/en/synodal-process/the-universal-phase/documents.html.

# Chapter 1

# Reading the Scriptures Together and Learning to Journey Together Again

If you want to understand what's at stake in the current synodal process, you need to start by probing the evangelical depth of the Greek word *syn-hodos*, which means "to journey together." With whom do we journey, and how do we live this experience day by day?

The Scriptures ask us these questions . . . and many more besides.

As a first approach to the process initiated by Pope Francis, we therefore let the Scriptures tell us about the march of God's people toward the Promised Land, trusting that, when the time comes, they will give us back the word so that we can follow it today on our human and ecclesial journeys.

First, we need to situate the term *synod* in a constellation of words that are highly significant in our human life, before searching for this set of elementary words in what we might call the "missionary travelogues" of the early Christians.

In reading them, we discover the meaning—very simple—and the stakes—perhaps more complex—of the current "journeying together" of our communities and churches.

## One Word and Its Evangelical Meaning

Let's not forget: Christian tradition does not rely primarily on a codified religious language but instead refers to our simplest ways of existing and living in space and time; it gives a recognizable form to our human experience through and within a set of fundamental images and metaphors. A *shared journey* is one such image.

Journeying together obviously implies a *path* or "way." Let's not forget that the very first designation Christians used to identify themselves was people of "the Way" (Acts 9:2; 19:9, 23; 22:4; and 24:14, 22), even before others called them "Christians" (Acts 11:26). We can see the metaphor that is at work here: the paths that our feet tread are taken to symbolize the path of life that each of us, in our human groups and our communities, travel.

Underpinning all New Testament texts is this human itinerancy in space and time, charged with spiritual depth. In his very first text, 1 Thessalonians, we see Paul, "bereft of you for a short time, in person, not in heart" (1 Thess 2:17), sending Timothy from Athens to the church of Thessalonica and praying that "[n]ow may God himself, our Father, and our Lord Jesus direct our *way* [*hodos*] to you" (1 Thess 3:11).

Luke's work follows this metaphor. Think of the seventy-two disciples, sent out on the roads (Luke 10:5) when Jesus is already on his way to Jerusalem (*poreuô*; Luke 9:51-56); or the two disciples on the road to Emmaus after his crucifixion: Christ joins them on their way (*syn-poreuô*; Luke 24:15), their eyes unable to identify him until they recognize him in the breaking of the bread and then discern his presence on their path (*hodos*; Luke 24:32, 35). Remember Philip on the road from Jerusalem to Gaza, when he approaches the Ethiopian eunuch sitting in his chariot, reading the prophet Isaiah. To his question, "Do you understand what you're reading?," the Ethiopian queen's high-ranking official replies, "How can I understand what I'm reading if I don't have a guide on the road (*tis hodègèsei me*)?" (Acts 8:26, 31, my translation). Let's not forget this second metaphor of the *hod-ègos* or "guide-path," which we will come back to later. Readers will be able to find many more examples,[1] not without re-

[1] Luke uses the term "*syn-hodia*" just once, in Luke 2:44: "Thinking that he [Jesus] was in the caravan, they [his parents] journeyed for a day and looked for him." Here the term is translated as "caravan," which calls to mind *Evangelii Gaudium* 87: "Today, when the networks and means of human communication have made unprecedented advances, we sense the challenge of finding and sharing a 'mystique' of living together, of mingling and encounter, of embracing and supporting one another, of stepping into this flood tide which, while chaotic,

membering that the Gospel of John identifies Jesus himself as "the way" that is also "the truth and the life" (John 14:6).

But the metaphor of the road is part of a whole *constellation* of fundamental *metaphors* for life; it calls first for the *border* to be crossed, and next the "threshold"—above all, the threshold of "home."

Home is a reserved, private space, and its threshold marks the boundary between a sanctuary and a more or less foreign "elsewhere," a vital, quasi-bodily boundary that exists within all cultures and between all peoples. Without homes in which to pause and retreat, places of protection and intimacy—"tents"[2] in the desert, or houses and apartments in our towns and cities—our common journey would hardly be viable and would ultimately dissolve our identities. It's worth noting that these elementary boundaries between "outside" and "inside" have been continually crossed since the beginning of human history. This can be done using force of arms (as is currently the case in Ukraine), through trade and negotiation, or by requesting hospitality—to name but three basic ways of crossing our borders. The Bible is familiar with all these situations, but it gives pride of place to hospitality: "Do not neglect hospitality, for through it some have unknowingly entertained angels," as the Letter to the Hebrews reminds us (13:2), no doubt referring to Abraham and Sarah under the oak of Mamre (Gen 18:1-16). And since it is unconditional, true hospitality produces social mixing: "There is neither Jew nor Greek, there is neither slave nor free person, there is not male and female; for you are all one in Christ Jesus," we read in Paul (Gal 3:28).

---

can become a genuine experience of fraternity, *a caravan of solidarity*, a sacred pilgrimage."

[2] The Working Document for the Continental Stage (October 24, 2022; text available at https://www.synod.va/en/highlights/working-document-for-the-continental-stage.html) 25–28, uses the metaphor of the *tent*, well matched to that of the *caravan*: *"Enlarge the Space of Your Tent" (Is 54:2)*: "Listened to today, these words of Isaiah invite us to imagine the Church similarly as a tent, indeed as the tent of meeting, which accompanied the people on their journey through the desert: called to stretch out, therefore, but also to move. At its centre, stands the tabernacle, that is, the presence of the Lord. The tent's hold is ensured by the sturdiness of its pegs, that is, the fundamentals of faith that do not change but can be moved and planted in ever new ground, so that the tent can accompany the people as they walk through history. Finally, in order not to sag, the structure of the tent must keep in balance the different forces and tensions to which it is subjected: a metaphor that expresses the need for discernment" (27).

The metaphor of the road and journeying together, then, calls forth the metaphor of *orientation* and *horizon*.

The latter structures the entire biblical corpus, especially its second book, Exodus. As its name suggests, this book retraces the journey from Egypt to the Promised Land, crossing a very special "threshold": the Red Sea, a place of death and life. The long desert crossing that separates this passage from arrival in the Promised Land shows that it is not enough to have been freed from the bonds of "slavery" to become truly free. Like the horizon, the Promised Land recedes as we go along the road, taking on multiple meanings, as expressed in the prophetic writings of the Bible. Justice and the reconciliation of companion travelers with one another and with all creatures are the most important expressions of this, not forgetting "rest," which once again recalls the desire for a house, or "dwelling," and orients the rhythm of creation (Gen 2:2; Ps 95:11; and Heb 4:4, 10).

In this messianic perspective, Jesus' journey—as a new Joshua (see the Book of Joshua)—takes him from the Jordan to Galilee (Mark 1:14), which, thanks to his beneficent presence with the Twelve and his disciples, is transformed into a promised land, a "Galilee" of the nations for "the people who sit in darkness" (Matt 4:14-16). And before suffering the fate of the prophets in Jerusalem, Jesus announced to his disciples that "after [he has] been raised up, [he] shall go before [them] to Galilee" (Mark 14:28; cf. 16:7). The Galilee of the nations can then happen anywhere on our planet, where disciples of Jesus or others (see Mark 9:38-41) heal those who no longer dwell in themselves, or grasp their hand and help them up (Mark 1:31).[3]

And so, on this path of salvation toward a promised land, another, somewhat ultimate metaphor presents itself to us: the upright posture of those who, treading the paths of the earth with their feet, raise

[3] In this context of healing, we can recall another metaphor that clarifies that of the hospitable house—namely, the church as a "field hospital," a metaphor used as early as 2013 by Pope Francis: "I see clearly that the thing the church needs most today is the ability to heal wounds and to warm the hearts of the faithful; it needs nearness, proximity. I see the church as a field hospital after battle" ("A Big Heart Open to God: An Interview with Pope Francis," *America*, September 20, 2013, https://www.americamagazine.org/faith/2013/09/30/big-heart-open-god-interview-pope-francis).

their hands toward heaven, from which they expect and receive blessing and life.

Situated in the biblical constellation of these few elementary metaphors, likely to reveal the human and evangelical depth of our existences, the term "synodality" loses its apparent abstraction: to be in synod, then, is quite simply to *journey* along the road of life, not alone but with others and *together*, in search of a *home* and offering hospitality to and receiving it from others, beyond all the borders that separate us from one another and that risk reducing our march to a business trip or turning it into a military operation. To be in synod is to constantly set out again toward a common horizon of justice, reconciliation, and peace, and to raise our hands to heaven, having rediscovered with others an upright posture, the ultimate sign of our human dignity.

## Gospel Figures and Missionary "Travelogues"

The Preparatory Document for the Synod 2021–2024 (= PD)[4] introduces several New Testament figures for whom "the Spirit of God . . . illuminates and vivifies this 'journeying together'" (PD 16). First is Jesus himself, then the crowd who encounters him ("the 'everyone' of the human condition"), and finally his disciples and apostles, not forgetting "the 'extra' actor, the antagonist, who brings to the scene the diabolical separation of the other three" (PD 16–21). This look back at Jesus' journey with others is complemented by a look at the nascent community and "the risk of placing unjustified limits on faith sharing" illustrated by the encounter between Peter and the centurion (PD 16 and 22–24). Readers may refer to this beautiful chapter III of the Preparatory Document. For my part, I'd like to present two other passages from Luke, which, as we progress along the synodal path, may take on a rich and beautiful meaning.

First, let's consider the aforementioned sending forth of the seventy-two disciples on the roads of Galilee (Luke 10:1-24). This text brings together all the biblical elements just outlined: the sending of the disciples out on the roads, two by two, unarmed and without

[4] Text at https://www.synod.va/en/documents/preparatory-document.html.

supplies, to be welcomed or turned away as they cross the threshold of this house or that town; these "dwellings" thus either become places of encounter among bearers of peace, or places of inhospitality and refusal—places where, as under the oak of Mamre and in Sodom (Gen 18 and 19), either the reign of God arrives or curses and judgments are manifested. For it is in the simplicity of everyday life, whether hospitable or inhospitable, that a "crisis," or decisive sorting, takes place.

The return of the seventy-two to the one who sent them out on the road is particularly telling in the context of the current synodal journey. Indeed, *the disciples review* what has just happened to them and report their deeds and successes to Jesus: "Lord, even the demons are subject to us because of your name."

He reminds them that *he* had experienced every possible temptation (Luke 4:13)—"I have observed Satan fall like lightning from the sky"—and that, having set out without sandals and leaving behind even the dust of their feet to those who did not welcome them, *they* were given the authority to trample underfoot snakes and scorpions and all the power of the enemy.

But they should not rejoice in their successes: they should rejoice that their names are written in heaven. And it is heaven and earth that come together "at that very moment" in Jesus' exultation under the action of the Holy Spirit: "I give you praise, Father, Lord of heaven and earth . . ." Despite all the mishaps along the way, those he sent, "the childlike," truly experienced—as he did—an "abundant harvest" (another metaphor that, following on from the parable of the sower [Luke 8:4-15], is included in the theme of the "way"). Jesus can then conclude his prayer and conversation with his disciples with a beatitude addressed to them and to those like them: "Blessed are the eyes that see what you see!"

This dispersal of the disciples, two by two, along the roads of Galilee and their return to the One who sent them does not represent a synodal experience in the strict sense of the term, but prefigures it or, better still, recounts its quasi-utopian horizon. The very first account of an assembly that could be called "synodal" is found in the Acts of the Apostles (15:1-35). The movement unfolds in the opposite direction: we are first told of the return—in this case to Jerusalem—and only later of the dispersion.

Paul and Barnabas, the two of them who set out on the road, can report their own story, "what God had done with them and how he had opened the door of faith to the Gentiles" (Acts 14:27). Once again, a tale of deeds, you might say. But this time, this "success" raises discussions and conflicts, even indoctrinations within the churches in the making: "Unless you are circumcised according to the Mosaic practice, you cannot be saved" (Acts 15:1b).

In the Jerusalem assembly examining this affair, Peter's testimony, referring to his encounter with the centurion, and James's speech, differently situated, have their importance. But it is above all the account of Barnabas and Paul, listened to in great silence, that seems to carry the conviction of the assembly. This assembly therefore sent two men from the Jerusalem community, Barnabas and Paul, to the very place where the conflict began and entrusted them with a letter addressed "to the brothers in Antioch, Syria, and Cilicia of Gentile origin" (Acts 15:23). No writing without face-to-face communication! When the seventy-two had returned to Jesus from their mission, their joy authenticated the presence of the Holy Spirit; in this case, the joy of the letter's recipients confirmed the assembly's decision after the event: "When the people read it, they were delighted with the exhortation" (Acts 15:31).

Judas and Silas return—after "some time" (Acts 15:33)—to those who had sent them, while Paul and Barnabas remain—"some time" (Acts 15:36)—with those who had sent them to Jerusalem. The meaning of the movement of dispersion and return is thus transformed into communication between churches . . . and Christians of Jewish and Gentile origin.

In meditating on this second passage from Luke, we didn't stray far from the initial metaphor of "the way" and "journeying together." After all, the conflict that gave rise to the Jerusalem assembly was precisely about whom to choose as companions: "Whom do we walk with, and how do we live this experience day by day?" we wondered at the outset. The debate about the need for circumcision and observance of the law of Moses is about the "barriers" that separate us and can prevent us from journeying together; it ultimately touches on our experience of God, the God whom Peter truly discovers "shows no partiality" (Acts 10:34; cf. Deut 10:17).

Like the story of the Jerusalem assembly, that of the meeting between Peter and Cornelius suggests that removing these "barriers" is not a matter of course. Divine impartiality can be recognized intellectually and attested to in the Scriptures—perhaps even more readily today, when the idea of election has become inconceivable to many. But the question of "barriers" comes up very concretely when it comes to "journeying" with Christians and others who don't share my sensibility or some of my convictions. A whole religious conception of purity prevents Peter from entering into a relationship with the Roman centurion until Peter's *conversion*, thanks to his spiritual experience of hearing a "voice" that, baffling his imagination, tells him of the purity of all God's creation and of the unexpected arrival of Cornelius's emissaries.

## When the Scriptures Help Us to Share God's Word

The transition from reading Scripture to sharing its word cannot be immediate. We see in the story of Peter's vision at Joppa that inner listening *and* listening to others are prerequisites. Peter was certainly accustomed not only to reading the Scriptures but above all to praying and listening to God's voice. We read in Acts that "Peter went up to the roof terrace to pray. . . . He was hungry and wished to eat, and . . . he fell into a trance" (Acts 10:9-10). He only understands what this enigmatic vision means after listening to Cornelius's envoys and, after a long journey, listening to the centurion himself. Indeed, the concrete situations of our own real-life experience can sharpen our inner ear and make us attentive to what others have to say about those same situations.

This is even clearer in the episode of the Jerusalem assembly, whose starting point is the conflict mentioned above. We hear first from Peter, and then Barnabas and Paul. But between these two interventions, a "great silence" settles over the whole assembly, taking the place of prayer and listening to God's voice. It is only after Paul and Barnabas have completed their account of their missionary journey that James speaks out to situate the "event" that has just taken place within the framework of the prophetic Scriptures (Acts 15:13-21). And as in the meeting between Peter and Cornelius, the process of reading and listening together, inwardly and mutually, ends in a decision: "Can anyone withhold the water for baptizing these people, who have received the holy Spirit even as we have? . . . Then the apostles and presbyters, in agreement with the whole church, decided . . ." (Acts 10:47, 15:22).

It is therefore remarkable that the Preparatory Document for the Synod 2021–2024 invites all the faithful to give voice to the Scriptures—the "journey" outlined in chapter III of the document "Listening to the Scriptures" (PD 16–24)—and to allow themselves to be generated by the Scriptures to a personal voice shared with others—the "journey" outlined in chapter IV, "Synodality in Action: Pathways for Consulting the People of God" (PD 25–30). In a way, these two "journeys" overlap and are called upon to make each other fruitful, here and now. So, it comes as no surprise that the summary of chapter IV reflects the questions posed to us by the Scriptures and begins by asking us about our journey companions, our ability to listen, and our ways of speaking with them: (I) "Who are the road companions, including those outside the ecclesial perimeter?" (II) "To whom does our particular Church 'need to listen to' "? And (III)"How do we promote a free and authentic style of communication within the community and its organizations, without duplicity and opportunism?"

A quick look at the Working Document for the Continental Stage *"Enlarge the Space of Your Tent" (Is 54:2)*, published in October 2022,[5] reveals that, on every continent, many Christians are considering the concept of "radical inclusion," or even social mixing in the Pauline sense of the term. Just as pagan converts to Judaism faced barriers related to circumcision and observed the law of Moses, so today divorced and remarried people, LGBTQ+ people, and other Christians belonging to marginalized groups face barriers to full acceptance.

As in the early days of Christianity in Antioch and Jerusalem, these issues give rise to discussion and conflict within the churches—which is normal—and sometimes even indoctrination—which is less fortunate. They therefore deserve to be examined together and by all, maintaining our faith in the impartiality of a God who manifests himself in the dignity of every human being and makes access to Christ Jesus unconditional.

[5] Text at https://www.synod.va/en/synodal-process/the-continental-stage/resources-and-tools/documents.html.

❖ ❖ ❖

Some people see the new synodality as complicated and abstract, and others view it as remote and threatening to the Catholic faith. This analysis has sought to situate it within our Scriptures and, at the same time, to root it in our experience as living itinerants, interacting with others on a daily basis.

We could characterize the spirit of this approach, as recounted by Luke, for example, in terms of "enlightened pragmatism," that is, a reflection nourished by what we do: we effectively start journeying together, the Scriptures in hand, letting ourselves be touched by the most basic questions that have been with us from the start, whether they come to us from the Scriptures or are addressed to us by journeying companions—close by, more distant, or even excluded. The sign that these questions really reach us is that our outer and inner ears perk up and invite us to take them seriously and let them disturb our certainties, to check whether we have heard and understood them properly, and finally to deal with them together and make appropriate decisions. This slow maturation, the inner work that takes place during this time, and the fruit that comes from dealing together with what concerns us all enable us to understand the "enlightened pragmatism" of the current synodal process in terms of "spiritual *practice*" or—in more technical language—"*practical* pneumatology." It's the joy of the seventy-two on their return from mission, or that of the recipients of the letter from the Jerusalem assembly, which in some way signals the hidden presence of the One who was at work from the start: the Holy Spirit, whose manifestation is finally experienced in a prayer of praise from the heart—that of Jesus on the return of the seventy-two.

Like the disciples interpreting what had just happened to them, and the Jerusalem assembly listening to the interpretations of Peter, Paul, and Barnabas before making its decision, we must now continue our own interpretation, extending it to the synodal process, convinced that reading of the Scriptures in common, experiencing inner and outer listening, and expressing joy and praise in no way exclude reflection, but on the contrary demand it.

A synodal pragmatism that allows itself to be truly enlightened by history and theology can indeed help us to listen to and understand one another better, to read the Scriptures more rigorously so that they inspire us in truth, and, finally, to taste more deeply the joy that the coherence of what has just been inaugurated brings us, while we relinquish, in thanksgiving, the results and fruits we already perceive.

# Chapter 2

## Synodality—A Constitutive Dimension of the Church?

We have just mentioned enlightened pragmatism and its spiritual dimension. They are perfectly summed up at the very beginning of the Preparatory Document for the Synod 2021–2024, already quoted several times:

> By journeying together and *reflecting* together on the journey that has been made, the Church will be able to *learn through Her experience* which processes can help Her to live communion, to achieve participation, to open Herself to mission. Our "journeying together" is, in fact, what most effectively enacts and manifests the *nature of the Church* as the pilgrim and missionary People of God. (PD 1; emphasis mine)[1]

This very precise formulation first recalls what has already been said in our first chapter on interpreting our experience referred to here by the term "reflecting." The second sentence of this short passage then takes us further, toward the question of the *identity* or *missionary nature* of the people of God who, effectively *journeying* together and *reflecting* on what they are experiencing, become aware of *who they are*.

[1] Text available at https://www.synod.va/en/documents/preparatory-document.html.

In his address commemorating the fiftieth anniversary of the institution of the Synod of Bishops, on October 17, 2015, Pope Francis already offered such a *reflection* on the church's missionary identity, adding a decisive aspect, expressed in the form of a double thesis: "*Synodality, as a constitutive element of the Church,* offers us the most appropriate interpretive framework for understanding *the hierarchical ministry itself.*"[2] This sentence links two facts in a way that is by no means self-evident: first, synodality is a constitutive dimension of the church, expressing its very identity—and let's not forget that means *everyone "journeying together" on an equal footing*; and second, it offers the best framework for understanding the church's hierarchical ministry. We are always tempted to invert this order and situate synodality more within the hierarchical or pyramidal architecture of the church. Francis instructed us to live these two aspects of our unique ecclesial itinerancy simultaneously and to think of them together.

If this instruction is effectively implemented, the ecclesial architecture, as laid down by Vatican I and Vatican II, begins to budge. To be sure, Pope Francis's synodal vision remains within the "dogmatic" perimeter of *Lumen Gentium*, the Dogmatic Constitution on the Church of the last council (1964). But it does direct the spotlight on an ecclesial and spiritual dimension that, while present in the text, is not its main focus. In fact, this new dimension corresponds to what we have learned from reading the Scriptures: the fundamental equality of all human beings before God and the baptismal equality of all Christ's faithful form the basis of a "journeying together," unafraid to confront the differences that threaten to separate us or to address the issues these differences raise. The limits of *Lumen Gentium* thus appear, calling for a critique of the council, but also revealing new potentialities in what it has delivered to us: spiritual and institutional "openings" that, until now, have not been perceived.

Some might ask why we are still interested in a council that took place sixty years ago, when we no longer live in the same era. We must, however, remind them of the importance of the conciliar assemblies in the Christian tradition, starting with that of Jerusalem:

[2] Text at https://www.vatican.va/content/francesco/en/speeches/2015/october/documents/papa-francesco_20151017_50-anniversario-sinodo.html (emphasis mine).

they have tackled the new questions that arise at a given moment in history; they have reestablished communion between divided faithful and their local churches and recreated a consensus on the Christian faith itself; they have laid down basic norms and rules for living together as baptized people; and sometimes, as at Vatican II, they have proposed a vision for the future of the entire world. The church moves forward in history, reinterpreting its tradition and continually adjusting itself to new interlocutors and unprecedented cultural situations. The Second Vatican Council was the last collective act of this kind, and it still binds us together.

The enlightened pragmatism and spiritual practice that was carried out by Vatican II oblige us to take a broader look at the history of the current synodal process, to place it in the footsteps of the two Vatican Councils and, as we shall see, in an even longer history. Recognizing the newness of the synodal vision of the people of God proposed by Pope Francis against the background of the last council, and acknowledging it as being adapted to the situation of today's society and church, is the very first step in the direction of peace of mind and a creative way of untangling the web of problems mentioned in the introduction.

Such a future-oriented rereading of Vatican II's *Lumen Gentium* and the work of the council concerns, as we have said, both sides of Francis's thesis: synodality and ministry. I will explain them step by step, starting with the pope's initial insistence on the equality of all the baptized.

## From Recognizing the Equality of All the Baptized to Experiencing Brother- and Sisterhood

Let's face it: this baptismal equality is by no means self-evident. The conflicts in the early church I mentioned in the first chapter, and those that are shaking the church today, are proof of this. As in our societies, equality all too often remains an abstract affirmation with no real consequences in practice, creating resentments that, when they last, are difficult to resolve. Calls for "fraternity" are therefore of little effect and remain useless if they are not based on recognition of the equality of those concerned.

1. In his opening address to the Synod on Synodality on October 9, 2021, Pope Francis makes this the principle of the participation of all. This is why, in his commentary on the three key words of the synod—"communion—participation—mission"—he insists on the centrality of the middle term:

> The words "communion" and "mission" can risk remaining somewhat abstract, unless we cultivate an ecclesial praxis that expresses *the concreteness of synodality* at every step of our journey and activity, encouraging real involvement on the part of each and all. . . . This is not a matter of form, but of faith. Participation is a requirement of the faith received in baptism. As the Apostle Paul says, "in the one Spirit we were all baptized into one body" (*1 Cor* 12:13). *In the Church, everything starts with baptism.* Baptism, the source of our life, gives rise to the *equal dignity of the children of God*, albeit in the diversity of ministries and charisms. Consequently, all the baptized are called to take part in the Church's life and mission.[3]

This reference to the centrality of baptism, and to the equal dignity of all Christ's faithful that is its consequence, gives a *new focus* to the interpretation of *Lumen Gentium* (= LG). This focus corresponds to the fundamental decision taken by the council to precede the two chapters of the text on the hierarchical structure of the church (chap. III) and the laity (chap. IV) by a new chapter on the people of God (chap. II).[4] But it also highlights the fact that this decision was not implemented consistently and to the end.

Thus, the idea of the equality of all the baptized, which should have found its place in this second chapter, appears only in the fourth chapter on the laity:

[3] Text at https://www.vatican.va/content/francesco/en/speeches/2021/october/documents/20211009-apertura-camminosinodale.html (emphasis mine).

[4] Let us remind the reader of the outline of this text, which has shaped the life of the Catholic Church for sixty years: chap. I: The Mystery of the Church; chap. II: The People of God; chap. III: The Church Is Hierarchical; chap. IV: The Laity; chap. V: The Universal Call to Holiness in the Church; chap. VI: Religious; chap. VII: The Pilgrim Church; chap. VIII: Our Lady.

> The chosen people of God is, therefore, one: "one Lord, one faith, one Baptism" (Eph 4:5); there is a common [*communis*] dignity of members deriving from their rebirth in Christ, a common grace as sons and daughters, a common vocation to perfection, one salvation, one hope and undivided charity. In Christ and in the church there is, then, no inequality [*inaequalitas*] arising from race or nationality, social condition or sex. . . .
>
> In the church not everyone walks along the same path, yet all are called to holiness and have obtained an equal [*coaequalis*] privilege of faith through the justice of God (see 2 Pet 1:1). Although by Christ's will some are appointed teachers, dispensers of the mysteries and pastors for the others, yet all the faithful enjoy a true equality [*vera aequalitas*] with regard to the dignity and the activity which they share [*dignitatem et actionem communem*] in the building up of the body of Christ. The distinction [*distinctio*] which the Lord has made between the sacred ministers [*sacros ministros*] and the rest of the people of God implies union, for the pastors and the other faithful are joined together by a close relationship. . . .
>
> As the laity by divine condescension have as their brother Christ [*fratrem habent Christum*] who, though Lord of all, came not to be served but to serve (see Mt 20:28), they also have as brothers [*fratres*] those who have been placed in the sacred ministry and who by Christ's authority, through teaching, sanctifying and ruling so nourish the family of God that the new commandment of love may be fulfilled by all. (LG 32)[5]

Even in this fourth chapter, the equality of all the baptized is relativized by the distinction between the "sacredness" of ministers (*sacri ministri*, etc.) and the "secular character" of the laity (*indoles saecularis*; LG 31). The difference between sacred and secular is also chronically confused with that between sacrality (*sacrum*) and holiness (*sanctum*), the former being closely linked to the exercise of power in the church

[5] In this text, as in other conciliar texts quoted in this book, I have kept some Latin terms, either to emphasize the coherence of the vocabulary or because they have a technical meaning. All quotations of Vatican II documents are taken from Austin Flannery, ed., *Vatican Council II: The Basic Sixteen Documents; Constitutions, Decrees, Declarations, A Completely Revised Translation in Inclusive Language* (Liturgical Press, 2014).

(*potestas sacra*);[6] it's a link that is broken only in a few places in this document, at least on a terminological level.[7]

This way of thinking, specific to the second millennium of the church in the Latin West and the result of an important reform—the so-called Gregorian reform of the eleventh century—is reflected in the distinction between *Lumen Gentium* and the Pastoral Constitution on the Church in the Modern World, *Gaudium et Spes* (= GS). Let's not forget that the council adopted two constitutions on the church, one—of "dogmatic" status—on the church in itself, and another—of "pastoral" status—on the church's presence in society. Separating these two views of God's people rooted in history and society, one looking inwards (*ad intra*) and the other outwards (*ad extra*), runs the risk of obliterating the necessary mutual relationship.[8] In the Dogmatic Constitution on the Church, this vision dominates the two chapters on the hierarchical constitution (*constitutio hierarchica*) of the church, or the "sacred power" of the bishops (chap. III), and on the laity, or their "secular" character (chap. IV).

To return to the second chapter, let us therefore remember that the concept of "equality" (*aequalitas*) is explicit. But it is taught *indirectly*, at least in part of the text, through the doctrine of the three ministries or tasks of Christ Jesus (*tria-munera*)—his priesthood, his prophetic ministry, and his kingship—communicated by the risen Lord to the whole people of God. This chapter certainly makes baptism the fundamental principle of this people (LG 9 §1). But when it introduces

[6] See Christoph Theobald, "Le sacré et le saint: Une confusion qui donne à penser," in Alexandre Escudier, Pierre Gisel, and Jean-Marc Tétaz, eds., *Le sacré en question* (Labor et fides, 2023).

[7] *Lumen Gentium* 10 and 18 use the term "sacred power" (*potestas sacra*), while the description of the magisterium in *Lumen Gentium* 25 uses the biblical term "authority" (*auctoritas*).

[8] In the Pastoral Constitution on the Church in the Modern World, *Gaudium et Spes*, "basic equality between all" is clearly affirmed, with particular mention of women's rights (29 §2). On this point, therefore, there is a tension between the two documents on the church, which will leave a lasting mark on the council's reception. GS 44, on "What the Church Receives from the Modern World," is the only text to indicate the historically evident reciprocal interaction of the two perspectives, a paragraph that would find its definitive form in the fourth and fifth versions of the text, written in November and December 1965 (see Christoph Theobald, *La réception du concile Vatican II: I. Accéder à la source*, Unam sanctam—Nouvelle série 1 [Éditions du Cerf, 2009, new ed. 2023], 310–15).

the common priesthood of all the faithful (*sacerdotium commune*) in the following section (LG 10), it immediately distinguishes it from the ministerial priesthood (*sacerdotium ministeriale*), clarifying this difference with the classic concept of "sacred power" (*potestas sacra*; LG 10 §2). Number 12, on the other hand, teaches that all the people of God—"from the bishops to the last of the faithful"—participating in Christ's prophetic ministry, "cannot be mistaken in belief" (*in credendo*). Received from the Holy Spirit, this messianic gift manifests itself as an "instinct" of faith, also called the "sense of faith" (*sensus fidei*), which enables us to "discern what is truly of God."[9] To justify his thesis that synodality is "a constitutive element of the Church," in his address commemorating the fiftieth anniversary of the institution of the Synod of Bishops (October 17, 2015), Pope Francis relies precisely on this conciliar text, which I will comment on below.

2. Only if we understand the structure and dynamics of *Lumen Gentium* without overlooking its limitations can we appreciate the importance of the change of perspective brought about by Pope Francis. While the Dogmatic Constitution on the Church recognizes the equality of all believers given by baptism (and makes this explicit in its fourth chapter), it remains committed to the post-Gregorian distinction between the "sacred power" or *potestas sacra* of ministers, and the secular character of the laity. It can therefore place those who exercise the "sacred ministry" at the service of "their brothers and sisters" (LG 13 §3 and 18 §1)—that's a big step—and, conversely, require the laity to welcome these sacred ministers as they would Christ—as "brothers" (LG 32 §4). But the path that leads from the principled equality of all the baptized to their brother- and sisterhood is never guaranteed from the outset, while it frequently passes through negative experiences of more or less conscious demonstrations of force or more or less violent exercises of power. However, this path, strewn with pitfalls and sometimes influenced by the "diabolical antagonist" (see PD 21), does not appear as such in the council's spotlight.

[9] *Evangelii Gaudium* 119 (text at https://www.vatican.va/content/francesco/en/apost_exhortations/documents/papa-francesco_esortazione-ap_20131124_evangelii-gaudium.html). In this issue, Pope Francis translates the technical terms of *Lumen Gentium* 12 into the language of experience.

Given Pope Francis's view of the equal dignity of all the baptized as the axis of his interpretation of the council, the church's pathological phenomena, systemic in nature because it is linked to the sacralization of the ministry—"clericalism"—can be placed and interpreted in a broader ecclesiological framework. At the same time, we are seeing the emergence of a path that leads from the principle of the equality of all the baptized to a sister- and brotherhood that is real because it is experienced: a path that must now be lived, reflected upon, and structured in a new way.

## The Church's Synodal Nature "in the Wake of Vatican II"

However, this task touches on the constitution, or very nature, of the church. Just as the third chapter of *Lumen Gentium* on the episcopate clarifies—"in the footsteps of Vatican I"—the *hierarchical constitution* of the church and places sacred ministers at the service of "their brothers and sisters" (LG 18 §1), Pope Francis's thesis demands—now "in the footsteps of Vatican II"—that the constitutive or constitutional status of the *synodality of the people of God* be recognized and that this status makes much more clear the equality of all the baptized and their effective sister- and brotherhood. It goes without saying that this new view of the unique reality of the church must therefore shape our understanding of *ecclesial ministry, which is also constitutive*. We will consider this further on.

1. Three years after the pope's address commemorating the fiftieth anniversary of the Synod of Bishops, synodality was addressed for the first time in a document by the International Theological Commission entitled "Synodality in the Life and Mission of the Church" (2018).[10]

The commission understands Pope Francis's instruction as an invitation to cross the "new threshold . . . in the wake of Vatican II" (9). Here again, we find not only the metaphor of the "path" and the "threshold" that we discussed in the first chapter but also the specific way the Second Vatican Council related to previous councils, situ-

[10] Text at https://www.vatican.va/roman_curia/congregations/cfaith/cti_documents/rc_cti_20180302_sinodalita_en.html.

ating itself in their "wake," which allows him to articulate fidelity to tradition and novelty, in a fairly open and metaphorical manner, without losing the necessary rigor.

There is no point in presenting the whole document here; a glance at the most important achievements of the commission's work may suffice to show how, on the basis of Pope Francis's twofold thesis, the historical rereading of the two Vatican councils has moved forward.

The first chapter anchors synodality in Scripture, tradition, and history.[11] Against this backdrop, the second chapter sketches out a theology of synodality whose source it recognizes as a trinitarian ecclesiology of communion, which it attributes to the Second Vatican Council (43–53).

The decisive arguments are in numbers 54 to 56 of the document. First of all, it reflects on the succession of the first three chapters of *Lumen Gentium*, on the topics of the mystery of the church, the people of God, and the hierarchical nature of the church. According to the document, this succession "stresses that the ecclesiastical hierarchy is at the service of the People of God in order that the Church may carry out her mission in conformity with God's plan of salvation, in the logic of the priority of the whole over its parts and of the end over the means" (54). Focusing then on chapter II of *Lumen Gentium* and returning to the three ministries of Christ Jesus shared with the whole people of God—already mentioned above—the text roots synodality in the church's priestly ministry (*munus saderdotale*; LG 10) and prophetic ministry (*munus propheticum;* LG 12) (55), before dealing, in an additional section, with the mission of all the baptized and of bishops (56). It therefore takes very seriously Francis's instruction to live and think together these two aspects of the common ecclesial journey—the role of all the baptized and that of ordained ministers. It is here, and only here, that the document refers to the "sense of faith" of all the faithful (*sensus fidei;* LG 12 §1 and *Evangelii Gaudium* [= EG] 119[12]), "the key to their 'walking together'" (56).

[11] This chapter deserves to be discussed from a historical and theological point of view, which is not possible here.

[12] Text at https://www.vatican.va/content/francesco/en/apost_exhortations/documents/papa-francesco_esortazione-ap_20131124_evangelii-gaudium.html.

The central passage of the text reads as follows:

> Synodality means that the whole Church is a subject and that everyone in the Church is a subject. The faithful are σύνοδοι, companions on the journey. They are called to play an active role inasmuch as they share in the one priesthood of Christ [LG 10], and are meant to receive the various charisms given by the Holy Spirit in view of the common good [LG 12 §2). Synodal life reveals a Church consisting of free and different *subjects*, united in communion, which is dynamically shown to be *a single communitarian subject* built on Christ, the corner-stone, and on the Apostles, who are like pillars, built like so many living stones into "a spiritual house" (*cf. 1 Peter* 2,5), "a dwelling-place of God in the Spirit" (*Ephesians* 2,22). (55; emphasis mine)

2. At first glance, this passage seems to complicate matters unnecessarily. In a rather descriptive style, however, it comes close to the constitutive status of synodality. This—and this is how the implicit argument of the text can be summed up—is born of the need to live and bear very concretely the tensions that result from the simple fact that the church as a whole is a "subject" and that all the faithful are equally so; for the people of God as a "subject" consists "of free and different subjects." There's no better way to describe the fundamental difficulties facing ecclesial life and the church's mission.

We can only regret that the first part of the text links too directly the reception of the multiple charisms, given by the Holy Spirit (LG 12 §2), to the participation of the faithful in the priesthood of Christ through the "common priesthood of the faithful" (LG 10)[13] without incorporating their "sense of faith" (*sensus fidei fidelium*). It is treated separately, although the text goes on to make it "the key to their 'walking together'" (56)! On this point, reflection must move forward,

[13] The intention of the text is undoubtedly to link the Christological and the pneumatological, the unity of Christ and the church and the charismatic diversity of the church. This reference to Christ *and* the Spirit is clearly present in LG 12, and it is sufficient to base synodality on Christ's "prophetic office" (*munus propheticum*), while the presentation of Christ's "priestly office" (*munus sacerdotale*), communicated to the people of God (in LG 10 §2), immediately highlights the difference between the "common priesthood" of the faithful and the "ministerial or hierarchical priesthood."

starting not from the "common priesthood of the faithful" but from their participation in Christ's "prophetic ministry." The pastoral and missionary implications of this move will gradually become clearer, and I will come back to them in more detail in the next two chapters. First, however, we need to read *Lumen Gentium*, chapter 2, number 12, on the "prophetic office" (*munus propheticum*) of the "holy people of God"; precisely the section on which Pope Francis bases his thesis that synodality is "a constitutive element of the Church."

3. I therefore invite the reader to this little exercise in patience (without shying away from a few Latin terms), an exercise whose fruits we will reap later:

> The holy people of God shares also in Christ's prophetic office: it spreads abroad a living witness to him, especially by a life of faith and love and by offering to God a sacrifice of praise, the fruit of lips confessing his name (see Heb 13:15). The whole body of the faithful [*universitas fidelium*] who have received an anointing which comes from the holy one (see 1 Jn 2:20 and 27) cannot be mistaken in belief [*in credendo*]. It shows this characteristic through the entire people's supernatural sense of the faith [*sensu fidei totius populi*], when, "from the bishops to the last of the faithful" [St. Augustine], it manifests a universal consensus [*universalem consensum*] in matters of faith and morals. By this sense of the faith, aroused and sustained by the Spirit of truth, the people of God, guided by the sacred magisterium which it faithfully obeys, receives not the word of human beings, but truly the word of God (see 1 Th 2:13), "the faith once for all delivered to the saints" (Jude 3). The people unfailingly adheres to this faith, penetrates it more deeply through right judgment, and applies it more fully in daily life.
>
> Moreover, it is not only through the sacraments and the ministries that the holy Spirit makes the people holy, leads them and enriches them with his virtues. Allotting his gifts "at will to each individual" (1 Cor 12:11), he also distributes special graces among the faithful of every rank. By these gifts, he makes them fit and ready to undertake various tasks and offices for the renewal and building up of the church, as it is written, "the manifestation of the Spirit is given to everyone for profit" (1 Cor 12:7). Whether these charisms be very remarkable or more simple and widely diffused, they are to be received with thanksgiving and

> consolation since they are primarily suited to and useful for the needs of the church. Extraordinary gifts are not to be rashly desired, nor from them are the fruits of apostolic labors to be presumptuously expected. Those who have charge over the church should judge the genuineness and orderly use of these gifts, and it is especially their office not indeed to extinguish the Spirit, but to test all things and hold fast to what is good (see 1 Th 5:12 and 19-21). (LG 12)

To explain the "prophetic office" of the "holy people of God," *Lumen Gentium* refers both to the "sense of the faith" of the faithful (*sensus fidei fidelium*, LG 12 §1) and to their "charisms" (*charismata*) in their present plurality and in history (LG 12 §2).[14] While the charisms given by the Spirit of God accentuate the church's diversity, it is up to the "sense of the faith," given to all by the same Spirit, to make possible—at the heart of this diversity and without abolishing it—a "universal consensus" (*consensus universalis*); a consensus that implies both the acceptance of " 'the faith once for all delivered to the saints' (Jude 3)"[15] and a "unique interplay [*conspiratio*] between the bishops and the faithful" (DV 10 §1).

The pastoral and missionary implications of these two paragraphs can hardly be overestimated. Although promoted by Vatican II, discernment of the multiple charisms of the faithful has yet to make a real mark on post-conciliar ecclesial practice. It requires a reversal of perspective, looking not primarily at what our churches lack—such as a sufficient number of ordained ministers—but at what is actually given to them on the ground. The current sense of "crisis" risks preventing us from perceiving these gifts of the Spirit that, when they are truly welcomed, discerned, and recognized as such, result in rich and fruitful differences, whereas we often reduce them to oppositions of "sensibility," or even ideological positions.[16]

Here we come back to what was said earlier about enlightened pragmatism and the spiritual practice of journeying together which,

[14] In EG 119 and 130–31, Pope Francis refers explicitly to these two paragraphs.

[15] LG 12 §1; see also Vatican II's Dogmatic Constitution on Divine Revelation *Dei Verbum* (= DV), 8 §1.

[16] See Christoph Theobald, *Urgences pastorales du moment présent* (Bayard, 2017), 307–21.

as at the Jerusalem assembly, requires that true otherness, offered by the Holy Spirit, be brought to the fore. What Pope Francis says in *Evangelii Gaudium* about the "sense of faith" of all the faithful offers criteria for advancing along this path, criteria that articulate difference and consensus (*conspiratio*). Not only does he remind us that the "instinct of faith"—this kind of spiritual sixth sense—is founded on "a certain connaturality" of all the baptized "with divine realities, and a wisdom which enables them to grasp those realities intuitively"; he also twice insists that this "sense" in no way depends on the ability to "find words to explain that faith" nor the "wherewithal to give them [divine realities] precise expression" (EG 119). It thus relativizes a certain hierarchy between an elite of "knowers" and an "ignorant" people and emphasizes the common life of the baptized. This is also expressed in the unprecedented link he establishes from the outset between the "sense of faith" and the call to evangelization given to all "missionary disciples" by the Spirit whose "sanctifying power" is at work in all the baptized (EG 119 and 120).

I hypothesize that in the history of Christianity, synodality—the "path" that, according to Pope Francis,[17] "God expects of the Church of the third millennium"—is manifesting itself as a "constitutive element of the Church" precisely at a time when the people of God is confronted, perhaps for the first time, with an ever-increasing diversity of charisms and, at the cultural level, with a world that has become "polyhedral." This is the image proposed by Pope Francis, who replaces the metaphor of the "sphere" (well known thanks to the terrestrial globe) with that of the "polyhedron." More difficult to visualize, this three-dimensional geometric object is made up of many-sided surfaces. It therefore reflects the confluence of many diverse elements, which nevertheless retain in it their originality.[18] Only synodality, then, can manage and overcome the inevitable misunderstandings, confusions, and conflicts, and thus keep alive the reality of the church's "prophetic ministry" (*munus propheticum*) "in belief" (*in credendo*): on the path, always to be taken again, toward

[17] See Address Commemorating the Fiftieth Anniversary of the Institution of the Synod of Bishops, October 17, 2015, https://www.vatican.va/content/francesco/en/speeches/2015/october/documents/papa-francesco_20151017_50-anniversario-sinodo.html.

[18] See *Evangelii Gaudium* 234–37.

an experienced brother- and sisterhood, of which "consensus" (*consensus Ecclesiae*) is the core, not imposed authoritatively or "from outside" (as was often the case during the second, post-Gregorian millennium), but by receiving what the Holy Spirit actually gives to the faithful.

As a constitutive element of the church, synodality can therefore be founded on the participation of the people of God in Christ's "prophetic ministry," provided that we understand the church's itinerant status in history—on the path of equality for all toward brother- and sisterhood, as explained above—as an essential condition for the exercise of this prophetic ministry, which belongs to all. Only an understanding of synodality as an essential aspect of the church's nature can take it beyond the classical framework of a characteristic that belongs only to "sacred" ministers.

## The Synodality of the People of God as the Most Appropriate Framework for Interpreting Ordained Ministry

This brings us to the ministerial side of Pope Francis's thesis: "Synodality, as a constitutive element of the Church, offers us the most appropriate interpretative framework for understanding the hierarchical ministry itself."

It is this aspect of synodality that has caused the most concern among a good number of bishops and priests, and, let's face it, has provoked considerable resistance from certain parts of God's people. This is understandable, for it would be naive to think that the establishment of a true synodality of all the baptized would not affect the *way* in which "hierarchical ministry" is exercised and understood. It is therefore important to understand what this second side of Francis's thesis really means.

1. To this end, we return once again to the prophetic ministry of the people of God, as interpreted by number 12 of *Lumen Gentium*. The constitution not only recognizes the special "characteristic" or property of the people of God, namely the "universal consensus [*consensus universalis*] in matters of faith and morals"—"from the bishops to the last of the faithful" (§1)—and the diversity of "gifts" (*charismata*), whether they "be very remarkable or more simple and

widely diffused" (§2). It also addresses the constitutive role of authority, referring in *both* paragraphs to the oldest text in the New Testament, 1 Thessalonians. The first paragraph situates the magisterium within the "entire people's supernatural sense of the faith." The reason for this can be found in 1 Thessalonians, to which *Lumen Gentium* 12 §1 makes reference: "And for this reason we too give thanks to God unceasingly, that, in receiving the word of God from hearing us, you received not a human word but, as it truly is, the word of God, which is now at work in you who believe" (1 Thess 2:13).

The most elementary and dogmatically necessary function of the apostolic ministry within the whole people of God and its sense of faith is therefore to make it possible to hear the Word of God himself in human words. In this capacity, the apostolic ministry is "endowed with the authority of Christ," an expression used in chapter III of the constitution (LG 25).

The second paragraph also refers to the First Letter to the Thessalonians. It is not enough to ensure that the Word of God is heard in human words, which is the task of the preaching and teaching mission. The ministry also presides over the discernment of charisms, which, even if constantly threatened by the occultation and distortion of the Spirit's manifestations, must remain the work of the whole ecclesial community. That's precisely what *Lumen Gentium* 12 §2 retains from 1 Thessalonians (see 1 Thess 5:12, 19-21) when it attributes "especially" (*speciatim*) to "those who have charge over the church" the authority of the judgment of authenticity (*iudicium de eorum genuitate et ordinato exercitio*) that is, for Paul, the responsibility of the entire community: "Do not quench the Spirit. Do not despise prophetic utterances. Test everything; retain what is good" (1 Thess 5:19-21).

While the first paragraph of *Lumen Gentium* 12 retains the post-Gregorian language of the "sacred" and speaks of being "guided by the sacred magisterium" (*sub ductu sacri magisterii*), the second refers to "those who have charge over the church," taking the functional and verbal term *praesunt* from the First Letter to the Thessalonians: "We ask you, brothers, to respect those . . . who are over you [*proistamenous hymōn*] in the Lord" (1 Thess 5:12). Number 25 of the constitution, which deals with the preaching and teaching mission, should be read in conjunction with the section on the prophetic ministry of the people of God (LG 12); it avoids the canonical term "sacred power" (*potestas sacra*) and uses instead the Gospel-rooted term "authority" (*auctoritas*), while number 32, quoted at the beginning on the equal dignity of all the baptized, combines the two sets of language. Criticized above, the ambivalence of the link between sacrality and the exercise of power in the church seems to have led, in recent Roman documents, to the abandonment of the vocabulary of *potestas sacra*: neither the text of the International Theological Commission on "Synodality in the Life and Mission of the Church," nor the Apostolic Constitution *Episcopalis Communio* on the Synod of Bishops (2018) uses this term; they prefer the term "authority."[19]

2. The "understanding of hierarchical ministry" sought by Pope Francis in his double thesis becomes clearer if we situate it *within* the framework sketched out by *Lumen Gentium* 12 and place it on the *way* that leads from the principled equality of all the baptized (*sensus fidei fidelium*) to their sister- and brotherhood and which, thanks to synodality as a constitutive dimension of the people of God, integrates the charismatic diversity of all. Within this synodality, as the "journeying together" of all, this ministry plays a specific role, and, as we have shown, a constitutive and non-delegable one: by enabling, in the exchange of words that are always human, the listening to the Word of God, and thus summoning the prophetic-synodal church, while ensuring its link with the emerging church (in a diachronic relationship) and with all the particular churches (in a synchronic relationship).[20] The Word of God has the unique ability to inspire genuine listening in the believer, which is always a stereophonic listening: listening to the voice of the other (especially the voices of the poorest) and the cry of creation, listening to the "inner master" (to use St. Augustine's magnificent expression, which refers to the conscience or heart) and, in all this, listening to the voice of God. I will come back to this in the next two chapters.

[19] See "Synodality in the Life and Mission of the Church" 16, 17, etc.; Pope Francis, Constitution *Episcopalis Communio* 2, https://www.vatican.va/content/francesco/en/apost_constitutions/documents/papa-francesco_costituzione-ap_20180915_episcopalis-communio.html.

[20] At this point, the foundation of synodality *and* ministry—as constitutive dimensions of the people of God—must integrate the concept of "tradition," explicated in chapter II of the Dogmatic Constitution on Divine Revelation (*Dei Verbum*), as does the Preparatory Document for the Synod 2021–2024 in nos. 12–14. I will come back to this in the final chapter of this book.

There is, moreover, a close relationship between this listening to the Word of God in the concert of human voices and creation, on the one hand, and thanksgiving, the *Eucharistia*, which responds to the *Euangelion*, the Gospel of grace, on the other. *Lumen Gentium* 10 and the beginning of *Lumen Gentium* 12 bring into play the "spiritual worship" (Rom 12:1) or "priestly ministry" of all believers. Similarly, the paragraph on multiform charisms urges the faithful to respond to these gifts "with thanksgiving and consolation" (LG 12 §2). Corresponding to this relationship between the community's prophetic vocation and its eucharistic response, the link established by tradition between the ministry of the Word and the presiding of the Eucharist can boast a beautiful "coherence." Finally, the ministry of government (*munus regendi*) is also rooted in the prophetic ministry (*munus propheticum*) of the people of God, as is made clear in the same paragraph on charisms, which entrusts "those who have charge over the church" with the judgment of authenticity, without, however, nullifying the discernment of the communities and correcting it extrinsically *a posteriori*.

It would be an illusion to believe that political patterns and habits do not play a role in the synodal process, a question I will address in the final chapter. It must remain clear, however, that whatever the concrete implementation of the synodal process, it is meant to respect the charismatic foundation of the church in its ever-growing diversity, the "sense of faith" (*sensus fidei*) oriented toward the fraternal/sororal consensus of all—even if this "sense" often remains at an intuitive stage (see EG 119)—and the mission of the church's magisterium and government within the constitutively synodal dimension of the church.

It has to be admitted that this new integration and reorganization of the data of Vatican II reveals the great fragility of the ecclesial subject, a fragility that, as in our democratic societies, appears first and foremost as the fragility of many ordained ministers. For this reason, Pope Francis introduces two experiential metaphors to illustrate the conversion discussed below: the vertical metaphor of an inverted pyramid—"in this Church, . . . the top is located below the base"[21]—and the horizontal metaphor of a common path offering

[21] Pope Francis, Address Commemorating the Fiftieth Anniversary of the Institution of the Synod of Bishops.

several positions—"So the Bishop is called to lead his flock by 'walking in front of them, showing them the way, showing them the path; walking in their midst, to strengthen them in unity; walking behind them, to make sure no one gets left behind but especially, never to lose the scent of the People of God in order to find new roads'" (*Episcopalis Communio* 5).

I dare to hope that this brief overview will help to reassure readers who are worried, or even anxious, not to lose the "Catholic" sense of ministerial authority in the progressive "synodalization" of the church. Let us repeat: for the reasons stated, ordained ministry is as constitutive of the people of God as synodality, but it is undoubtedly invited to transform itself in practice and on a theoretical level. For, as I stated at the beginning of this hypothesis-like chapter, the architecture of the church, fixed by the two Vatican Councils but often frozen, cannot fail to understood anew if Pope Francis's instructions are actually put into practice. We have yet to present this question.

## From Primacy through Collegiality to Synodality

When we look back on the three steps we've just taken—the recognition of the equality of all the baptized, the synodal constitution of the church that follows, and the place that the ordained ministry must find within it—the evolution of the church's self-understanding on its journey through human history reveals a new coherence that challenges both the spiritual life of the people of God and its way of thinking about itself.

1. Let us start with a few brief historical reminders. It may come as a surprise today that, against the resistance of a significant minority, the First Vatican Council (1869–70)—which was interrupted by the Franco-Prussian War and never completed—anticipated the debate on the Petrine ministry and gave precedence to its constitution *Pastor Aeternus* (1870) "on the institution, the permanence, the nature, and the force of the sacred primacy of the Roman Pontiff and his infallible teaching office,"[22] while its constitution on the church was already under discussion. This can obviously be explained by the context of the time. Faced with a triumphalist European modernity

[22] This is summarized in *Lumen Gentium* 18 §2.

and in an anti-Protestant, anti-Gallican context,[23] it consisted of presenting the Petrine ministry as the ultimate bulwark of a church that found itself set in opposition to "the gates of hell" (see Matt 16:18).

Vatican II again presents this doctrine to all the faithful (*firmiter credendam rursus proponit*) in the now-global context of the *universal church* and completes it—"following in the steps of the first Vatican Council" and "continuing with this same undertaking"—with the doctrine of episcopal collegiality (LG 18). The main difficulty then lies in articulating these two doctrines (LG 22 and 23 and the "Preliminary explanatory note" by the council's Doctrinal Commission). After the Second World War, the ecumenical consciousness born outside Catholicism also developed within the Roman Catholic Church and manifested itself in the council's fundamental decision to give *precedence* to the equality of all the baptized over the hierarchical structure, without consistently applying this decision or detaching it from the sacral framework of the post-Gregorian church.

The convocation of the Synod on Synodality takes place in a new context: according to Pope Francis, the world and the universal church are going through an "epochal change"[24] in which the tension between a globalized world and the diversity of its cultures can no longer be understood using a spherical model but instead should be pictured as a polyhedron.[25] A "new threshold" must be crossed and a new beginning made, this time "in the wake of Vatican II" (International Theological Commission 9). The synodalization of the church initiated by Pope Francis coincides, moreover, with the global growth of the ecumenical movement, which requires a similar change of outlook and can no longer be viewed solely from a Roman perspective, but asks all partners to "walk *together* on the path towards full communion" (9; emphasis mine).

[23] For the historical background to this decision, see Klaus Schatz, *Vaticanum I. 1869–1870*, Vol. II: Von der Eröffnung bis zur Konstitution *"Dei filius"* (Ferdinand Schöningh, 1993), 197–205, and Christoph Theobald, "Première Constitution sur l'Église du Christ *Pastor aeternus* du concile de Vatican I," in Bernard Sesboüé and Christoph Theobald, *Histoire des dogmes*, vol. 4: *La Parole du salut* (Desclée, 1996), 316–44.

[24] Pope Francis, Address to the Fifth Convention of the Italian Church, Florence, November 10, 2015, https://www.vatican.va/content/francesco/en/speeches/2015/november/documents/papa-francesco_20151110_firenze-convegno-chiesa-italiana.html.

[25] See *Evangelii Gaudium* 234–37.

2. The conciliar texts and Pope Francis's statements seem to presuppose ongoing doctrinal development. But in reality, the church's internal conflicts clearly show that both the ecclesiology of Vatican II and the synodal ecclesiology of Pope Francis operate a change of perspective known as a "paradigm shift," which is not self-evident and which concerns—each time and on a new scale—the whole ecclesial architecture. This means that the church's synodality, if recognized as a constitutive dimension of the people of God, brings with it a new understanding of episcopal collegiality and papal primacy. This change of perspective is at least sketched out in the pope's address commemorating the fiftieth anniversary of the institution of the Synod of Bishops (2015) and in his apostolic constitution *Episcopalis Communio* (2018).[26]

Let us start with episcopal collegiality, as defined at Vatican II.

In its opening paragraphs, the apostolic constitution *Episcopalis Communio* (= EC) describes the link between episcopal collegiality and the institution of the Synod of Bishops (1–4), before explaining in the next two paragraphs the *principle* already mentioned of the change of perspective: "Underpinning this work of renewal [of the Synod of Bishops] must be the firm conviction that all Bishops are appointed for the service of the holy People of God, *to whom they themselves belong through the sacrament of Baptism*" (5; emphasis mine). The two issues concerned proceed by induction, dealing first with the episcopal ministry in the local church, then with the Synod of Bishops, each time combining a doctrinal formulation with reference to experience, in line with what has already been said of a new interest in "spiritual practice."

As far as the bishop is concerned, the text maintains a *bipolar tension*:

> *It is certainly true*, as the Second Vatican Council teaches, that "when Bishops engage in teaching, in communion with the Roman Pontiff, they deserve respect from all, as the witnesses of divine and catholic truth; the faithful must agree with the judgment of their Bishop on faith and morals, which he delivers

[26] Text at https://www.vatican.va/content/francesco/en/apost_constitutions/documents/papa-francesco_costituzione-ap_20180915_episcopalis-communio.html.

> in the name of Christ; they must give it their adherence with religious assent of the mind." *But it is also true* that "for every Bishop the life of the Church and life in the Church is the condition for exercising his mission to teach."[27]

The same constitutive tension is found at the level of the synod of bishops as an expression of episcopal collegiality and is explained here using the ecclesial and political concept of "*representation*." Still quoting John Paul II (*Pastores Gregis* 58), the following section thus asserts: "The Bishops assembled in Synod *represent* in the first place their own Churches" (EC 6; emphasis mine). However, within each constitutive tension, the emphasis is on the link to be effectively experienced between those who collegially represent their churches and those whom they must represent, an experience that consists, for both the bishop and the Synod of Bishops, of learning and spiritual listening: "Although structurally it is essentially configured as an episcopal body, this does not mean that the Synod exists separately from the rest of the faithful. On the contrary, it is a suitable instrument to *give voice to the entire People of God*, specifically via the Bishops, established by God as 'authentic guardians, interpreters and witnesses of the faith of the whole Church'" (EC 6; emphasis mine).

What is outlined in this text remains open to further clarification, no doubt as a result of the synodal process. Other texts of the Second Vatican Council should be reread in this context, which is not the place to do so here: number 23 of the Dogmatic Constitution on the Church, the Decree on the Eastern Catholic Churches and, of course, the Decree on Ecumenism—texts which, precisely, highlight the historical diversity and plurality of the particular and local churches and which root their diversity, at least in part, in the charismatic structure of the church and in the mutual exchange of gifts (LG 13 §3, cf. 1 Pet 4:10).[28] "Representation" (*representatio*), both personal and collegial, and the related listening and learning made possible

[27] EC 5. The internal quotations are from LG 25 and Pope John Paul II's post-synodal apostolic exhortation *Pastores Gregis* 28.

[28] On the relationship between collegiality and synodality from an Orthodox and Roman Catholic perspective, see Amphilochios Miltos, *Collégialité et synodalité: Vers une compréhension commune entre catholiques et orthodoxes*, Unam sanctam, Nouvelle série, 7 (Éditions du Cerf, 2019).

by the Holy Spirit—on the road to a *consensus universalis*—thus become much more complex and (in my terminology) "stereophonic"; we will have to come back to this later.

3. Finally, the Petrine ministry, too, is affected by the paradigm shift brought about by the emphasis on synodality, as Pope Francis emphasizes in his address commemorating the fiftieth anniversary of the institution of the Synod of Bishops as "the urgent need to think about 'a conversion of the papacy.'" Already Vatican II summarized the teaching of Vatican I in a succinct formula—"The Roman Pontiff, as the successor of Peter, is the perpetual and visible source and foundation of the unity both of the bishops and of the whole company of the faithful"—and associated it with the analogous statement that the individual bishops, however, "are the visible source and foundation of unity in their own particular churches" (LG 23 §1). In his speech, Francis repeats this principle, but he points to the "listening process conducted at every level of the Church's life":

> The Synod process culminates in listening to the Bishop of Rome,[29] who is called to speak as "pastor and teacher of all Christians" [*Pastor Aeternus*, chap. 4], not on the basis of his personal convictions but as the supreme witness to the *fides totius Ecclesiae*, "the guarantor of the obedience and the conformity of the Church to the will of God, to the Gospel of Christ, and to the Tradition of the Church."

However, the hierarchical metaphor of the summit and a famous fifteenth-century formula corresponding to it—"with Peter and under Peter" (*cum Petro et sub Petro*)—are immediately "undermined" from a biblical perspective[30] and, through the image of an inverted pyramid, subjected to a "distancing effect."

[29] Translations of the text interpret the genitive either as *genetivus objectivus* (all listen to the bishop of Rome), or as *genetivus subjectivus* (it is the bishop of Rome who listens to all, before he pronounces).

[30] "Let us never forget this! For the disciples of Jesus, yesterday, today, and always, the only authority is the authority of service, the only power is the power of the cross. As the Master tells us: 'You know that the rulers of the Gentiles lord it over them, and their great men exercise authority over them. It shall not be so among you; but whoever would be great among you must be your servant, and whoever would be first among you must be your slave' (*Mt* 20:25-27). *It shall not be so among you*: in this expression we touch the heart of the mystery of the

The paradigm shift is outlined. In the background is the shift, already made by *Lumen Gentium*, from a vision of the church unilaterally centered on Christ and oblivious to the Spirit, toward an understanding where the Holy Spirit and spiritual experience—in technical terms a "practical pneumatology"—play a decisive role. According to Vatican II, the people of God forms a "complex reality comprising [*coalescit*] a human and a divine element" (LG 8 §1): if "the social structure of the church serve[s] the Spirit of Christ who vivifies it, in the building up of the body" (LG 8 §1; cf. Eph 4:16), then Christ's presence cannot be fulfilled in a hierarchically fixed set of roles, but must always allow itself to be subjected to a "distancing effect."

Pope Francis wished to make this spiritual effect of distancing possible within the people of God by introducing the constitutive difference—between its synodal representation and those who are represented—into a "dynamic of stereophonic listening" by all, and by understanding the "visible social structure" of the synod as a "process."

❖ ❖ ❖

In this second chapter, we have ventured deep into the current debates sparked by the convocation of the Synod on Synodality. We have tried to take account of the concerns raised by this convocation. Let us not lose sight of the fact that everything we have just explained and developed on a doctrinal and theological level is part of an "enlightened pragmatism"; I wanted to explore its spiritual or pneumatological dimensions (to use the language of theologians): it's by actually journeying together, without fear of our differences and conflicts, that we learn from each other and can gradually enter into true "stereophonic listening," enabling us to hear God's "voice" today. However, this experience, both individual and collective, bears lasting fruit only if it is accompanied by rereading and even rethinking. On a more practical level, I will come back to this in the next chapter. First, I want to bring out the historical side, which is particularly decisive for understanding the current conflicts surrounding

Church, and we receive the enlightenment necessary to understand our hierarchical service" (Address Commemorating the Fiftieth Anniversary of the Institution of the Synod of Bishops).

synodalization in the Roman Catholic Church and for helping to overcome them.

We have therefore briefly reviewed the history of the Latin Church's understanding, going back to the two Vatican Councils and even further back to the Gregorian reform of the eleventh century. We have observed a kind of inversion movement: the ecclesiology of the second millennium culminated in 1870 with the declaration of the jurisdictional and magisterial "power" of the supreme pontiff. At Vatican II and under Pope Francis, however, a reverse movement of "incarnation" began to take shape, attempting to reach out, in ever finer and more concrete ways, to Christian and ecclesial existence on the ground: with the definition of an episcopal collegiality in connection with the plurality of particular churches and, today, with the insistence on the baptismal equality of all the faithful and on the synodality of the entire people of God, which involves all in its advance. Far from abolishing what has been learned by those who have gone before us and which has been acquired and forms the normative heritage of the people of God, the new experiences of the baptized on the road of history, provoked by changes in times, invite us to take another look at the "architecture" of the church. We need to realize that the church cannot be confined to the buildings of the past (which, of course, are always a joy to inhabit), but it must be transformed into the lightweight "tent" of God's dwelling in the midst of a "pilgrim and missionary People of God" (PD 1).

However, the history of human beings is marked by moments of great acceleration. This is undoubtedly the case today. At the same time, uncertainty about the future is growing: We don't know what kind of world and what kind of church will "emerge" from the current crises. In this trying situation, we can be guided by Pope Francis's four principles of social coexistence, made explicit in his exhortation *Evangelii Gaudium*, especially the first one which affirms the superiority of time to space: "Giving priority to time means *being concerned about initiating processes rather than possessing spaces*" (EG 223; emphasis mine). The convocation of the Synod on Synodality is a response to this principle. It is therefore the processual form of synodality that will be dealt with in the next chapter.

# Chapter 3

# From Celebrating Exceptional Events to Learning New Ways of Listening to Each Other and Making Decisions

Announced in May 2021 and officially launched in Rome on October 10 of the same year, the Synod on Synodality concluded on October 27, 2024. Understanding its biblical roots and Pope Francis's synodal vision against the backdrop of the ecclesiology of the Second Vatican Council and the great tradition is certainly enlightening and can help us to live the process underway with greater zest and lucidity and reap some of the fruits. That's what the first two chapters were designed to encourage, while also listening to the concerns of some and the skepticism of others. But coherence of a vision, be it biblical or pontifical, is one thing; another is actual experience, with its surprises, its bogging down, and its revivals.

Presenting and analyzing this ongoing experience is the aim of this chapter, in which I would like to flesh out the spiritual practice and "enlightened pragmatism" referred to several times in the preceding pages.

In particular, we need to measure the pastoral implications of extending the process over time and the ambition to bring about a profound transformation of the ecclesial "culture," introducing new ways of listening to one another and making decisions. Clearly, this new style is expressed in different ways in the world's major cultural and continental spheres. This sets in motion another aspect of ecclesial architecture already mentioned in chapter 2, namely the presence of the universal church in a plurality of particular churches, each of which is truly the church of God on the spot, and all of which are in mutual relationship with the church of Rome and its bishop, who at the same time exercises the Petrine ministry. This "polyhedral" differentiation of the churches—to use Pope Francis's image, which replaces the metaphor of the "sphere" with that of the "polyhedron"—obviously raises the question of their "consensus"; this has already been discussed. This major challenge was perceived by the Second Vatican Council, even though it took place in a still relatively homogeneous cultural universe. But for the first time, the council fathers reflected on their way of proceeding and their way of agreeing, putting the spotlight not on the content of Christian doctrine, but on the relationship between those who proclaim the Gospel—in relation to Scripture and the great tradition—and the many recipients of this proclamation, of course differently situated—an interest they called "pastoral" or "missionary." We shall see that the Synod on Synodality reactivated this interest, while at the same time extending the conciliar mode of agreement—between the churches and their bishops—to the whole of the faithful.

To identify these new facets of the current synodal process, we first need to take stock of the various stages of the "journeying together" (*syn-hodos*), already completed or still to be completed, and then, after analyzing the issues we have just identified, we need to take a closer look at the concrete desiderata of the people of God, from the smallest ecclesial units up to the universal assemblies that met in Rome in October 2023 and October 2024.

This initial assessment will enable us to say whether or not the complex web of questions that emerged during the early twenty-first century is beginning to be untangled.

## Journeying Together and Stops Along the Way

To present the current synodal process, we need to briefly go through its stages, show its institutional structure and, above all, become aware of its spiritual dynamics.

1. The various phases of the process are well known: following its convocation by Pope Francis on October 10, 2021, the synod began at the diocesan level, inviting the local churches to rely on a team to help

parishes and movements get together and answer the very simple questions posed by the synod's General Secretariat in Rome; I will come back to this in the final part of this chapter. The first novelty is that this "consultation," a classic in the synodal tradition, took place for the first time in a synodal form. The real impact of this step, accompanied by methodological advice to which I shall also return, is difficult to measure, not least because of the huge differences among local churches: What do dioceses such as Paris or Los Angeles have in common with a church in Amazonia?

In any case, before the summer of 2022, the diocesan syntheses were collected by the bishops' conferences and compiled into a national synthesis. This was discussed at an ecclesial assembly, bringing together the bishops of a country or region with their flocks, and then approved by the episcopate alone. Did any filtering or censoring of opinions occur? It's hard to say now. Historians will get to the bottom of it, and I will come back to it at the end of this chapter when I present some of the texts and their contents.

Thus, in August 2022, the General Secretariat of the synod received the syntheses of 112 of the 114 bishops' conferences and all 15 Eastern Catholic Churches, in addition to the reflections of 17 of the 23 dicasteries of the Roman Curia, as well as those of religious superiors, institutes of consecrated life and societies of apostolic life, associations and movements of the lay faithful; in short, quite a considerable group of institutions and individuals. It is therefore easy to understand the enthusiasm with which those in charge of the secretariat spoke at their press conference on August 26, 2022, of "a dialogue unprecedented in the history of the Church, not only for the quantity of responses received or the number of people involved . . ., but also for the quality of participation."[1]

This is the main source of the Working Document for the Continental Stage, published on October 24 of the same year under the biblical title: *"Enlarge the Space of Your Tent" (Is 54:2)*. At the same time, each particular and diocesan church was invited to reread this new document and to hear not only its own voice but also and above all

[1] All the documents cited in this chapter can be found on the website of the General Secretariat of the Synod: https://www.synod.va/en/resources/documents.html.

those of other local churches. This is yet another novelty in the process, the aim of which is to gradually broaden the churches' ability to listen to what the Spirit is saying to each and every one of them. Once again, it is difficult to assess the extent to which this new instruction was actually put into practice.

Between February and March 2023, seven continental assemblies met in the Middle East, Europe, Asia, North America, Latin America with the Caribbean, Africa with Madagascar, and Oceania: representative "ecclesial assemblies" of the people of God, made up of bishops, priests, and other members of the faithful, including consecrated men and women, all of whom were tasked with rereading the Working Document together, identifying "resonances" within their particular contexts, pointing out the continent's specific "tensions" and "issues," and formulating priorities, recurring themes, and calls to action (Working Document for the Continental Stage 106). Each assembly recorded the fruits of its deliberations in a final document.

Thus ended the first phase of the synodal process. The second phase began on June 20, 2023, with the publication of the *Instrumentum Laboris* (= IL) for the first of the universal assemblies to be held between October 4 and 29, 2023, in Rome.

2. Under current law, which dates back to the institution of the Synod of Bishops by Paul VI in 1965, it is the pope who convenes the synod. In addition to the fact that Francis had already celebrated several synods—the one on the vocation and mission of the family (in two sessions); the one on young people, faith, and vocational discernment; and the one on Amazonia—a series of texts already cited gradually gave shape to his conviction that synodality is the "path" that "God expects of the Church of the third millennium": above all his now-famous address on October 17, 2015, commemorating the fiftieth anniversary of the institution of the Synod of Bishops and his apostolic constitution *Episcopalis Communio* on the Synod of Bishops (2018), a document that redraws the legal framework of this institution.

Its main body is the General Secretariat of the Synod, directly dependent on the pope, headed in his name by the secretary general (Cardinal Mario Grech) and two undersecretaries, one of whom is a woman (Sister Nathalie Becquart), and, in its important decisions, linked to a permanent council, elected by the previous assembly, the Ordinary Council of the Synod. Four specific commissions accompany the current process: the Theological Commission, the Methodological Commission, the Spirituality Commission, and the Communications Commission. As a member of the Theological Commission, I can testify to the fraternal/sororal—that is, quite simply synodal—style adopted by the Synod Secretariat.

Other institutions came into being as a result of the new perspectives of the process: diocesan and national teams that made possible and accompanied the synodal form of consultation of the people of God and, within the continental councils of bishops' conferences, specific bodies that set up the continental assemblies. These have revealed a wide variety of functions, depending not only on the very specific cultural situation of each continent but also on its history. Latin America already has a long continental experience, dating back to the Medellín assembly (1968) and even well before the council (1955). Being a minority and widely dispersed, the churches of Oceania are also accustomed to meeting together. This is more difficult for the older European churches, which are certainly in crisis, but are aware of their particular "personality" and are perhaps too close to the church of Rome to "dare" to take charge of their continental specificity within the communion of the world's churches. However, at the continental assembly in Prague (February 5–12, 2023), a fresh start was made, with another assembly set for 2025![2] For its part, the General Secretariat of the Synod took particular care to maintain links with each of these continental assemblies, with visits by its secretary or one of the undersecretaries, as well as providing methodological assistance and setting up important training courses led by some members of the various commissions.

Two important institutional decisions were taken during the process. The first, which has gone almost unnoticed, is the change of name of the secretariat in autumn 2022: since 1965, it has been known as the Secretariat of the Synod of Bishops, and it is now called the General Secretariat of the Synod. This change is explained by a second one concerning the composition of the Roman assembly. The official communiqué from the General Secretariat of the Synod states: "On 17 April 2023, the Holy Father approved the extension of participation in the Synodal Assembly to 'non-bishops' (priests, deacons,

[2] See Arnaud Join-Lambert, "Une nouvelle étape pour l'Église catholique: L'Asemblée continentale de Prague," *Études* 4305 (June 2023): 79–90.

consecrated men and women, lay men and women). This choice is in continuity with the progressive appropriation of *the constitutive synodal dimension of the church* and the consequent understanding of the institutions through which it is exercised" (emphasis mine). Our second chapter, in particular the few developments on the church's synodal constitution as the most appropriate framework for interpreting ordained ministry, helps to measure what is at stake in this decision by Pope Francis.

Drawing on the history of the Synod of Bishops, instituted by Pope Paul VI, the Secretariat's press release gives the reasons for this change: "It is in this perspective that one must understand the Holy Father's decision to maintain the specifically episcopal nature of the Assembly convened in Rome, while *at the same time* not limiting its composition to bishops alone by admitting a certain number of non-bishops as full Members." The following clarification, which argues for a better integration of the consultative phase and the Roman assembly, is subtle:

> It is therefore in the *role/function of memory* that the presence of non-bishops is included, and *not in that of representation*. In this way, the specifically episcopal nature of the Synodal Assembly is not affected, but rather is confirmed. This is shown first of all by the numerical ratio between bishops and non-bishops, the latter being less than 25% of the total number of Assembly members. But above all this is shown by the way in which the non-bishops are appointed: in fact, they are not elected by some *demos* or *coetus*, whose representation they would take on, but are appointed by the Holy Father on the proposal of the bodies through which episcopal collegiality is realised at the level of continental areas, rooting their presence in the exercise of pastoral discernment. (Emphasis mine.)

To this restrictive statement (which in no way detracts from the effective status of all assembly members), the press release adds: "The Assembly will have the opportunity to reflect on its own concrete experience with a view to formulating proposals on how to proceed in the future." The apparently clear distinction between the register of memory and that of representation is not without its problems, for we must ask whether "non-bishops" (who are not delegates of the one who called them, the pope) do not also have a function of ecclesial "representation," a concept which indeed requires further clarification.

Two further details concerning the participation of non-bishops are worth mentioning: "It is requested that 50% of them be women." They will therefore make up just over 10 percent of the members of the assembly. Admittedly, this is not a large number. All things considered, however, these women form a significant group, especially considering that their participation as full members is a historic first. The text adds: "and that the presence of young people also be emphasized." The other clarification concerns the criteria for appointing the 70 "non-bishops": "In selecting them, account is taken not only of their general culture and prudence, but also of their knowledge, both theoretical and practical, as well as their participation in various capacities in the synod process. As members, they have the right to vote." It should be noted that we're talking here about a certain "elite," excluding the so-called "poor" (whom we will, however, talk about), and that the identification, by the continental assemblies, of those who will be on the list of persons proposed for the pope's choice is relatively non-transparent.

Compared with national and continental assemblies, and in view of the apostolic constitution *Episcopalis Communio*, this new regulation represents a significant evolution. For continental assemblies were "*ecclesial* assemblies," bringing together the baptized and, among them, consecrated persons, priests, and bishops; assemblies, however, were always followed by meetings of bishops alone from a country or continent (thus maintaining the specificity of episcopal collegiality). Admittedly, these "episcopal assemblies" did not modify the final documents of their "ecclesial assemblies" but received and commented on them—a procedure not without its share of confusion. In any case, the new legislation of April 17, 2023, attempts to avoid them by situating the "non-episcopal" presence *within* the synodal assembly of bishops, perhaps at the cost of a lack of satisfactory clarity as to the articulation between the synodality of the church and episcopal collegiality. This question, it should be remembered, has already been addressed in the previous chapter.

3. These few elements of institutional regulation introduce significant changes but should not overshadow the breadth of the process

underway, a few decisive markers of which should now be recalled. Too little attention has been paid to the indications given in the aforementioned Preparatory Document on the dimensions and different levels of "journeying together," and to the *Vade mecum* drawn up by the Methodological Commission.

The Preparatory Document recalls that the church's synodality comprises "two different perspectives, which are strongly interconnected." The first concerns the internal life of particular churches, the relationships among the individuals who make them up and among the communities of different kinds (including religious and monastic communities), including ecumenical relations with members of other Christian churches (PD 28).

The second perspective looks at how God's people interact with the whole of humanity and how Christians live out their relationships with believers of other religions and with people far removed from the faith, as well as with specific social environments and groups and their institutions (PD 29). At the end of this chapter, and in a future assessment, we must ask ourselves whether these two views—"internal" and "external"—of a single, constitutive missionary ecclesial reality have really been honored.

The same question will arise with respect to the three levels of synodality, already distinguished in the International Theological Commission's "Synodality in the Life and Mission of the Church" (no. 70):

- the level of the style with which the Church ordinarily lives and works, which expresses its nature as the people of God that journeys together and gathers in assembly "summoned by the Lord Jesus in the power of the Holy Spirit to proclaim the Gospel." This style is realized through "the community listening to the Word and celebrating the Eucharist, the brotherhood of communion and the co-responsibility and participation of the whole People of God in its life and mission, on all levels and distinguishing between various ministries and roles";
- the level of ecclesial structures and processes, determined also from the theological and canonical point of view, in which the synodal nature of the church is expressed in an institutional way at the local, regional, and universal levels;

- the level of synodal processes and events in which the church is convoked by "the competent authority," according to specific procedures determined by the ecclesiastical discipline (PD 27).

The current process focuses on the first of these three levels. Synodal structures have always existed in the Catholic Church (second level). The Second Vatican Council gave particular prominence to the "presbyteral council"—the "senate of the bishop"—and placed alongside it a "diocesan pastoral council," both of which operate on the principle of "representation." Other councils, such as the "diocesan economic council" or the "college of consultors," which intervenes in particular when an episcopal see becomes vacant, are also important; and we have already mentioned national and continental bodies in all their diversity. Synodal life is by no means nonexistent in the Catholic Church.

Yet all these structures are in danger of losing their vitality, especially when it becomes difficult to renew their membership, as the churches of Western Europe suffer from chronic shrinkage and, due to sexual abuse, a significant loss of credibility. For this reason, and in a very lucid manner, the Preparatory Document insists on the articulation of the three levels as a condition of the church's credibility: "In fact, if it is not embodied in structures and processes, the style of synodality easily degrades from the level of intentions and desires to that of rhetoric, while processes and events, if they are not animated by an adequate style, turn out to be empty formalities" (PD 27).

In the next chapter, I will return to this delicate and difficult balance between the "spiritual" and "institutional" sides of the current synodal process, since the work of the Holy Spirit can never be reduced to either. But first, a word about the method (*met-hodos*) that has enabled us to experience the synodal breath in a concrete way, and not just a protocol or a rite: "spiritual dialogue," also known as "conversation in the Spirit."

This procedure was first presented in the *Vade mecum*, drawn up by the General Secretariat's Methodological Commission, and explained again in the *Instrumentum Laboris* for the first session (IL 32–40).[3] This

[3] This document can be found on the website of the General Secretariat of the Synod: https://www.synod.va/en/synodal-process/the-universal-phase/documents.html.

method, which has several variants, consists of giving each participant in a relatively small group (six or seven people maximum) the opportunity to express their views on a specific question, requiring each person to listen attentively and to enter, with an open mind and heart, into the world of the other. Once this first round has been completed, a moment of silence allows everyone to listen inwardly to what the other members have said that has resonated with them, astonished them, or raised new questions or challenged them—elements that can be freely shared in a second round. A further period of silence prepares participants for the exchange of ideas on what they should remember and pass on to the assembly, whether local, national, continental, or universal. This is the third round of spiritual conversation.

The form of "debate" is by no means excluded, and may even become necessary, when argumentation and "pros and cons" come into play to move from conversation to decision. But, let's face it, debate can easily turn into confrontation and power-grabbing, privileging some over others who are less adept at expressing themselves but who have a true spiritual sense, the "*sensus fidei*" referred to in the previous chapter. If, on the other hand, the debate takes place in a climate of spiritual conversation, it can be a great help in learning how to listen and how to speak in a way that is likely to advance a common feeling and intelligence about the questioning submitted for exchange.

Clearly, these "stops" along the way—at once local, national, continental, and, ultimately, universal—are situated on the daily journey of God's people. They are related to it, inviting us to remember the road we have traveled and helping us to navigate it, as in the account of the Acts of the Apostles commented on in the first chapter.

These communal "stops" are guided by basic questions. I mentioned them at the start of the book: With whom do we walk, and how do we live this experience day by day? The Preparatory Document summarizes them as follows: "How does this 'journeying together,' which takes place today on different levels (from the local level to the universal one), allow the Church to proclaim the Gospel in accordance with the mission entrusted to Her; and what steps does the Spirit invite us to take in order to grow as a synodal Church?" (PD 2 and 26).

The invitation to answer these questions by listening to one another obviously presupposes a climate of prayer and a slight ritualization, which all the texts and practices of the General Secretariat emphasize. It's a question of hearing what the Spirit is saying to the churches (see Rev 2:7); a listening—which I have called "stereophonic listening"—that involves reading the Scriptures and also the ancient rite of the enthronement of the Evangeliary to signify that it is Christ Jesus who presides over the assembly, and which culminates in the eucharistic thanksgiving.

4. When one considers the complexity of this process, the sequence of its various phases, its institutional structure, and, above all, its spiritual stakes, one cannot help but be aware of the extreme fragility of what has been undertaken and admire the courage shown by the person who convened this synod and those who are accompanying its realization. The questions I have formulated in this brief presentation are intended to draw attention to the fact that the outcome of the process is by no means guaranteed. Legitimate doubts may therefore be raised about its implementation in local churches and about the circulation of experiences among churches and at local, national, and continental levels. Some feel that the process is not just complex, but downright complicated; others are bothered by the inevitable wavering, accusing the organizers of treating Catholicism's proverbial canonical and doctrinal precision too lightly, thus joining the camp of worriers and skeptics discussed in the previous chapter.

The pedagogy of church reform developed by the General Secretariat will certainly have to be evaluated later. But we must recognize right now that the real fragility of the process stems from the fact that it appeals to the "pneumatological" or spiritual side of our existence and ecclesial being, and thus to the freedom and maturity of Christians and the capacity of communities to enter into spiritual practices (such as "conversation in the Spirit") that cannot be imposed. It's hardly surprising, then, that the first part of the *Instrumentum Laboris* of the first session ends with an invitation to formation:

> Bearing in mind the significance of conversation in the Spirit to animate the lived experience of the synodal Church, *formation in this method, and in particular of facilitators capable of accompanying communities in practising it, is perceived as a priority at all levels of ecclesial life* and for all the Baptised, starting with ordained

> Ministers in a spirit of co-responsibility and openness to different ecclesial vocations. Formation for conversation in the Spirit is formation to be a synodal Church. (IL 42)

The future will show whether the current Synod on Synodality will succeed in bringing about a profound transformation of "ecclesial culture," which remains its primary objective. To achieve this, it is not enough simply to describe what is happening. We also need to be aware of the conditions—and there are three of them—which, over and above what has already been said in the previous chapter on the critical and prospective reception of the ecclesiology of the Second Vatican Council, will enable us to make progress toward this ambitious goal.

## The Synod—From Event to Process

The first and undoubtedly most important condition is to remove from the synodal experience its character as a singular, exceptional event without trivializing it—which, let's face it, is what happened to most of the advisory/synodal bodies prompted by Vatican II. The distinction between the word "synod" and the more recent concept of "synodality" marks this move toward a constitutively synodal understanding of the church: the understanding of the church as a gathering of the baptized cannot be expressed only in exceptional, one-off events, but must also and above all be manifested at "the level of the style with which the Church ordinarily lives and works" (PD 27) on a daily basis, thus making her missionary presence in society credible.

While John Paul II's aforementioned post-synodal apostolic exhortation *Pastores Gregis* (2003) still regards the synod as an "event" (58), Pope Francis integrates it into a global "process" that includes *all dimensions of* the church and, above all, places each assembly in a series of several assemblies (EC 6). This is not just a process of consultation, as has already been noted, but a process of discernment aimed at a *consensus* of all as an expression of "common obedience to the Spirit of Christ" (EC 7), while understanding, adds Francis, that the *sensus fidei* must be distinguished "from the changing currents of public opinion." It is remarkable that—in the spirit of 1 Thessalonians (5:12,

19-21)[4] and developing the guidelines of *Episcopalis Communio*—it no longer reserves this process of discernment for the assembly of bishops but integrates it into the process of consultation of the whole people of God, precisely by having given this process a synodal form. This is clearly evident in the first phase of the synod, which is summarized at the beginning of its *Instrumentum Laboris*, inviting all to "engage in *ongoing* synodal discernment" (IL 6; emphasis mine).

The processual nature of synodality opens up a new relationship with *time*. It should be remembered here that the problem of the rhythm of ecclesial assemblies arose as early as the fifteenth century, under the pressure of reform that arose during the Great Schism, when Christendom had to emerge from the rivalry between three popes, each claiming legitimacy for himself. The decree *Frequens* of the Council of Constance (October 9, 1417) attempted to institute the regular convocation of councils by the pope (every five, then seven, then ten years). In the background was the need for permanent reform. After the Council of Basel (which began in 1431), the historical trend was to leave it up to the pope to discern the "favorable moment" (the *kairos*) for convening a council. The processual nature of the synod—"which is 'in some manner the image' of an Ecumenical Council" (EC 8)—does not deprive the pope of this prerogative. It does, however, lead to a different understanding of Christian temporality, insofar as all participants in the "journeying together" are now called upon to distinguish their own communal "favorable moments" (*kairoi*), on a local, national, and regional level. This "moment" is then divided, so to speak, into numerous *kairoi*, to be integrated into the universal discernment process. Realizing this is by no means self-evident; neither is the "dynamic of listening" mentioned above.

As long as the synod was seen as a one-off "event," this constitutive fragility of the synodal institution was not necessarily apparent. On the other hand, if we move from a simple consultation to a synodal consultation, the never-guaranteed transition to a spiritual experience of listening, free and frank speech, and shared discernment, as well as

[4] In chapter 2, above, p. 33, I analyzed the adoption of this text by *Lumen Gentium* 12 §2, which maintains discernment by the whole community, reserving judgment of authenticity to "those who preside" "in a particular way" (*speciatim*).

the absence of such an experience, can be more easily recognized. Conversely, deepening this spiritual perspective requires us not to limit it to a particular "event" but to entrust it to a medium- to long-term process of spiritual and institutional reform. I have already noted that this shift from "event" to "process" corresponds to the first of the four principles of social cohabitation developed by Pope Francis in his apostolic exhortation *Evangelii Gaudium*: "*Time is greater than space*" (EG 222–25). "Giving priority to space," he writes, "means being concerned about *initiating processes rather than possessing spaces*" (EG 223). What emerges is a whole new worldview, based not on a metaphysics dependent on Western culture but on a processual and stylistic conception of human life on planet earth.

## Synodality in the Intercontinental and Intercultural Exchange of Gifts

Far from being devalued, the church's spatial architecture thus acquires a new significance, above all a cultural one. What's at stake is the difficult transition from post-Gregorian—as we've already discussed—and above all "colonial" standardization of the Latin Church to its geographical and cultural differentiation. The continental assemblies of the post-conciliar era, first in Latin America and then, under John Paul II, on all continents, are the first attempts to respect and integrate this internal diversity. This is the second condition for an in-depth transformation of everyday "ecclesial culture."

Vatican II's Dogmatic Constitution on the Church and its Decree on the Church's Missionary Activity provide essential theological pointers along this path. At the end of the second chapter, I already referred to *Lumen Gentium* 23 on the composition of the *one* church in the form of a historical and cultural diversity of particular churches. This text must be read in the context of the church's catholicity as an exchange of gifts, defined in the second chapter of the constitution: "In virtue of this catholicity, each part contributes its own gifts to other parts and to the entire church, so that the whole and each of the parts are strengthened by the common sharing of all things and by the common effort to achieve fullness in unity" (LG 13).

The 2023 *Instrumentum Laboris* refers to these two council texts in its review of the continental stage (IL 4–6). Here is the most significant passage:

> First of all, we have experienced the joy expressed in the *sincere and respectful encounter between brothers and sisters in the faith: to meet each other is to encounter the Lord who is in our midst!* Thus, we were able to touch with our own hands the catholicity of the Church, which, in the variety of ages, sexes and social conditions, manifests an extraordinary wealth of charisms and ecclesial vocations, and is the custodian of a treasure trove of differences in languages, cultures, liturgical expressions and theological traditions. In effect, this rich diversity is the gift of each local Church to all the others (cf. LG 13), and the synodal dynamic is a way to appreciate and enhance this rich diversity without flattening it into uniformity. Similarly, we have discovered that there are shared questions, even if synodality is experienced and understood in a variety of ways in different parts of the world on the basis of a common inheritance of the apostolic Tradition. Part of the challenge of synodality is to discern the level at which it is most appropriate to address each question. Equally shared are certain tensions. We should not be frightened by them, nor attempt at any cost to resolve them, but rather engage in ongoing synodal discernment. Only in this way can these tensions become sources of energy and not lapse into destructive polarisations. (IL 6)

It is only in the final period of the council that the challenge of hearing the Gospel, of interpreting it and making it heard in each geographical and cultural context in a very specific way, comes to the fore. The Missionary Decree *Ad Gentes* (= AG) situates this diversity in the divine plan of salvation between the "dispersion of Babel" and the Pentecost of "the church of the New [Covenant] . . . which speaks every language" (AG 4, 8, and 9). The third chapter of this text, as well as *Gaudium et Spes* (44), outline this ever-problematic mission of translation and interpretation for the entire people of God. "To achieve this [goal], it is necessary that in each of the great socio-cultural regions, as they are called, theological investigation should be encouraged and the facts and words revealed by God, contained in sacred scripture, and explained by the fathers and magisterium" (AG 22).

The current synodal process is still far from assuming this task in its ultimate consequences. But it will certainly lead to a new consistency, at an institutional level, for the "great socio-cultural regions"; according to the fourth principle of social coexistence formulated by

Pope Francis: "Here our model is not the sphere, which is no greater than its parts, where every point is equidistant from the centre, and there are no differences between them. Instead, it is the polyhedron, which reflects the convergence of all its parts, each of which preserves its distinctiveness. Pastoral and political activity alike seek to gather in this polyhedron the best of each" (EG 236).

## The "Return" of the Council's Pastoral Approach

But this diversity raises a fundamental problem, already perceived by Vatican II: *How* can we make the transition from this plurality to a communal *consensus* for all, if the doctrine of the faith no longer always directly exercises its classic unifying function due to its form of expression historically and culturally situated in the Mediterranean and Western world? Of course, listening to the Word of God remains dependent on common and irreducible reference points, such as the classical creeds, sacramental rites, and so on. However, as in the case of Scripture, we are now faced with a diversity of expressions of faith that cannot be reduced to a common catechism.

The answer lies in conciliar or synodal methodology, the first expression of which is the pastoral orientation of Vatican II.[5] Apostolic tradition is pastoral in essence, insofar as it not only seeks to reach and transform its historically and culturally situated recipients, but at the same time allows itself to be touched and penetrated from within—in all its practical, doctrinal, and liturgical expressions—by what it learns and discovers in the encounter with and by its interlocutors. The term "reform," already used several times, designates precisely this "work," which consists of a permanent refiguration of tradition, in the act of receiving and delivering (1 Cor 11:23 and 15:1-4), an act which, under the guidance of the Spirit, reconstitutes this tradition each time in its astonishing polyhedral plasticity.

At this point, several conciliar texts introduce the distinction between, on the one hand, the church's discourses and practices, historically and culturally situated, and, on the other, a second level of

[5] See Christoph Theobald, "La 'pastoralité' de l'enseignement du concile Vatican II. Bilan d'une réception controversée," in Theobald, *Le courage de penser l'avenir: Études œcuméniques de théologie fondamentale et ecclésiologique*, Cogitatio fidei 311 (Éditions du Cerf, 2021), 35–58.

reflection—a *meta-reflection*—on "method" (*met-hodos*), a reflection that shows *how* or by *what path* (*hodos—via*, in Latin) such discourses and practices have appeared and can still appear, while preserving the interpretive competence of all participants in the search for truth, that of some more specifically. Behind this way of proceeding lies Jesus' own itinerary, his own "way of living with" his disciples and contemporaries: his style or *modus conversationis*, already presented by St. Thomas (*Summa Theologica*, Part III, question 40) and evoked in *Dei Verbum* (7) as well as in the Declaration on Religious Freedom, *Dignitatis Humanae* (11). This brings us close to the "conversation in the Spirit" mentioned above. But, let us face it, there's a great danger that we will forget to engage our own contemporaries in "conversations" that honor the two different perspectives—external and internal—of synodality, which are "strongly interconnected" (PD 28 and 29).

In the pastoral and missionary orientation of a church that is constantly moving off-center, the synodal process is a specific way of implementing the council's *modus pastoralis* and, above all, of engaging it at all levels of the people of God. Its common march, its *syn-hodos*, requires a *met-hodos*, a method. But the current synodal process also places this pastoral methodology of the council in a new perspective: the widest participation of all the faithful is the expression of their identity as "missionary disciples," founded on their baptism; Pope Francis never ceased to underline this and to put this participation in direct relation to the *sensus fidei fidelium*[6] discussed in the previous chapter. The council encouraged the laity in the apostolate (Decree *Apostolicam Actuositatem*) and gave them a pastoral method in the "see, judge, act" of Catholic Action (*Apostolicam Actuositatem* 29), which is also the basis of *Gaudium et Spes*. But the synodal process goes much further, introducing a change of perspective. It not only involves all the baptized in the church's pastoral mission, but it also invites them—precisely in terms of this commitment—to initiate and constantly reinitiate a process of discernment in common—listening to each other, listening to those who are otherwise situated, listening to creation—and, in so doing, to hear the voice of the Spirit, opening the way to *consensus* for all.

[6] See EG 24, 40, 50, and more especially, 119 and 120.

Doctrine and dogma do not, however, lose their function, as shown in the previous chapter, synodal ecclesiology remaining within the ecclesiological framework of the Second Vatican Council. On the other hand, the pastoral and synodal approach of parishes, local churches, and the church as a whole becomes *the* "place" referred to in time and history where doctrine threatened with abstraction can be concretely manifested in an incarnate and, therefore, entirely new form. It is, so to speak, surrounded by a "practical pneumatology" or "enlightened pragmatism" and centered on the conversion experience that underpins it; this will be discussed in the next chapter.

But before doing so, we need to return from the three conditions for a profound transformation of ecclesial culture, analyzed just now, to the current synodal process, and ask ourselves about the concrete "results" that are taking shape.

## An Ambitious Questionnaire

So, finally, we turn from the synodal way of proceeding to the contents or *desiderata* that emerged from the first phase of the Synod on Synodality. Three terms mark out the whole process: "communion—participation—mission" (terms often forgotten in the field). Not only do they trace a mission-oriented path, but they also open up a complex interplay of relationships, raising questions and issues. Enumerated in the Preparatory Document, these questions were echoed more precisely in the national syntheses and continental documents before being incorporated into the first *Instrumentum Laboris*.

One might be tempted to content oneself with this last text, which would be a way of short-circuiting all that has just been said about the novelty of the current process and of depriving oneself of the highly differentiated ecclesial experience to which it bears witness. So, even if we have to accept a few repetitions, we're now going to take a selective look at this synodal journey, bearing in mind the complex web of questions that have been accumulating for decades. As I mentioned in the introduction: yes or no, are we starting to see things more clearly?

Admittedly, many Catholics were uncomfortable, even disturbed, by the theme given to this synod, which was clearly out of step with specific topics dealt with in previous synods (the Eucharist, the Word of God, the family, young people, and so on). However, a single question guided the entire process: "How does this 'journeying together,' which takes place today on different levels (from the local level to the universal one), allow the Church to proclaim the Gospel in accordance with the mission entrusted to Her; and what steps does the Spirit invite us to take in order to grow as a synodal Church?" (PD 2 and 26).

The Preparatory Document explains this single question in terms of "ten thematic nuclei." Following an inductive logic, these "nuclei" articulate the individual and relational side of the spiritual process and its social and institutional side. Thematic fields I to III are devoted to very elementary anthropological and spiritual data—companions on the journey, listening, and the ability to speak frankly—after which field IV integrates listening to the Word of God and celebrating the Eucharist.

The following five fields develop the institutional aspect of the synodal process: the principle of co-responsibility in the church and society and its realization in the participation of all in the church's mission (V), concrete ways of living dialogue within the church and society and of managing conflicts (VI), relations with other Christian confessions (VII), the new relationship to be defined between the co-responsibility of all and the authority of some in the church (VIII), and discernment and decision-making processes (IX). A final field concerns formation, which is necessary and already underway thanks to the stylistic change brought about by the current synodal journey (X).

What has become of this range of explanations of the single initial question on a national level (assuming that, in principle, each national document is already the fruit of discernment, carried out by the country's local churches, alone and in concert)? Showing this is the role of the first stage of this succinct investigation, which can only remain highly selective and therefore partial.

## The Churches of Poland and France

Indeed, a huge field of research is opening up here. For the documents at our disposal represent a multitude of "snapshots" of the particular styles of all the churches on the planet. They need to be compared and reintroduced into the intercommunication between churches, which has been the task of continental assemblies. I will focus here on Europe, and in particular on two very different syntheses: France[7] and Poland.[8] The challenge is to make differences in climate appear, even if, as we will see when we move on to the continental and universal level, questions are at least partially converging, not only within Europe but also on other continents.

However, all the European reports underline the relatively limited participation in the process: in France, more than 150,000 people took part (out of the 29 percent of the French population who identify themselves as Catholics), which is not negligible if we compare this figure with that put forward by the Polish bishops, who mention 100,000 participants (out of the 91.9 percent of Poles who identify themselves as Catholics), or that of the Spanish episcopate, with 220,000 participants (out of the 80 to 90 percent Catholics).

All also mention the various kinds of resistance encountered by the consultation: the difficulty of hearing the voice of the poorest, of reaching young adults, and, above all, the disinterest shown by many priests. The national synthesis of Polish Catholics, significantly entitled "Hopes, Fears, and Anxieties," is particularly frank and realistic (in contrast to much more enthusiastic syntheses, such as the one from Italy; more sober ones, such as the one from Switzerland; or darker ones, such as the one from Belgium, whose initial diagnosis stresses the negative image of the church in society). From the outset, the Polish synthesis distinguishes four attitudes: "(1) enthusiasm and gratitude for creating space and giving the opportunity to speak out in the Church, especially by the laity; (2) fear, distance, and distrust of embarking on the synodal path associated, for example, with the so-called 'German way' ([e.g.,] proposals for doctrinal changes)" and with the outbreak of demands on the church, especially on the part of the laity[9]; "(3) fear and disbelief as to whether we, as ordinary Christians, have anything to say to the Pope and whether the voice

[7] Text at https://eglise.catholique.fr/conference-des-eveques-de-france.

[8] English text at https://synod.org.pl/poland-polish-episcopal-conference/.

[9] The Polish synthesis is the only one to mention—in a negative way—the German synodal path (with the obvious exception of the synthesis of the church of Germany, which virtually reproduces the main lines of this path).

of the lay faithful will be heard at all; (4) a noticeable lack of interest among many priests, laity, and even among thriving communities whose members did not feel the need to become personally involved in the synod or only delegated representatives to attend." All the reports, however, emphasize and even make tangible the joy of those who actually took part in the process.

1. While most of the summaries more or less follow the order of the ten "nuclei" of the Preparatory Document, as is the case with the Polish church's text, others adopt their own particular structure, as, for example, the church of France: while stating in the introduction that "it makes no theological judgement," it organizes the ascents according to a very particular theological pattern. The first part, entitled "Immersing Ourselves in the Word of God," evokes both existing practices and particularly significant *desiderata*: "Expectations are high when it comes to homilies: many are the disappointments expressed when preaching is not sufficiently based on the Word of God and does not nourish the daily life of the baptized. A recurrent request is that preaching at the Eucharist be extended to the laity, and specifically to women's voices. . . . Many syntheses invite us to propose and promote celebrations of the Word of God."

The second part invites us to "give credible signs of God's goodness and of the equal dignity of the baptized," focusing on five wishes (always with quotations drawn from several national syntheses): (1) "Pursuing the experience of synodality," with a very fine comment on the diverse rhythms of listening and discernment; (2) "Ministries at the service of encounters with God and people," with a long, well-nuanced paragraph on the ministry of priests, without glossing over the problems of their relationships (e.g., authoritarianism, difficult relations with women, etc.), personal balance, and health ("It is regularly hoped that the celibacy of priests will be left to their free choice"); (3) "Men and women: living the equal dignity of baptism," evoking, on the subject of the place of women, "an urgency as well as innumerable wounds" ("We also read many requests for women to be able to receive diaconal ordination. . . . A little less often, even if it is largely recurrent, we find the request that women be able to be ordained priests"); (4) "Governance: recognizing and valuing charisms"; an emphasis that appears too rarely in the synodal process as a whole and in the national texts ("The syntheses express many tensions on this subject, for example the recurrent experience of abuse of power, the 'pyramidal' aspect of governance, the fear of conflict that invites one to hide problems rather than deal with them, the arrival of a new parish priest who imposes a direction contrary to that which has prevailed in a parish until now"); and significantly at the end, (5) "The liturgy: articulating depth and fraternity"; a shared desire that does not overlook numerous "tensions" ("between pastoral flexibility and attachment to rituals, between esteem for the richness of liturgical symbols and questions about a language that has become unintelligible for many").

Finally, the third part expresses the ultimate aim of "living as brothers and sisters in Christ," emphasizing the expectation of closeness ("Serving fraternity") and the spiritual necessity of "cultivating listening and dialogue."

In a way, the conclusion gives the "theological" key to this structuring of the text:

> In the syntheses, we find two particularly stimulating promises, closely linked to each other: they have as their object the Word of God (part I) and fraternity (part III). . . . To proclaim the Word of God through and in fraternity, the Church needs credible signs of God's closeness (part II). These signs do not end in themselves but help to make the whole ecclesial body a "sacrament" of God's call to humanity. There are already many ways in which this "dream" can become reality: they nourish our hope, and now invite us to new conversions.

The bishops of France, meeting in conference after the ecclesial assembly, expressed delight with the results in their *Document d'accompagnement de la collecte des synthèses synodales*,[10] adopted on June 15, 2022, while making what some saw as a correction:

> At this stage, we are aware of the absence of certain topics: one of the three central terms of the synod, mission, is not very present. . . . We have to listen to other calls, less expressed or reported, but nonetheless urgent, where Christians have a witness

[10] Text at https://eglise.catholique.fr/conference-des-eveques-de-france.

to give: the major challenges facing society, the various anthropological models proposed, integral ecology, international solidarity. We also have to ask ourselves why certain Christian spiritual riches are either ignored or devalued, for example, the Eucharist as the sacrifice of Jesus, the sacraments, the consecrated life, the celibacy of priests, the diaconate. We also note that the family as a place for learning about fraternity is not mentioned.

2. As for the national synthesis of the church in Poland, titled "Hopes, Fears, and Anxieties," we've already discussed its overall approach; right from the introduction, it reports "a clear contestation of the synod, or at least an underestimation of its significance." The first paragraph, however, reports the positive appreciation of those who actually took part, "the very act of meeting [being] the first fruit of the synod." This emphasis is maintained right to the end, when, in the final paragraph, the editors acknowledge that "the synod has brought out our *expectation for change in the Church*," adding, "*concerning the way it functions, not doctrine or structure*" (emphasis mine). Once again, it's the "German synodal method" that serves as a foil, as it is said to have reinforced the fear of change. The basic thrust of the text becomes clearer here: the distinction between, on the one hand, the doctrine and structure of the church, and, on the other, its functioning, makes it possible to send back to back those who prefer "to maintain the status quo and preserve the existing forms, which would be a response to contemporary problems and the crisis of the universal and local Church" and those who, in the spirit of the German method, make proposals for doctrinal and structural change. In-depth training in synodality, on the other hand, is presented as a prerequisite for operational change, which ultimately depends on "personal conversion."

From the second paragraph onwards, the synodal synthesis follows the order of the ten nuclei of the Preparatory Document, treating them precisely from the angle of *dysfunctions*, courageously designated, and proposing, here and there, concrete desires for change. The first four themes ("accompanying," "listening," "speaking," "dialogue") bring together "nuclei" I to III and VI, dealing with the interplay of relationships within the church, largely identified with the parish system (apparently little affected by the restructuring seen in Western Europe, particularly in France). It is in this group that we find most of the questions also addressed in other summaries:

> People seeking an experience of faith, those hurt by the clergy and by their anti-testimony, people living in non-sacramental relationships, LGBT+ people, people caught up in addictions, and refugees were particularly pointed out. A sense of remoteness on the common path is also expressed by people representing the traditionalist trend. People with disabilities, who have difficulties with mobility and are thus unable to participate fully in the life of the Church community, also sometimes feel excluded. There is also a lack of intergenerational connectivity in the parish. Outside the community are people who are guided by a false and stereotypical image of the Church and Catholics, as well as non-practitioners for whom remaining on the periphery is convenient and a personal choice. These groups and circles are clearly of concern to us. At the same time, we ask ourselves whether pastors and committed lay faithful are too quick to give up on courting those with faith difficulties and crises. ("Hopes, Fears, and Anxieties")

In the paragraph on the exchange of words, we find "a picture of a Church wounded, affected by scandals and human misery," but we also find contrasting experiences of priests:

> In the consultations and syntheses, the harsh criticism of priests, based primarily on their own parish experiences, was heard very clearly. We perceive the pastor as an absent and uninvolved person, while on the other hand we are aware that we need him very much and are looking for guides on the paths of our faith. Our attitude toward priests clearly reveals the tension between expectations and desires on the one hand and unpleasant realities on the other.
>
> The laity notice and highly appreciate in their priests a consciousness of vocation, deep faith, true piety, living according to principles, attention to worship and teaching, concern for people, love for the Church, apolitical while engaging in social issues, selflessness, and above all, authenticity and witness. Examples were cited of zealous priests, especially parish priests, thanks to whom the pastoral ministry and parish community are develop-

> ing. At the same time, the lay faithful perceive in priests a lack of faith and authentic piety, materialism, violation of moral principles, lack of sensitivity to people's needs, poor quality of relations with the parish and local community, an erroneous anthropological vision, revealed in an extremely negative understanding of the human being, and, finally, a lack of building relationships among themselves and neglect of their own formation. ("Hopes, Fears, and Anxieties")

Other harsh observations follow: the discrepancy between assertions about the "Church of dialogue" and the day-to-day difficulties of dialogue between clergy and laity/parishioners, the absence of spaces for dialogue and, above all, the use of inaccessible and incomprehensible language. Even the paragraph on celebration, which goes into great detail, highlights serious dysfunctions, in particular "the problem of the low level of homilies," their "moralistic tone": "Celebrants not infrequently read other people's texts, downloaded from the Internet." The paragraph on mission tries to understand why, despite a real desire for evangelization, this theme is so little addressed, and blames the absence of relationships that allow faith to be discussed and the lack of "proper formation and basic religious knowledge." Again, the text refers to the fact that "in [the] Church, the laity are rarely treated as partners in evangelization." As for ecumenism, the synthesis admits that it is virtually absent, for fear of "Protestantization," acknowledging, however, that the war in Ukraine and the arrival of many refugees has brought new ecumenical challenges.

Finally, the lengthy paragraph on "Authority and Responsibility" confirms the tenor of the synthesis as a whole. It strongly reaffirms the hierarchical structure of the church and at the same time castigates its dysfunctions.

> The Synod confirmed that we respect and value hierarchical authority in the Church. We are convinced that decisions in the Church should be made by those who are called to do so, and they should take responsibility for them. The faithful understand and do not question the role that the pope, bishops and all clergy play in the Church. We express respect to those who have received the sacrament of Holy Orders or the gift of consecrated

> life. We do not want to take over the authority of bishops and presbyters. On the contrary: we want to have confidence in them and treat them as shepherds. We feel responsible for them. We are aware of the need to support our shepherds with prayer, since their mission is not easy.
>
> Authority is not only responsibility, but above all service. Authority, responsibility and service must be formed by love. ("Hopes, Fears, and Anxieties")

That said, the document is scathing in its criticism of the distance and lack of contact between bishops or priests and their people, a logic of "top-down planning," the absence of creativity, "the dominant role of the priest in everything," and the absence of parish councils, but also the presence of a passive attitude in many of the faithful.

3. The difference between the two syntheses, French and Polish, is obvious. The context is not the same: Poland (still) sees itself as a Catholic country with a tightly knit parish network and influential institutions, whereas French-style secularism and a de-Christianization or differentiation of relations to Christian tradition among Catholics and other citizens create a completely different cultural climate. It is also significant that neither the Polish synthesis nor that of the church of France includes a situation analysis, as is the case with the texts of the Belgian dioceses and the Swiss churches. The difference is also theological (or even ideological), as shown by the Polish distinction between doctrine and structure, on the one hand, and ecclesial and pastoral functioning on the other. It's no coincidence that the Polish episcopate strongly opposed their German neighbor's synodal path, taking up the baton from Roman critics. The same scenario will be repeated at the European Assembly in Prague. As for the dysfunctions or problems to be addressed, the two French and Polish "lists" largely concur. One might even say that the Polish list is more realistic and cruder, except that the question of the presence and role of women at all levels of ecclesial life is not mentioned once.

Let's recall once again that this first survey is far from representative, either of Europe as a whole or, even less so, of other continents. The continental assemblies we will now be discussing, prepared by the Roman synthesis, will give us a more accurate picture.

## Africa and Europe

1. The Working Document for the Continental Stage (DCS) with its beautiful biblical title *"Enlarge the Space of Your Tent" (Is 54:2)*[11] begins with a realistic rereading of the experience of the synodal process, without silencing "the weeds" alongside "the fruits and seeds," and recalling from the outset the common baptismal dignity: "This foundational reference to baptism—not as an abstract concept but as a felt identity—immediately brings into focus the link between the synodal form of the Church and the possibility of fulfilling its mission" (DCS 22).

The second chapter of the document focuses on "Listening to Scripture." It's worth noting that, in the national syntheses, Scripture doesn't really play a structuring role, whereas the Preparatory Document had devoted a long development to it, focusing (as I showed in the first chapter of this book) on the "characters" or "figures" of the Gospel stories and the Acts of the Apostles. On the other hand, a synthesis such as that of the church in the Philippines is very attentive to the many symbols and metaphors adapted to this culture, for example, that of the "boat" and the "crossing of the storm" (Mark 4:35-41), other than the synodal symbolism of the "way." The brief biblical chapter of the Working Document (DCS 25–28) introduces yet another metaphor, linked to that of the Exodus people's journey through the desert; it thus comments on the title of the text: "Enlarge the space of your tent, spread out your tent cloths unsparingly, lengthen your ropes and make firm your pegs" (Isa 54:2). I quote here the two essential passages:

> 26. To the people in exile the prophet's words evokes the experience of the exodus, when they dwelt in tents, and announces the promise of the return to the land, a sign of joy and hope. To prepare, it is necessary to enlarge the tent, acting on the three elements of its structure. The first is the tent cloth, which protects from the sun, wind and rain, delineating a space of life and conviviality. They need to be spread out, so that they can also protect

[11] This document can be found on the website of the General Secretariat of the Synod: https://www.synod.va/en/synodal-process/the-continental-stage/resources-and-tools/documents.html.

> those who are still outside this space, but who feel called to enter it. The ropes that hold the cloths together are the second structural element of the tent. They must balance the tension needed to keep the tent from drooping with the softness that cushions movement caused by the wind. That is why if the tent expands, the ropes must be stretched to maintain the right tension. Finally, the pegs are the third element: they anchor the structure to the ground and ensure its solidity, but remain capable of moving when the tent must be pitched elsewhere.
>
> 27. Listened to today, these words of Isaiah invite us to *imagine the Church similarly as a tent*, indeed as *the tent of meeting*, which accompanied the people on their journey through the desert: *called to stretch out, therefore, but also to move*. At its centre, stands the tabernacle, that is, the presence of the Lord. The tent's hold is ensured by *the sturdiness of its pegs*, that is, *the fundamentals of faith that do not change but can be moved and planted in ever new ground*, so that the tent can accompany the people as they walk through history. Finally, in order not to sag, *the structure of the tent must keep in balance the different forces and tensions to which it is subjected*: a metaphor that expresses the need for discernment. This is how many reports envision the Church. (DCS 26 and 27; emphasis mine)

The heuristic force of this metaphorical play is apparent in the third chapter of the text, which, reviewing all the national syntheses, organizes them under the angle of "*five* generative *tensions* that are intertwined with one another." The text simplifies and concentrates the "ten nuclei" of the Preparatory Document, while maintaining the inductive logic of that text, moving from everyday relationships and exclusionary tendencies to mission and from mission to institutional issues and, finally, to the source and summit of Christian life, the liturgy. I quote the summary of these tensions, forming the framework for continental discernment:

1. listening as openness to welcome: this starts from a desire for radical inclusion—no one is excluded—to be understood in a perspective of communion with sisters and brothers and with our common Father; listening appears here not as an instrumental action, but as the assumption of the basic attitude of a God who listens to his People, as the following of a Lord whom the Gospels

constantly present to us in the act of listening to the people who come to him along the roads of the Holy Land; in this sense listening is already mission and proclamation;

2. our outgoing drive toward mission. This is a mission that Catholics recognize as needing to be carried out with brothers and sisters of other confessions and in dialogue with believers of other religions, transforming human actions of care into authentically spiritual experiences that proclaim the face of a God who cares to the point of giving his own life so that we may have it in abundance;

3. carrying out the mission requires assuming a style based on participation, this corresponds to the full assumption of coresponsibility of all the baptized for the one mission of the Church arising from the common baptismal dignity;

4. the construction of concrete possibilities for living communion, participation and mission through structures and institutions inhabited by people properly formed and sustained by a living spirituality;

5. the liturgy, especially the Eucharistic liturgy, the source and summit of Christian life, which brings the community together, making communion tangible, enables the exercise of participation, and nourishes the momentum toward mission with the Word and the Sacraments. (DCS 11)

The dysfunctions and problems as well as the *desiderata* formulated in the national syntheses are all integrated into this framework. In the first paragraph on "Welcoming Listening," we find the people and categories who feel neglected and excluded, including, in many situations, ordained ministers and—an unexpected mention—the family circle of those who have abandoned the ministry.

> Despite the cultural differences, there are *remarkable similarities between the various continents regarding those who are perceived as excluded,* in society and also in the Christian community. In many cases their voice has been absent from the synod process, and they appear in reports only because others speak about them, lamenting their exclusion. (DCS 40; emphasis mine)

Entitled "Sisters and Brothers for Mission," the second paragraph stresses the intertwining of the fullness of life and the kingdom of God: positively in terms of evangelization, but also negatively: "The wounds of the Church are intimately connected to those of the world" (DCS 44). Numerous excerpts from national syntheses from every continent are quoted to point out exclusions (tribalism, sectarianism, racism, gender inequality, etc.) and to enumerate open and little-advanced mission projects such as ecumenism, the increase in the number of interfaith and interreligious families, the inculturation of the Gospel and its contextualization in secularized or secularizing societies, and the urgent need to develop intercultural approaches.

The important third paragraph on "Communion, Participation, and Co-responsibility" begins with a statement of principle, again based on the syntheses as a whole:

> The mission of the Church is realized through the lives of all the baptised. The reports express a deep desire to recognise and re-affirm this common dignity as the basis for the renewal of life and ministries in the Church. They affirm the value of all vocations in the Church, and above all, invite us to follow Jesus, returning to his style and way of exercising power and authority as a means of offering healing, reconciliation and liberation. "It is important to build a synodal institutional model as an ecclesial paradigm of deconstructing pyramidal power that privileges unipersonal managements. The only legitimate authority in the Church must be that of love and service, following the example of the Lord" (CE Argentina). (DCS 57)

On this basis, the text makes positive reference to—"The tone of the reports is not anti-clerical" (DCS 58)—a possible "beyond" of clericalism, and above all invites us to rethink women's participation, evoking the sadness of many of them. The following extract shows that none of the difficult questions are censored:

> Almost all reports raise the issue of full and equal participation of women: "The growing recognition of the importance of women in the life of the Church opens up possibilities for greater, albeit limited, participation in Church structures and decision-making spheres" (EC Brazil). However, the reports do not agree

> on a single or complete response to the question of the vocation, inclusion and flourishing of women in Church and society. After careful listening, many reports ask that the Church continue its discernment in relation to a range of specific questions: the active role of women in the governing structures of Church bodies, the possibility for women with adequate training to preach in parish settings, and a female diaconate. Much greater diversity of opinion was expressed on the subject of priestly ordination for women, which some reports call for, while others consider a closed issue. (DCS 64)

The concluding section on "Charisms, Vocations, and Ministries" (DSC 66–70) provides a few brief indications, without glossing over the hesitations, even terminological ones, that weigh heavily on this issue.

The fourth paragraph then returns to the *tensions* that run through all the syntheses, inviting the churches not to be afraid of them but to consider them as "a source of energy" and fields for discernment. This is where "synodality takes shape." In this spirit, the text addresses structures and institutions, recalling the newness of the continental stage and the need to review the synodal style of all decision-making bodies, at all levels of the church: "Many reports show the need for these bodies to be not only consultative, but places where decisions are made on the basis of processes of communal discernment rather than on the majority principle used in democratic regimes" (DCS 78). Clearly, these changes in institutional culture require training and must be supported by a "synodal spirituality" "from accentuating the individual dimension," this spirituality is called upon to shift "to the collective dimension: a spirituality of 'we,' which can enhance the contributions of each person" (DCS 85). I will come back to this in the next chapter.

A final paragraph deals with the relationship between "Synodal Life and Liturgy" (DCS 88–97). It stresses that because liturgy is rooted in the culture of a particular people, it clearly exposes the tensions currently running through the church, including the suffering caused by the exclusion of certain categories of people from communion. The limits of celebrations in contradiction with a synodal style are clearly indicated, and the possibilities offered by the variety of ritual traditions and symbolic forms, specific to different cultures, are recalled.

The final chapter of this document outlines the next steps for the people of God, distinguishing between "the long-term horizon," that is, the in-depth transformation of "ecclesial culture," and "the next steps" of the continental stage (DCS 98). The above summary of questions and *desiderata* cannot replace reading the document which, thanks to numerous quotes from national summaries, considerably broadens the perspective and scope of the "cloth of the tent of encounter" (see DCS 26 and 27), even if, to the astonishment of many, the tensions identified in the third chapter are more or less the same on every continent. The document therefore instructs the seven continental assemblies to address them.

Three questions (already mentioned above) should mark out their work: (1) identify, in a climate of prayer, the *intuitions* that resonate most strongly with the lived experience and realities of the church on a given continent, and also ask about experiences that seem to be new and enlightening; (2) discern which substantive tensions or divergences emerge as particularly important from a continent's point of view; and consequently, which issues or problems should be addressed and considered in the next stages of the process; and (3) gather together, from what emerges from the previous two questions, *priorities*, recurring themes, and calls to action that can be shared with other local churches around the world and discussed at the first session of the synod assembly in October 2023.

To observe the implementation of these instructions, I am once again obliged to make a choice. In order to convey the diversity of the contributions, I will focus on the continental assemblies of Africa and Europe.

2. The Introduction to the Document of the African Synodal Continental Assembly[12] takes stock of the African process, which began with two preparatory sessions in Ghana and Kenya, and culminated in the Addis Ababa assembly (March 1–6, 2023). The document notes the significant fact that the "spiritual conversation" method was unfamiliar to most of the participants. It therefore had to be taught

[12] Text at https://www.synod.va/content/dam/synod/common/phases/continental-stage/final_document/AFRICA-EN.pdf.

and then practiced. With regard to this methodological axis, the Addis Ababa report notes the many obstacles encountered, including the difficulty of entering into a listening experience, the lack of time, and the difficulty of applying this method to a large text such as the General Secretariat's Working Document.

In response to the first question in this text, twenty *intuitions* are listed. These form the outlines of a rereading, targeted in a very specific way.

It first points out that, since Vatican II, the church in Africa has been a point of focus several times in the church's synodal experience, culminating in several documents (in particular, John Paul II's *Ecclesia in Africa* [1995] and Benedict XVI's *Africae Munus* [2011]). The document then goes on to challenge the image of the tent as the main image, since many Africans associate it with "warfare, displacement and refugee situations. The assembly preferred the image of the 'Family of God' where everyone has his or her place and responsibilities according to 'family values' (though there is no homogeneity on what the latter includes in all countries)" (Intuitions 2). On several occasions, the text refers to Ephesians 2:19 in order to highlight the image of the church as the "family of God," referred to often on the African continent since *Ecclesia in Africa*: "So then you are no longer strangers and sojourners, but you are fellow citizens with the holy ones and members of the household of God." (See also the third part of the text: Conclusion 1 and 2.)

The attitude of listening is the third intuition. The document notes, however, the difficulty that "family, church, national issues, social problems, spiritual problems, etc., often vary in interpretation or social importance." It is within this framework that we also find the synodal invitation "to listen to the cultural practices that have been either ignored, condemned or suppressed by the Western culture through which the Gospel was preached to Africans," a problem raised in other places in the text. (Intuition 16, for example, refers to numbers 55 and 56 of the General Secretariat's Working Document on Local Cultures: "There is the need to reread the history of the indigenous people and then recover, promote and integrate their cultural practices into the liturgy. This is a proper inculturation which enhances diversity, moving from multi-culturality to inter-culturality where different practices complement and enrich one another.")

As for the "participation of all," the African document mentions three more specific groups of people: women, "many of whom feel that they do not occupy a sufficiently important place in the Church's decision-making structures"; young people—"the idea of a preferential option for young people" is put forward, and we are invited to take an interest in the problems they face, beyond their relationship with religion (see Intuitions 14)—and disabled people (Intuitions 4). We speak of the care and protection of children and vulnerable people (Intuitions 11) and of welcoming "those who feel marginalized, for example, people in polygamous marriages, divorced and remarried, and single parents. Many people expressed the desire to revisit the position of the Church on those that considered themselves officially marginalized due to irregular family situations" (Intuitions 12).

In another series of intuitions, we perceive a certain concern with regard to the synodal approach: the risk that, through ideological, economic, and political influences, the synodal church will be put under pressure when it should remain focused on the Word of God and the church's firm tradition (Intuitions 5). A similar tone is found in other intuitions: the need to learn to balance attention to spiritual matters and material problems (Intuitions 7), the aim of evangelization which implies conversion (Intuitions 8), and the obligation to discern and explore new ideas (Intuitions 10).

Questions of co-responsibility and clericalism are little addressed (Intuitions 6 and 13), the problem being more on the side of the laity, who have internalized this culture by not playing their proper role in the church. Three intuitions focus on liturgy (Intuitions 16, 17, and 18), with particular emphasis on "people's cultural ways of worship" and their active participation. The text also calls for a greater awareness of African solidarity, also in the relationship of the churches to political leaders: "To be able to ask questions and try to resolve problems without removing our capacity to reflect and achieve what we need by ourselves" (Intuitions 19 and 20).

This contextualized rereading of the Working Document for the Continental Stage is followed by a list of six questions and issues, without the conflict potential that probably underlies them being made explicit as such. I simply list them without comment, drawing attention, however, to the fact that their formulation is relatively general and may therefore also apply to other continental situations:

1. What mechanism do we put in place to cater for the respect for diverse cultures?
2. How is the Synodal Church more empathetic and what are her means of promoting concrete Solidarity?
3. There is a tension between a strong understanding of truth and the principle of mercy (particularly the accommodation with difference, minority views and dissent), between belonging to the Church and not living as a full member of the Church, between autonomy and co-responsibility. How do we deal with it?
4. Where is Synodality taking us as we listen to the voices of diverse people? Is this not leading us to democracy? Thus, there is only a thin line between dialogue, listening and decision making and the rule of the majority.
5. Everything we have raised is important. How would the local Church make use of all the points that are being raised in our discussions?
6. In listening to others, to the Holy Spirit and to the Word of God, what are the criteria for discernment and judgement?

These intuitions and questions lead, finally, to eight *priorities* on which the African synodal assembly calls for further discernment at the level of the universal church. They largely reproduce the *intuitions*, reordering them and giving them a more incisive form.

The first associates the deepening of the synodality of the church "as Family of God" with a way of nurturing life and reaching out to the entire human family and all creation—and the text adds: "from the Small Christian Communities to the Vatican level." The second takes up the question of "African voices and values," terminology already present in the first priority—especially "values such as family, solidarity, communitarian life, reverential dialogue, hospitality and co-responsibility"—but adds a remark that can also be understood as an African demand: "Africans have equal responsibility for the doctrines and teachings of the Church in collaboration with other local Churches (Eph. 2:19). Accordingly, it is paramount that their experiences and ever-evolving cultural values be taken into consideration and their problems be always equally considered. This will help them to own the teachings and to be committed to living them out."

The third priority brings together the classic investments of the post-conciliar church in society, perfectly adapted to the African context: "The commitment of the Church, Family of God (*Africae munus*, 1), to conflict resolution, the fight against economic colonialism and illegal exploitation of resources in Africa, and the promotion of Good Governance, Justice and Peace" must be strengthened and intensified; without forgetting, as religion is also a cause of conflict in Africa, the need to promote ecumenism and interreligious dialogue. The last of the eight priorities focuses on ecological justice, making it clear to the universal church that "Africa bears the brunt of the current climate crisis, although it contributes the least to it."

Other priorities concern the internal life of the church: inculturation and liturgical renewal (Conclusion 4), the urgency of formation "as a means of making the synodal model a pastoral model of the Church's life and practice" (Conclusion 5), the implementation of the principle of subsidiarity (Conclusion 6)—here we find the questioning of the place of women, young people, and people with disabilities—and the pastoral care of the family, sensitive to all the "irregular" situations already mentioned above (Conclusion 7).

It should be noted that the specific "personality" of the church as "Family of God" in Africa emerges clearly from this contextualized, albeit succinct, rereading of the Roman Secretariat's Working Document. Even so, the Addis Ababa assembly is perfectly aware that its final document cannot capture the full richness of ecclesial experience on the continent. A reading of this text reveals the difficulties the delegates encountered in trying to apply the method of spiritual conversation and in coming up against the very open nature of the synodal process. Problems and tensions are named not explicitly, but by allusion, suggesting a different relationship to speech and conversation than that to which Europeans or Americans are accustomed. The organization of themes respects the framework laid down by the General Secretariat but fulfills it according to a different, less Cartesian logic.

It is undoubtedly respect for this *otherness—one of seven—*that will enable the Roman process to reach a successful conclusion.

3. Alongside the African text, the Final Document of the European Continental Assembly,[13] held in Prague from February 5 to 12, 2023, takes on a new dimension: that of *another*, equally discerning rereading of the General Secretariat's Working Document. While the text from the "young" churches of Africa emphasizes the continent's synodal tradition, the "old" churches of Europe are delighted with this first meeting of the people of God "to listen to one another and dialogue in an atmosphere of prayer and listening to the Word of God" (introduction 2). From the outset, the Final Document lists a few characteristics of the context for the churches in Europe, starting with recent events such as the earthquake in Turkey and Syria, the war in Ukraine, and the wounds caused by sexual and other abuses. The text takes a look at the continent's "spiritual geography" between west and east and north and south, overcoming traditional stereotypes of large, opposed, and homogeneous blocks, and brings in the two striking phenomena of secularization and migration, without hiding the fact that the churches of Europe are also churches of martyrdom (introduction 12–18). The introduction ends with a call to action: "Amidst such complex challenges, there is a need to revitalise listening to the Word of God" (introduction 19).

As instructed by the General Secretariat, the introduction is followed by a series of seven common *intuitions*, identified during the discussion of the Working Document, with a view to "building a synodal Church in a European perspective." It suffices to list them here, accompanying some of them with a few brief comments:

1) the spiritual dimension of synodality, in a perspective of ongoing conversion to Christ;
2) the rediscovery of the common baptismal dignity and its implications;
3) the essential link between synodality and mission;
4) dialogue as a way of life of the Church;
5) the commitment to overcome prejudices and reconcile memory;

[13] Text at https://www.synod.va/content/dam/synod/common/phases/continental-stage/final_document/en-newdoc/Europe-EN.pdf.

6) preferential attention to families, women and young people;

7) the adoption of the synodal method for all ecclesial processes. (20)

While the first three points of reference outline the theological, sacramental, and missiological framework of synodality, the other four points clarify the pastoral and spiritual issues at stake.

The fourth point deals with relations within and among local churches; ecumenical, interfaith, and societal relations; and relations with marginalized and wounded people, each time according to the very different contexts on the continent. The fifth point is particularly significant: "Facing open wounds, overcoming prejudices, reconciling memories" (39–44). Here we find the specific groups already mentioned several times in previous documents: "the poor people, the marginalized people, those who feel left out or not welcome, the LGBTQ community, divorced and remarried people, migrants, and people whose lives did not turn out as they hoped for (The Netherlands)" (40). The following paragraphs of this resonance mention, with great frankness, the "differences of opinion" and "mutual accusations" that arose during the assembly, as well as the "differences in worldview." The report from Luxembourg mentions "the great gap between those who seek reform or even transformation and others who are afraid of change to the point of rejecting it. May these gaps make us curious to discover each other's arguments, may they make us vigilant to respect each other in order to build the future of our communities together, and not against each other, seeing in diversity a wealth" (40–42).

The sixth and seventh points are not without African resonances. The sixth names families, women, and young people, and the seventh testifies to the fruitfulness of the method of spiritual conversion; a point that poses a difficulty in the African synodal document, despite the fact that it makes the "synodal model" a pastoral model for the life and practice of the church (Conclusion 5).

The next chapter of the document lists seven *tensions* highlighted by the Prague assembly, introducing them with a reflection on how to either let them degenerate into hurtful polarizations or to overcome them by carrying them together:

1) the relationship between proclaiming the truth of the Gospel and witnessing to God's infinite mercy;

2) the articulation between fidelity to tradition and *aggiornamento*;

3) the liturgy in the life of the Church;

4) the pluralism of understanding mission;

5) the ability to exercise co-responsibility of all in the light of the diversity of charisms and ministries;

6) the forms of exercising authority in a synodal Church;

7) the articulation and unfolding of diversity and unity and the local-global dynamic. (53)

While well contextualized, these seven tensions, or at least the formulation of their titles, are sufficiently general to be compared with those found on other continents. This is clear when we juxtapose European and African tensions: the latter are more sensitive to cultural issues, while the former are more refocused around theological issues, precisely formulated in an alternative way to highlight their conflicting nature. Thus, liturgy (the third tension) is not treated for its own sake, but as a mirror of the lively tensions within several European churches of an ecclesiological nature that concern the understanding of mission (the fourth tension): "We are being convoked for what? Some might mix belonging to the Church with retreating into a comfortable cocoon. Others can imagine it more of a space where everyone can mix and match without any sense of commitment or conversion. For some of us, it's not clear what mission entails. And if it's all ministerial, how are we to understand the specific gifts of the ordained within the one holy People of God? (Malta)" (70).

Tensions concerning the co-responsibility of all, charisms, ministries (the fifth tension), and forms of exercising authority within a synodal church (the sixth tension) all echo issues already addressed in the national syntheses. By way of example, I quote just one extract:

> Some contributions also point to the existence of questions concerning the limits of access to ordained ministry: The historical

> variability of the figure of the priest must be open to debate about the ordination of married men (Czech Republic). Another concern is the ordination of women to the diaconate, even though this is not a simple topic. There are also tensions concerning so-called divisive issues, such as women's access to the sacrament of Orders [and] ordination of married men (Portugal). In particular, opinions are divided on the ordination of women to the diaconate/priesthood (English-language working group). According to Luxembourg, the question of women's access to ordained ministries must be studied in depth. (75)
>
> More broadly, the question of the place of women in the exercise of authority came up in many delegations. (76)

The final chapter of the text sets out some European priorities for the Roman assembly in October 2023:

- deepen the practice, theology, and hermeneutics of synodality. We need to rediscover something that is ancient and belongs to the nature of the Church, while always being new. This is a task for us. We are taking the first steps along a path that opens up as we walk it;
- address the meaning of an all-ministerial Church as a horizon in which to place the reflection on charisms and ministries (ordained and non-ordained) and the relations between them;
- explore forms for a synodal exercise of authority, namely the service of accompanying the community and preserving unity;
- clarify the discernment criteria for the synodal process and at what level, from local to universal, decisions are to be made;
- take concrete and courageous decisions on the role of women within the Church and on their greater involvement at all levels, including in decision-making and taking processes;
- consider the tensions around the liturgy, so as to consider, from a synodal perspective, the Eucharist as the source of communion;
- care for a synodal related formation of the entire People of God, with specific attention to discerning the signs of the times, with a view to carrying out the common mission;

- renew the living sense of mission, overcoming the rift between faith and culture in order to once again bringing the gospel to people's heart, finding a language that can articulate tradition and renewal, but above all that can walk with people instead of talking about them or to them. The Spirit asks us to listen to the cry of the poor and the earth in our Europe. In particular the desperate cry of the victims of war call for a just peace. (92)

In addition to the themes also found in other continental assemblies, the insistence on the theology and hermeneutics of synodality (at the top of the list); the question of the level of decision-making, from local to universal; and the lengthy final development on the gap between faith and culture are among the specific emphases of the European continent.

4. Other continental syntheses could also be considered in the comparison just begun here. We must realize that today, we cannot be Christians without a genuine interest in different styles of Christian and ecclesial life marked by the cultures of other continents, although we often circle around our own steeples, literally and figuratively. However, to take this comparison between the seven continental assemblies to its logical conclusion is not possible within the limited scope of this chapter.

It's clear, however, that the three new conditions for the exercise of synodality—its processualism, contextuality, and pastoral rootedness—have taken shape over the past two years. This is an unexpected and important fruit of this first phase. Indeed, many threads have been unraveled, revealing an initial set of questions, organized differently on each continent but common enough to be deliberated together. This "list" of tensions, questions, and priorities relates to all the essential relationships of the baptized faithful: each individual with him- or herself, with others, and with the planet. It is a participative relationality that is pastoral and at the same time ecumenical and missionary. From this whole, certain groups of people emerge with greater force: women, young people, and those we might call the "poor" and excluded. In the background, and perhaps more explicitly in the European document, questions of a theological nature are posed—questions that are more complex and also more conflictual, and without their treatment, the synodal process risks stagnating.

It remains for us to verify this "feedback" by comparing it with the *Instrumentum Laboris*, published on June 20, 2023, to open the first synodal phase.

## The *Instrumentum Laboris* of 2023

1. The foreword to this new document begins by recalling the road traveled to date and presenting the challenges of the *Instrumentum Laboris*: "The IL takes a step beyond the DCS, drawing from the insights of the first phase and now the work of the Continental Assemblies, *articulating some of the priorities that emerged from listening to the People of God*, but avoids presenting them as assertions or stances. Instead, it expresses them as *questions addressed to the Synodal Assembly*. This body will have the task of discerning the concrete steps which enable the continued growth of a synodal Church, steps that it will then submit to the Holy Father" (IL 10).

The text is divided into two sections, corresponding to the two missions given to the continental assemblies. Entitled "For a Synodal Church," section A first lists a series of fundamental characteristics or distinguishing features of a synodal church (IL 19–31), emphasizing that it "is founded on the recognition of a common dignity deriving from Baptism, which makes all who receive it sons and daughters of God, members of the family of God, and therefore brothers and sisters in Christ, inhabited by the one Spirit and sent to fulfil a common mission" (IL 20). The same section goes on to present—once again—"a way forward for the synodal Church," namely "conversation in the Spirit" (IL 32–42). As the dynamics of the assembly are spelled out in the introduction to the "Worksheets for the 2023 synod assembly"—to which I will return later—we learn that the first step will be to work on this section A. In the spirit of rereading, "The Assembly is asked to conduct its work in an integral manner considering the experience of the People of God as a whole in all its complexity" (IL, Worksheets).

Entitled "Communion, Mission, Participation," section B expresses in the form of questions the three *priorities* that emerge most strongly from work on all continents. The change in the order of appearance of the three terms, now grouping "communion" and "mission," is motivated by the interweaving of these two perspectives, one reflected in the other (IL 44). This is obviously a choice induced by the synod's subtitle; perhaps it also points to the difficulty, noticeable in all syntheses, of considering the two internal and external perspectives as intrinsically linked. Five worksheets are proposed for each of these priorities, enabling them to be approached from different perspectives. This was the focus of the second stage of the assembly that began in October 2023, operating in group work (*circuli minores*, according to synodal jargon) and general assembly. To this end, each card first indicated the guiding question and made it explicit; it then formulated the discernment question proposed to the assembly and, finally, gave suggestions for prayer and preparatory reflection. The *Instrumentum Laboris* rightly notes that

> [a] term as abstract or theoretical as synodality has thus begun to be embodied in a concrete experience. From listening to the People of God a progressive appropriation and understanding of synodality "from within" emerges, which does not derive from the enunciation of a principle, a theory or a formula, but develops from a readiness to enter into a dynamic of constructive, respectful and prayerful speaking, listening and dialogue. At the root of this process is the acceptance, both personal and communal, of something that is both a gift and a challenge: to be a Church of sisters and brothers in Christ who listen to one another and who, in so doing, are gradually transformed by the Spirit. (*IL* 18)

A number of fundamental issues are, however, touched upon without weighing the text down.

First, I note that the *Instrumentum Laboris* makes it clear that the "synodal Church" is first and foremost a "vision," a term that appears here in the church's discourse and in the right place:

> The commitment asked of the Assembly and its Members will be to sustain a dynamic equilibrium between maintaining an overview, which characterises the work outlined in section A, and the identification of practical steps to be taken in a concrete and timely fashion, work which is the focus of section B. On this will depend the fruitfulness of the discernment of the Synodal Assembly whose task will be to open the whole Church to welcome the voice of the Holy Spirit. An inspiration for this work

> might come from reflection on the articulation of the Pastoral Constitution *Gaudium et Spes*, which "consists of two parts," different in character and focus, but becoming "a unified whole" (*GS*, footnote 1). (IL 16)

This simple yet complex vision, based on the experience of listening, does not exist outside or independently of a "way of proceeding" or a "method"; this is a second achievement that must be kept in mind. Here we find again the central hypothesis of this volume, namely that Pope Francis extended to all the baptized the way of proceeding—the *modus procedendi*—of the Second Vatican Council, refining it by integrating the so-called "spiritual conversation," whereas the council adopted the classic genre of debate—the *disputatio*—driven by the art of argumentation. This is not excluded, of course, but must be grafted onto "conversation in the Spirit," as the relationship between these two forms has not yet been clarified in the General Secretariat's document.

However, the *Instrumentum Laboris* does raise—rather discreetly—several problems of "language" and questions of substance involving the synod's relationship with tradition and the magisterium; this is a third point to bear in mind, already mentioned more or less explicitly by some continental assemblies. In its foreword, the Roman document affirms that "this focus on local Churches requires taking into account their variety and diversity of cultures, languages and modes of expression. In particular, the same words—think, for example, of authority and leadership—can have very different resonances and connotations in different linguistic and cultural areas, especially when in some contexts a term is associated with precise theoretical or ideological approaches" (IL 12). In the introduction to Part B, the text happily acknowledges that "priorities" "need to be addressed from the point of view of theology and canon law, as well as from that of pastoral care and spirituality" (IL 43). And the worksheets introduce two examples to show how to move forward on the synodal path, when such and such a question has already been addressed by the magisterium. This highly significant text deserves to be quoted in full:

> Some of the questions that emerged from the consultation of the People of God concern issues on which there is already magisterial and theological teaching to be considered. To give just two

> examples, we can note the acceptance of remarried divorcees, dealt with in the Post-Synodal Apostolic Exhortation *Amoris laetitia*, or the inculturation of the liturgy, the subject of the Instruction *Varietates legitimae* (1994)[14] of the Congregation for Divine Worship and the Discipline of the Sacraments. The fact that questions continue to emerge on issues like these should not be hastily dismissed, rather, it calls for discernment, and the Synodal Assembly is a privileged forum for so doing. In particular, the obstacles, real or perceived, that have prevented the steps indicated by previous documents from being realised should be considered and reflections offered on how they can be removed. For example, if the block stems from a general lack of information, then improved communication will be needed. If, on the other hand, the problem stems from the difficulty of grasping the implications of the documents in ordinary situations or an inability of persons to recognise themselves in what is proposed, a synodal journey of effective reception by the People of God could be the appropriate response. Another instance could be the reappearance of a question which emerges as a sign of a changed reality or situations where there is a need for an "overflow" of Grace. This requires further reflection on the Deposit of Faith and the living Tradition of the Church. (IL worksheets, introduction)

It should be noted that these highly sensitive issues—touching on "doctrine"—are not excluded from synodal deliberation, the synod even being described as a "privileged forum for so doing." The three interpretations given here of a stalemate on a given issue open up a new possibility, desired more or less clearly by several continental documents, for understanding the church's "doctrinal development."

The very last paragraph of the *Instrumentum Laboris* confirms this central concern for linguistic creativity and communication, a paragraph which, however, has no counterpart in the worksheets and is therefore in danger of being forgotten during the first Roman session:

[14] Surprisingly, the example refers to the fourth of the *Instructions for the Proper Application of the Constitution on the Sacred Liturgy of the Second Vatican Council* and not to the fifth: *Liturgiam Authenticam* (2001).

> Numerous contributions highlight the need for a similar effort to renew the language used by the Church in its liturgy, preaching, catechesis, sacred art, as well as in all forms of communication addressed to the Faithful and the wider public, including through new or traditional forms of media. Without demeaning or debasing the depth of the mystery that the Church proclaims or the richness of its tradition, the renewal of language must instead aim to make these riches accessible and attractive to the men and women of our time, rather than an obstacle that keeps them at a distance. The inspiration of the freshness of the language of the Gospel, the capacity for inculturation that the history of the Church exhibits, and the promising experiences already underway, even in the digital environment, invite us to proceed with confidence and resolution in a task of crucial importance for the effectiveness of the proclamation of the Gospel, which is the goal to which a missionary synodal Church aspires. (IL 60)

Does the *Instrumentum Laboris* honor all the issues raised at local, national, and continental levels of the synodal process? The document reassures its readers on this point: "The fact that the synodal process has highlighted certain points as priorities does not mean that other issues are less important" (IL, worksheets, introduction). From the outset, it also affirms, and reiterates at the beginning of the worksheets, that the earlier documents of the process are part of the textual heritage of the Roman assembly (IL 9). This is a fourth point to bear in mind. If, to give just one example, the highly controversial question of women's ordination to the priestly ministry is not named, the text recalls the request of most continental Assemblies and many Episcopal Conferences (worksheets, B 2.3).

Let us conclude this succinct presentation by adding that the final part of the assembly's work was devoted to harvesting the fruits, that is, to working out the paths along which we can continue to walk together. The worksheets in Part B on "Participation, governance, and authority" lead more specifically to this, asking at the end this question: "*How should we evaluate the experiment of extending participation to a group of non-bishops in the first session of the XVI Ordinary General Assembly of the Synod of Bishops? (October 2023)*" (IL, worksheets, B 3.5).

2. Let us return, at the end of this chapter, to the question posed in the introduction to this book: namely, whether the complex web of problems accumulated over decades—resembling a knot of threads difficult to untangle—is becoming somewhat organized. A cautious, provisional assessment can be based on several observations.

If we look at the various stages in the process of listening to the "sense of faith" of all the baptized, and if we read, albeit selectively, the local, national, and continental summaries and documents, we have to admit that a real *decanting of* many—not all—problems has taken place. In any case, it would be dishonest to talk of filtering out "irritating issues"—a procedure, it's true, that has often been applied in the past.[15] The framework—indeed, the global "vision"—in which these issues are situated has broadened, and section A of the *Instrumentum Laboris* provides an initial formalization, revealing their depth, and often their complexity (section B), especially if we take into account the great diversity of local contexts.

At the same time, awareness of the fragility of the synodal process has grown: resistance and skepticism have asserted themselves, and a certain indifference is evident from the participation figures (particularly among the clergy), the "empty chair policy" also existing in Catholicism. An observer might lament the low percentages of participation and blame the factors just named. But the observer can also point out—with modest and joyful pride—that this process is a historic first and ask what other global institution has the capacity to initiate such a deliberative process, at once local, national, continental, and intercontinental. We are left with the classic question of the active participation of all Christians in the future of their churches and of the church, classic because it concerns the (by definition) porous "frontiers" of Christian universalism, giving rise to more exclusivist, even elitist, or more inclusivist attitudes. The current synodal

[15] It suffices to recall here the Instruction on Diocesan Synods (1997): "In view of the bonds uniting the particular Church and her Pastor with the universal Church and the Roman Pontiff, the Bishop has the duty *to exclude from the synodal discussions* theses or positions—as well as proposals submitted to the Synod with the mere intention of transmitting to the Holy See 'polls' in their regard—discordant with the perennial doctrine of the Church or the Magisterium or concerning material reserved to Supreme ecclesiastical authority or to other ecclesiastical authorities" (IV.4).

approach is intended to be rigorously inclusive, but it inevitably comes up against the question of motivation and even spiritual capacity to get involved and put oneself on the line.

This brings us to a third point. The process has succeeded in clarifying the question of synodal and pastoral "method" (*met-hodos*), and in bringing to the fore, along with the two central practices of Christian tradition—listening to the Word of God and celebrating the Eucharist—that of "conversation in the Spirit." The stakes in this clarification are high, for it is on this clarification that the synodal transformation of the church's everyday culture in local churches and communities will depend. Let's not forget that this is the main aim of the Synod on Synodality. So it is easy to see why the *Instrumentum Laboris* places so much emphasis on the training and practical application of this method by all the people of God, at every level of the church (IL 42, 58, and 59). This method is indeed more than just a "method"! More on this later.

❖ ❖ ❖

This long third chapter has brought us to the heart of the current synodal process. The reader will have understood its complex workings and will, I hope, already have gathered the first fruits of the process, "results" that are ultimately relatively straightforward: the assertion that synodality is a "constitutive element of the Church" has begun to take shape; the three themes—"a communion that radiates," "co-responsibility for mission" and "participation, governance, and authority"—have gradually become clearer, crystallizing a wide range of issues raised during the first phase of the synod; and, above all, a new "way of proceeding" is being accredited at all levels of the church. For this to happen, a number of conditions had to be met, and this has been and remains the role of the General Secretariat: a new emphasis on the importance of *process* in carrying out a synod; the new emergence of continental identities, to be put into dialogue; and the "return" of the pastoral approach of the Second Vatican Council. I explained these conditions after the presentation of the process and before looking at the *desiderata* and initial results.

Let's not forget that the first chapter drew attention to the play of elementary metaphors in our human life and to the spiritual geography that these metaphors outline in the micro- and macro-units of our Scriptures. During the first phase of the synod, this metaphorical interplay was both clarified and modified: first of all, there were variations on the metaphor of the "way" (*hodos*), of "journeying together" (*syn-hodos*), of "the way forward together" (*met-hodos*); and, with the questioning of governance and authority to be exercised in the church, the metaphor of the "guide on the way" (*hod-ègos*) was given new relevance.

The metaphors of the "threshold" and the "house" were enriched by that of the "tent." But we've also noticed the resistance provoked by the image of the "tent" which, in certain contexts, evokes war, the countless displaced people on our planet, and refugee camps. Some texts introduce other metaphors, such as that of the "boat," adapted to geographical configurations such as Oceania, or that of the "family" which, as in Africa, clarifies that of the "house." The "return" to these linguistic "elementals" of our human condition—"elementals" that are both the commonalities of our earthly existence and the matrices of differentiation of the cultural worlds we inhabit—is a great asset in the search just begun for a new way of speaking the Gospel and . . . of letting God speak.

Two more fundamental questions have emerged from the journey we have just completed, and they will accompany us in the final chapters of this book. First we need to return to the question of "method" and reflect on the difficult articulation of the two inseparable aspects of the Holy Spirit's work in our history: personal conversion and its collective or institutional aspect, known as "reform." We have also noticed, from national and continental feedback, that many of the tensions, indeed most of the current conflicts, concern the church's relationship with its tradition. Fears have been expressed on this subject: will the church that emerges from its synodal "reform" remain the Roman Catholic Church? Assertions in high places that the Synod on Synodality will not touch "doctrine" are an attempt to reassure those concerned on this point. And we will see in our progress report in chapter 5 and in our presentation in chapter 6 how the synod fathers and mothers heard this concern during the two sessions in October 2023 and 2024. But at the same time, it is becoming increasingly clear that the epochal change we are witnessing cannot fail to have the effect of ushering Christianity into a new phase, undoubtedly the third in its history. This realization and the fears it raises are in the background of all the commentary and analysis and will have to be addressed in chapter 7.

# Chapter 4

## A Path of Spiritual and Institutional Conversion

Faced with the unpredictable outcome of the crisis in the church and in our societies, the progress of the synodal process is giving rise to strong hope for a possible reform of Roman Catholicism, but it is also encountering a great deal of skepticism, resistance, and indifference, as I have constantly observed. However, whether these reactions are positive, reserved, or downright negative toward such a reform, which was advocated by Pope Francis from the outset of his pontificate, they are above all driven by contrasting, even contradictory, expectations. Some formulate these *desiderata* in terms of "conversion": the church's crisis is said to reveal a lack of spirituality and personal commitment on the part of many Christians, and thus addressing that lack is all that must be done to overcome it. On the other hand, some observers believe that only a serious and more or less thorough revision of the institutional structures of Catholicism, linked to a bygone civilization, could lend credibility to its will to reform and give it a future.

Here we touch on a fundamental problem that has accompanied the Latin Church since the eleventh century, when its own reformation first became a major preoccupation. It was then that the concern arose to articulate the individual conversion of each Christian and the collective response to the call addressed by Christ Jesus to each and every person: "This is the time [*kairos*] of fulfillment. The kingdom of God is at hand. Repent, and believe in the gospel" (Mark 1:15). It is this complex relationship between the individual and institutional sides of conversion, underlying the expectations just mentioned, that will occupy us in this chapter.

A brief historical and theological detour is necessary to better understand this link before addressing its consequences in the pastoral management of the expectations raised by the current synodal process. The aim is to gain a better understanding of the types of resistance mentioned above, and to assess whether and under what conditions this synod can inaugurate a path of reconciliation between opposing sensibilities and creativity.

## The Inseparable Link between Reform and Conversion

The concept of "reform" and its equivalents appeared in the Middle Ages and became a decisive theme at the Council of Constance (1414–18). We have already mentioned the Great Schism and the rivalry between three "reigning" popes, one of whom was called John XXIII (!). Understandably, this council worked toward a "reform of the head and members" (*in capite et in membris*) of the ecclesial "body." Since then, the term "reform" has haunted not only the ecclesiastical sphere but also the socio-political space of many nations.[1]

If we assume that the idea of "reform" (*reformatio*) is an extension and transfer of the biblical *metanoia* or "conversion," always singular, to the collective and institutional level of ecclesial existence, the problem of the relationship between these two sides of the same reality inevitably arises. Since the reform councils of the Middle Ages (celebrated four times in Rome at St. John Lateran and then twice in Lyon), this question has been addressed at the level of ecclesial "discipline": one or more decrees on the doctrine of faith are followed by disciplinary "canons." This structure is particularly evident in the Fourth Lateran Council (1215), which laid the foundations for a Western church that was recognized and maintained until the Second Vatican Council. The Protestant reform and the Tridentine reform of the sixteenth century also assumed that new practices could promote

[1] See the classic: Yves Congar, *True and False Reform in the Church*, trans. Paul Philibert (Liturgical Press, 2010 [orig. 1950]); also Joseph Famerée and Gilles Routhier, *Penser la réforme de l'Église*, Unam sanctam—Nouvelle série 8 (Éditions du Cerf, 2021).

inner conversion, although Martin Luther was probably more aware that they could never guarantee it. Today, the accumulation of problems in the Roman Catholic Church brings with it the risk—the temptation—of tackling the necessary reforms with leaders who are predominantly institutional or committed to an institutional structure. Perhaps this is a historical and cultural limitation of the Synodal Way of the German dioceses, which has also borne good fruit. To be content with a call to conversion, without considering genuine institutional reforms, would be to succumb to the opposite temptation of spiritualization, which is much more widespread than we think. The "revolutionary" challenge of the current synodal process is to make us aware of the intrinsic link between conversion and reform, in the name of a broader and more precise vision of the "spiritual" that carries and inspires Christian tradition. When the temporal and spatio-cultural dimensions within the synodal process become more differentiated and complex, and when all the baptized are called upon to participate (and not just a few hierarchical leaders), being invited to journey together and to relearn how to listen and speak freely, it is, in an unprecedented way, the theology of the Holy Spirit that emerges on the surface of ecclesial consciousness and requires more nuanced and refined attention. In technical terms, we can also speak of the emergence of an integrative "pneumatology," inspiring an inclusive ecclesiology. The Spirit's main role is to maintain an inseparable link between the "tensions" that make up human and ecclesial existence—each person's relationship to self and others, the collective and institutional aspect of social life, our way of living in the common house of our earth . . . and, in all this, our relationship with the God of Christ Jesus—and to enable us to resolve these tensions in a process of reform and conversion. It's worth recalling here the Pauline metaphor of the "temple of the Holy Spirit," used in the council's Constitution on the Church: "The Spirit dwells in the church and in the hearts of the faithful" (LG 4; cf. 9 and 17). This metaphor, and the doctrinal affirmation already quoted above about the people of God as "one complex reality" at the service of "the Spirit of Christ who vivifies it, in the building up of the body (see Eph 4:16)" (LG 8 §1), point to the theological origin of the "tensions" revealed by the synodal process. They were not envisaged by the council at the time, and today they require both individual and collective discernment.

Only insofar as this complex interplay of relationships, with its inevitable tensions and conflicts, is taken seriously can the synodal church become, in the words of Pope Francis in his address commemorating the fiftieth anniversary of the institution of the Synod of Bishops, "a standard lifted up among the nations (see Isa 11:12) in a world which—while calling for participation, solidarity, and transparency in public administration—often consigns the fate of entire peoples to the grasp of small but powerful groups." Indeed, it's no coincidence that at the very moment when our Western democracies in crisis are working to revitalize their public spaces, introducing new ways of deliberating on issues of general interest,[2] Catholicism becomes aware of its synodal constitution. The analogy between these two situations shall be clarified in the final chapter, as the church is not founded, as are our democratic societies, on a "social contract," but receives its identity from the summons of the one we call God. It trusts the Spirit's work in each human being's freedom of conscience while reforming its own institutions so that they can effectively encourage everyone to listen to what the Spirit is saying to the churches. This way of proceeding can have a real, transformative effect within our human communities.

What, then, are the concrete consequences of this complex articulation between what is absolutely singular and what is common to all in the pastoral management of the contrasting expectations in relation to the synodal process? We need to think about this now.

## The Limits of Institutional Rules—and Yet the Need to Take the Institution Seriously

The high standards demanded of a synodal church should be accompanied by the modest recognition that the synodal rules discussed in the previous chapter (*Episcopalis Communio*, etc.) and the summary documents can certainly guide the process but can neither reflect what is *actually* happening nor automatically produce a syn-

[2] See Jacqueline Lagrée, *Délibérer: L'expérience des comités éthiques*, Épures (Presses universitaires de Rennes, 2023); Lagrée, "La délibération en comité bioéthique," *Études* 4302 (March 2023): 43–54. Also see Jürgen Habermas, *Espace public et démocratie délibérative: un tournant* (Gallimard, 2023).

odal style that requires a long-term change in the church's internal culture.

In other words, the institutional convocation of the synod in no way guarantees that it will actually turn into a spiritual experience of conversion *and* reform. Possible shortcomings can certainly result from the very conception and problematic management of the process. But let's also recognize that, given its spiritual purpose, it could and still can be expected to meet with disinterest and resistance—we've already talked about this—and to come up against what our Scriptures call "hardened hearts."

This is the crux of the synodal process. What is ultimately at stake is the *daily* capacity of the baptized to allow themselves to be interrupted by the Word of God. In the first chapter, we gave several examples of this interruption, taken from the works of Luke; it would be easy to multiply them. In the third chapter, I reported on what is said in the *Vade mecum* and other instructions from the Roman Secretariat about the spiritual climate that should underpin the process. In particular, we pointed to the importance of "conversation in the Spirit."

1. Taking up this basic question again, we can distinguish three practices likely to encourage listening to what the Spirit is saying to the churches.

The synodal process began with a prayer to the Holy Spirit called *Adsumus Sancte Spiritus*, attributed to St. Isidore of Seville. Since the seventh century, this prayer has introduced and accompanied numerous conciliar processes:

We stand before You, Holy Spirit,
as we gather together in Your name.
With You alone to guide us,
make Yourself at home in our hearts;
Teach us the way we must go
and how we are to pursue it.
We are weak and sinful;
do not let us promote disorder.

Do not let ignorance lead us down the wrong path
nor partiality influence our actions.
Let us find in You our unity
so that we may journey together to eternal life
and not stray from the way of truth and what is right.
All this we ask of You,
who are at work in every place and time,
in the communion of the Father and the Son,
forever and ever.
Amen.

Saying this prayer together at the start of every synod meeting, at whatever level, is a way of being ready to listen. Along with the two hymns *Veni Creator Spiritus* and *Veni Sancte Spiritus*, the *Adsumus Sancte Spiritus* is one of the few prayers addressed to the Holy Spirit, who is here called "Counselor"[3] in connection with the circumstance—"as we gather together in Your name"—a particular situation in which we need not only good (human) "counselors" but also the One who is *the* "Counselor" par excellence in each and every one of us, collectively. That's why this prayer of petition is so insistent, tracing the path of the Spirit's coming from without to within: come to us, dwell among us, and deign to dwell within our hearts.

The synodal path can then rise to the surface of prayer: where to go from here, and how to orientate ourselves and walk together? The road is indeed strewn with pitfalls: weakness and sin, the danger of provoking disorder, ignorance that risks leading us down blind alleys, and, above all, partiality. Those who become aware of these temptations ask even more earnestly to find unity in him, the Counselor, the Holy Spirit, without straying from the path of truth and justice. For they know that, in the expectation of one day arriving together in

[3] This reference is not clear in the English version of the prayer published by the synod secretariat, but it is in some of the other language versions—for example, in the Spanish edition, which reads "Tú que eres nuestro verdadero consejero" ("You who are our true counselor"), where the English has "With You alone to guide us."—Trans.

eternal life and the communion of Father and Son, justice and truth are realized only provisionally—they ask not to be led "down the wrong path"—and that the Spirit whose coming they implore at the start of each synodal session acts far beyond that particular place and time, indeed, "in every place and time."

A second practice, particularly highlighted by the first session's *Instrumentum Laboris*, is "conversation in the Spirit," which follows the opening prayer. The challenge of the three rounds of this conversation is to let each participant speak as freely as possible, on an equal footing and without fear of being stopped by someone else who speaks more easily or more forcefully (provided, of course, that everyone respects the time limits). The ability to listen is mobilized during the first round, and even more so during the second, when it's time to tell others what has been heard. It's then that we can see whether we've learned anything new from listening. It's only in the third round that the "we" of the group emerges, at the precise moment when the group synthesizes what has been retained by all, without silencing weaker, more minority and perhaps less promising "voices." The art of "weighting" comes into play here, requiring both an individual and collective act of interpretation. Conflicts are bound to arise. Perhaps they are simply misunderstandings that need to be cleared up. When different, even opposing, views, conceptions, and interpretations emerge, the process becomes slower and more difficult to manage. Arguments "for and against" need to be formulated and, above all, expert information provided, for example, on a particular point of church tradition.

In the current process, the transition to this more argumentative stage of the dialogue, which then becomes a "debate," has not yet been clarified, but it will undoubtedly be in the future.

"Conversation in the Spirit" risks losing its soul if it is not accompanied, or even guided, by a reading of the Scriptures. From the very beginning of the Preparatory Document, Scripture has played a structuring role, and, in principle, each new session begins with a moment of liturgy of the Word. We may well ask, however, whether the articulation of these two sides of the *same way of proceeding* is already well in place and reflected as such. Let's face it, there are many difficulties involved, both practical and substantive. How can we prevent the Scriptures from simply being read according to the themes of our conversations and thus instrumentalized? Conversely, how can we avoid letting them simply take the place of our human exchanges, always historically and culturally situated, making us mere "repeaters" or "guardians" of a spiritual heritage from the past? In other words, how can we, in our readings and rereadings, let them have the Word until they give it back to us, here and now?

As on our shared journeys, along our "paths" of life, when questions of direction arise, the "method" (*met-hodos*) of reading and conversing requires that we first distance ourselves to let another, broader perspective intervene—in this case, that of the nascent church to which we owe our Scriptures—before a movement of interiorization occurs and we succeed in speaking freely "face to face" with the biblical text and with others. Expertise must intervene here, directly or indirectly, to avoid "fundamentalist" confusions between the "world" of the Bible and our own situations. In the final analysis, however, there is the rule that "Sacred scripture must be read and interpreted with its divine authorship in mind" (DV 12).[4] And by returning to the articulation between "conversation in the Spirit" and the reading of Scripture, we can complete this traditional formula today: "Holy Scripture must be read and interpreted in the sacred spirit in which it was written and which gives us the opportunity to converse today."

Realizing that the episode or pericope read together at the start of a synodal session does not exhaust the Scriptures—far from it!—and realizing that even the texts of the liturgical cycle give us only a limited view of the whole of the "biblical world" (we sensed this in the first chapter when we spoke of the messianic orientation of the *biblical corpus*) enable us to situate the fragment of our "spiritual conversation" today in an infinitely wider perspective: in a "place" half open to the whole of our planet and at a "moment" in the succession of generations, grappling with their unpredictable future.

The ultimate challenge is to hear God himself speak to us, and even to hear what his Spirit is saying to the churches (see Rev 2:7). This is only possible if we sharpen our ears and learn to enter into "stereophonic listening." For we hear the very Word of God, as it resounds in the Gospel of his reign, proclaimed and lived by his Only-Begotten,

[4] Translation available at https://www.vatican.va/archive/hist_councils/ii_vatican_council/documents/vat-ii_const_19651118_dei-verbum_en.html.

Christ Jesus, when we perceive the echo of this voice in what others communicate to us of their own experience, when at the same time we allow ourselves to be joined by the many human voices around us and to be reached right to our very core by the cry of some "loved one" who has fallen on the road, and when we finally listen to the silent suffering that rises from the earth and from the living.

We are thus led toward a third practice, which is the response of participants in the synodal process to what they have heard. To the *Euangelion*, the Gospel of the Father's unfathomable goodness and inexhaustible grace, responds the *Eucharistia*, the thanksgiving of Christ Jesus—integral to his itinerary and the ultimate Word of God—into which the assembly enters with the whole church it represents. If the enthronement of the Evangeliary at the start of every assembly already signified that Christ Jesus is the "president" of the assembly, he makes himself mysteriously present in the celebration of the Eucharist. Here, as on Easter Sunday, he reveals himself to his disciples in the breaking of the bread and makes them realize that the experience they have just had—their way of sharing on the road, of listening and speaking—is a gift from God for which they give thanks together.

It should be added that these three practices form a single unit, a single "*met-hodos*," a single way of proceeding, *constitutive of* the synodal march.

2. The individual and collective conversion that consists of letting God and his Spirit speak and allowing ourselves to be interrupted by this Word cannot be commanded. It is a matter for the spiritual freedom of individuals and communities, a freedom which is by no means self-evident, but which can be received as an ever-surprising gift and fostered by the three practices we have just presented.

The temptation then is to be content with a call to conversion and even to downplay the prospect of institutional reforms, on the grounds that they cannot in any case guarantee the unique necessity of conversion and that institutions as they exist are sufficient or even embody Catholic identity.

While recognizing the limits of our institutional rules and, more generally, of the institutional side of the church, we must maintain, along with the entire Western tradition, that the ecclesial institution can more or less accomplish the mission it has received. This "more or less" is precisely the first area where the need for reform comes into play. Frequently, we resort here to a set of sociological and administrative considerations, valid for all institutions and their reforms; to be content with this would be to miss the specificity of the ecclesial institution, recalled above.

Founded on the sending forth of Christ Jesus, the church and its various canonical, dogmatic, and liturgical expressions have the unique mission of making it possible to listen to the Word of God which, here and now, simultaneously summons the whole of humanity and, within it, the church, the universal sacrament of salvation, thus enabling the reception and sending forth of new baptized persons and maintaining on our planet the eucharistic response of the people of God, dispersed and constantly to be led toward unity. The reform of several institutional parameters, "more or less" adjusted to their mission, is concerned with the current synodal process.

With this in mind, it should first be noted that the configuration of the three practices presented above is already the result of an institutional reform. As mentioned in the previous chapter, the pastoral orientation of Vatican II was very largely carried by the pedagogy of Catholic Action ("See, judge, act"), which fell more or less into disuse after the council. The various "movements" of renewal—biblical, liturgical, catechetical, diaconal, and so on (named in number 6 of the Decree on Ecumenism *Unitatis Redintegratio*)—have nevertheless continued to work within the church, in a somewhat disorganized way and not without giving rise to conflicts. The current synodal process, which, as I have shown, is perfectly in line with the pastoral approach advocated by Vatican II, takes a further step toward a new institutional integration of these practices. They are in fact at the junction of what, on the one hand, is a nonprogrammable conversion, both individual and communal, and what, on the other hand, concerns the institutional reform of the church.

With these new practices, three other parameters of ecclesial institutionality are drawn into a reform movement. Named and deployed in part B of the *Instrumentum Laboris* of 2023, they concern first and foremost ecclesial communion in all its facets, including thorny issues such as the inclusion of polygamous, and LGBTQ+, and divorced and remarried people. They then focus on co-responsibility in mission, a question that also touches on the architecture of the church, the relationship between the local and the global, and the continentalization of the ecclesial structure. Finally, they cover the issues of participation, governance, and authority within a synodal church, with the difficult question of the identity of participants in ordained ministry.

It should be remembered that in these three institutional areas, the 2023 *Instrumentum Laboris* summarized questions that arose during the first phase of the synod and introduced them into a process of discernment for participants of the assembly while they met in October 2023 in Rome (while the October 2024 Roman assembly was guided by a new *Instrumentum Laboris* of its own).

3. We can reasonably hope that this will indeed be a discernment that, in line with the "revolutionary" challenge I described above, unifies conversion and reform from a pneumatological perspective that does not separate the individual and institutional sides of Christian tradition. The peace and joy already experienced by many participants in the process is a first sign of the presence of the Holy Spirit. It obliges the synodal church to take very seriously the resistance that has been mentioned on several occasions.

## Resistance—Hardened Hearts and the Enemy's Nocturnal Work

1. Several national and continental summaries of the first synodal phase refer to this resistance or indifference. In the previous chapter, I presented the document by Polish Catholics that goes furthest in analyzing these reservations toward the Synod on Synodality. This document, we saw, distinguishes four attitudes: (1) enthusiasm and gratitude; (2) mistrust of the synodal approach, associated in particular with the German Synodal Way; (3) the difficulty of ordinary Christians either to feel authorized to say something to the pope or to believe that their voices as lay faithful will be heard; (4) a notable lack of interest among many priests, lay people, and especially among residents of prosperous communities.

This realistic diagnosis calls for several comments. First of all, it reveals a perennial problem of Christian tradition: the central challenge of the baptized lifestyle—namely, "to be *in* the world without being *of* the world"—and the permanent conversion it implies is, in fact, carried out by a "little flock" (Luke 12:32; LG 5 and 9). Hence the difference between those who try to enter into this lifestyle and those who, as early sociologists like Ernst Troeltsch put it, "compromise." The post-Gregorian church had no qualms about distinguishing between two types of Christians: those who follow the evangelical "counsels"—religious men and women and priests—and those who live by the precepts, laws, and commandments of the church. From Vatican II to Pope Francis, the church has tried to go beyond this distinction, defending "the universal call to holiness" (LG, chap. V) and insisting on the participation of all the baptized in the synodal process. At the same time, however, we see a wide variety of ways of belonging to Christian tradition and the church, including what is known today as "patrimonial Catholicism." It's perfectly understandable that, especially in Christian societies whose traditional structures continue to function, the inclusive "utopia" comes up against lay people who, fully engaged in secular life, don't believe they have the right to speak up or, if they do, assume they won't be heard. This incredulity is also the consequence of a number of aborted reforms—an attitude less closed-minded, however, than the simple lack of interest of those who are satisfied with the status quo or who don't see why a reform of the church may be necessary. The enthusiasm of some, also evoked by the Polish bishops, is not always helpful, for if it is the expression of a desire to convince the resistant or the indifferent, it risks becoming counterproductive.

Another difficulty, raised by the Polish synthesis document, is expressed through opposition to the German Synodal Way, which is suspected of wanting to modify the doctrine and structure of the church rather than simply reforming its "workings." Here we come up against a confusion that has been widespread since the Second Vatican Council. The council's clear insistence on the pastoral nature of doctrine—that is, doctrine's function of regulating the dynamic relationship between the Gospel of God, the church, and the historically and culturally situated "recipients" of its mission, within an apostolic tradition in constant adjustment—is far from being received. As a result, in a relatively tense situation, some loudly insist that the synodal process may touch neither the doctrine nor the structure of the church, when in fact the Catholic Church has never ceased to evolve and continues to adjust to the plurality of cultures, an evolution that necessarily implies doctrinal and structural "reframings." I showed this in the second chapter.

In the background of this questioning of fundamental theology, which is apparently frightening in the changing times in which we live, are the difficulties arising from a vague vocabulary. When we speak of the "doctrine" or "teaching" of a council or the bishops, or of the "teachings of the Church," what do we mean? The Nicene Creed or the *Catechism of the Catholic Church*? These two documents are linked by what the Second Vatican Council calls the "hierarchy of truths": "When comparing doctrines with one another, one should remember that in catholic doctrine there exists an order, or 'hierarchy,' of truths, since they vary in their relation to the foundation of the christian faith" (*Unitatis Redintegratio* 11). Moreover, the historical context in which these texts were written inevitably marks them; it does not take away their normative status but requires that, in each new situation, what binds the church is a matter for new discernment.

This is clearly stated in the 2023 *Instrumentum Laboris*, which also takes up an affirmation of *Gaudium et Spes* (44) and *Ad Gentes* (22): "What tools do local Churches use to read the cultures in which they are embedded? How can they, in the light of the Gospel, respect and value the cultures of the different local contexts? What opportunities can they create to re-read the teachings of the Church in the light of local cultures?" (IL B 1.5, Suggestions, 1).

The fears and resistance to the synodal process are therefore of different kinds. However, they all manifest themselves on an emotional *and* an intellectual level; they are, in fact, dependent on different visions of the church, more or less marked by a relationship to our past as a European Christianity and to current cultural mutations, experienced differently according to a specific context. I will come back to this in the next chapter.

2. The individual and ecclesial discernment required here need not fear opposition and conflict. In his apostolic exhortation *Evangelii Gaudium*, Pope Francis gives them a real place, while at the same time pointing the way to overcoming them. We have already discussed his four bipolar principles, which are likely to reach the roots of human conflict and open the door, at the heart of our epochal turning point, to a new humanity (EG 221–37). The first principle—"initiating processes rather than possessing spaces"—lies at the heart of the synod's processual form, while the fourth concerns the "polyhedral" architecture of the church as a communion of churches, within which the synodal process must fit. The second and third principles, on the other

hand, have not yet been mentioned. The second principle states that "unity prevails over conflict," and the third says that "realities are more important than ideas." The range of resistance and disinterest outlined above is likely to be confronted by the two criteria outlined here. Are the protagonists of the synodal process driven by a desire for unity? Are they ready to let their conceptions be challenged by a "reality" that resists being forced into any preconceived ideology?

This discernment is certainly complex, as we have just seen. It can be based on the conviction that the Holy Spirit is guiding it in the background, but it must also be aware that what the Scriptures call "hardening of the heart" is manifesting itself at the same time. Indeed, the church is called to accept and acknowledge that, on her journey, she remains a "mixed body" (*corpus permixtum*), as St. Augustine put it, citing the parable of the field where the servants discover weeds, "the enemy" having passed by, while the good seed has been sown by the master (Matt 13:24-30). In rereading the biblical part of Jesus' itinerary, the Preparatory Document distinguishes among several actors—Jesus, the crowd, the disciples and apostles—and adds a fourth:

> Then, there is the "extra" actor, the antagonist, who brings to the scene the diabolical separation of the other three. Faced with the perturbing prospect of the cross, there are disciples who leave and mood-changing crowds. The insidiousness that divides—and, thus, thwarts a common path—manifests itself indifferently in the forms of religious rigor, of moral injunction that presents itself as more demanding than that of Jesus, and of the seduction of a worldly political wisdom that claims to be more effective than a discernment of spirits. In order to escape the deceptions of the "fourth actor," continuous conversion is necessary. (PD 21)

According to Jesus' parable, the servants are not allowed to pull up the weeds, lest they uproot the wheat at the same time. The attitude to adopt is therefore paradoxical: it consists in combining lucidity about the actions of the "antagonist," the invitation to all to conversion and reform, and the search—indicated by two of Pope Francis's four principles—for unity and a readiness to let ourselves be instructed by "reality."

## A Path to Pacification and Creativity: A Method That's More Than a Method

Only by taking seriously the various levels of resistance listed above can we hope to transform the current synodal process into a path of pacification, even reconciliation, and creativity at the service of the church's missionary presence in our societies and on our planet.

But pacification and creativity are mutually dependent. The simple juxtaposition of opposing sensitivities and conceptions, unexpressed and in latent conflict, hinders creativity; the creativity of a group, or even of a personality, that advances without taking into account those who, while belonging to the same church, are otherwise situated, leads to the reinforcement of oppositions and conflicts. The diversity of today's Catholicism can tempt one to settle for the lowest common denominator among all, and to gradually settle down to an average level. How often do we hear church leaders simply say to some person or group: "Yes, you have your place and that's good. But be careful. Others are doing it 'this way' or 'that way,' like you, and are involved in 'mission,' for example. You know that," we sometimes add, to soften what could be taken as a warning. The real points of conflict, if there are any, then remain implied, and "the new," raised by the creativity of some, is immediately put into perspective.

1. In this context, the synodal process presents itself primarily as a path to pacification, which obviously requires that all or as many Christian individuals and groups as possible actually enter into it, that they "play the game," as we also say. This is not self-evident—as we have seen—because the synodal way of proceeding already implies a vision of the church that some of those who remain at a distance refuse to accept. We can reply that, since the very beginnings of the church and as far back as the Council of Jerusalem, the synodal way is the only one that has always made it possible to settle conflicts—that's why it's "constitutive"—and that by agreeing to it, we can hope that all positions can be freely expressed—of course, within a framework in which the normative data of tradition are not only present in their diversity (linguistic and cultural) but also, without being absolutized, integrated into the common discernment.

Accepting and implementing this very first manifestation of respect for others and of Jesus' way of relating to others is the beginning of a possible path to peace and reconciliation. It is for this reason that the first part of the October 2023 assembly was dedicated to "focusing with greater clarity on the fundamental characteristics of a synodal Church" (IL, worksheets, introduction), a way of ensuring together, at a time of epochal change, the fundamental rule of a common ecclesial journey begun two thousand years ago.

It is then that conflicting issues can be addressed peacefully. Synodal conversation and debate—in the Spirit—inevitably brings to the fore a *new point of discernment*, namely, the distinction between what should remain common to all and what belongs to the charismatic diversity of churches, groups, and individuals within the whole church. This was already discussed in the second chapter, when I dealt with the charismatic constitution of the church and the sense of faith of all, "from the bishops to the last of the faithful" (LG 12). Here, I'd like to underline that the distinction between what is common, belonging to the unity of the church, and what is accepted as being diverse because it is recognized as a charism of the Spirit is mobile and has always been so to a greater or lesser extent. The gradual ecumenical awareness of the churches, the difficult internal diversity of Catholicism—with its divisions, some of which are at least as deep as those between the major "confessions"—and the continentalization of ecclesial structure all militate in favor of a discernment of the mobility of the cursor. The Second Vatican Council introduced the principle of the "hierarchy of truths" (*Unitatis Redintegratio* 11) and adopted the "Meldenius" rule, already asserted by Pope St. John XXIII: "In essentials, unity; in doubtful matters, liberty; in all things, charity" (*In necessariis unitas, in dubiis libertas, in omnibus caritas*) (see *Unitatis Redintegratio* 4 §7).

Taking this principle into account does not guarantee the disappearance of all divisions. The history of Christianity teaches us as much: addressing the Corinthians, the apostle Paul states: "[T]here have to be factions among you in order that also those who are approved among you may become known" (1 Cor 11:19). John XXIII abandoned the imposition of canons and anathemas that have characterized the church's conciliar tradition since Nicaea (325). This is not to say that heresies and schisms have disappeared; they have instead become more insidious and harder to spot. Indeed, Pope Francis became more sensitive to them, regularly denouncing Gnosticism and Pelagianism as two ways of circumventing the Gospel of grace, either through an intellectualism or ideology that believes it can master everything, or through strategic action, incapable of perceiving the work of the Spirit and the interruptions it produces. The text of the Preparatory Document echoes this, speaking of "religious rigor, of moral injunction that presents itself as more demanding than that of Jesus," or "the seduction of a worldly political wisdom which claims to be more effective than a discernment of spirits" (21). If, in late antiquity and during the second millennium of Christianity, doctrinal delimitation and exclusion became common practice, reflecting a church that understood itself as a "society," or even as a "perfect society," the history of heresies and schisms makes us more aware, not only of the context in which they appeared, but also of the challenging role they played. It is important for the synodal church to remain attentive to the appeal, often expressed emotionally or ideologically, of those who, in one way or another, have distanced themselves from the current process of conversion and reform—*in omnia caritas*—without entering into an open-ended relativism in which everything and its opposite are allowed.

It should be noted that the creativity involved here is not given to everyone. It is a "charism" that can manifest itself in different forms, sometimes linked to that of the "peacemaker," or a person who works to reconcile opposing points of view or sensitivities, and sometimes to that of the visionary or a prophetic anticipation of another figure of the church better suited to the epochal turning point that we are currently experiencing. The decisive criterion is the relationship of these charisms to the good of all (see 1 Cor 12:7) and to the "universal consensus" toward which the "sense of faith" given to each person in baptism tends; as set out in number 12 of *Lumen Gentium,* which I commented on in the second chapter of this book.

The current synodal process frees up and considerably broadens the possibilities for manifesting charisms of creativity, given by the Holy Spirit to be discerned. By abandoning the limitation of synodality to the episcopal college and to specific moments in the history of the church, Pope Francis in fact summoned *all* to become sensitive to the plurality of charisms and to recognize them, one in another and one to another. Thus, sixty years after the council, this pastoral discernment could finally become a practice, destined to enter the daily life of the churches.

At the same time as the exercise of synodality was being concentrated in the hands of the bishops, the classic distinction between "deliberation" and "advice" was intended to maintain the hierarchy's freedom of decision, with neither "advice" nor "deliberation" binding on a higher authority, such as the bishop or the pope. However, another distinction is emerging: between *"decision-making"* and *"decision-taking."* It safeguards the ultimate responsibility of the ordained ministry by giving full scope to responsible synodal work at all levels of the church. The boundary between discernment and decision is indeed porous, since consultation and deliberation are already punctuated by mini-decisions, while the ultimate decision remains suspended on the discernment of all those who, being concerned, must receive it. Only a good articulation of these two sides of the same process will make it transparent and enable all concerned to answer clearly for their decisions, in the knowledge that "all transparency" is dangerous and that, for example, personal issues must be handled with discretion by those in power.

Will this new system put an end to the more or less widespread feeling that "councils" can always be convened and "deliberated," but that in the final analysis it's a small group, or even a single person, who decides, without anyone knowing the ins and outs? This goes to the heart of the problem of so-called "clericalism." It's not just the abuse of power by a few that is the problem; it's the most visible side of the phenomenon. The long-term effect of conscious or unconscious clericalism, on the part of the faithful and clerics alike, is the sterilization of initiative. How many people have left our assemblies from the back door because their creativity, often linked to a particular charism, was not respected and received? This creativity is intimately linked to the experience of responsibility. It is only insofar as the inventiveness of each individual is truly recognized and integrated into a larger whole in which all are co-responsible that it can develop and even surpass itself. As for authority, it is already present in this process of co-responsible "decision-making," based on conversation in the Spirit and debate, while having to and *being able* to trust that its ultimate "decision-taking" will be followed by a creative reception.

Synodality as a path to reconciliation and creativity cannot therefore be reduced to a conversion that is always singular, since it is a process of *decision-making* and *decision-taking*, which implies a transformation of the church's institutional structures. But neither can it be limited to structural reforms, for it is founded on trust and respect for the charism of each participant—respect and trust that are always the fruit of individual and collective conversion. Synodality liberates the particular gifts of each individual and brings them into a mutual recognition and sharing that succeeds insofar as it makes all co-responsible. Let's face it: the realization of this "vision" presupposes a "miracle," that of emerging from our ever-recurring conflicting confrontations, so that the cooperative liberation of each person's creativity can be recognized—with the joy already mentioned—as a sign of the Holy Spirit's action.

2. This ever-surprising "journeying together" of God's people—the *syn-hodos*—requires a very specific *met-hodos*, which I've tried to grasp more closely in this chapter. It is certainly a method, but *a method that is more than "just" a method*, for it brings to life all the dimensions of our life as Christians. This is clearly demonstrated by the three essential practices of prayer (the *Adsumus*), conversation in the Spirit with moments of debate, and the Eucharist.

But we have to take seriously the conflicting dimensions of our human lives, which are often hidden when we journey together. Catholicism doesn't like to confront it too much and take into account what prevents the transformation of the equality of all the baptized into brother- and sisterhood. In an address given in Florence on November 10, 2015, Pope Francis directs the contemplative gaze of the people of God toward the image of the *Ecce homo*—"Behold the man"—which is the merciful face—*misericordiae vultus*—of an "emptied" God, "similar to that of so many of our brothers and sisters, humiliated, rendered slaves, emptied," and "we know that the best response to conflicts of human beings, from the well-known *homo homini lupus* of Thomas Hobbes is the '*Ecce homo*' of Jesus who does not recriminate, but welcomes and, paying in person, saves."[5] Referring to the lifestyle of Christ Jesus—the *Ecce homo*—synodality is a way of confronting human violence, including its nocturnal or diabolical dimension. In the very midst of our ever-recurring conflicts

[5] Text at https://www.vatican.va/content/francesco/en/speeches/2015/november/documents/papa-francesco_20151110_firenze-convegno-chiesa-italiana.html.

and exclusionary tendencies, it consists in constantly reinstating *co*mmunion, *co*-responsibility, and participation for all, and in making "*co-*" or "*syn-*" (with) the aim of the three practices we might forget are a "Christ-like" way of achieving victory over evil, violence, and death, and of participating in the Spirit's creativity. Gradually integrating this path of pacification and creativity into the church's everyday culture is, we recall, the aim of the current synodal process.

Allow me to refer on this point to a personal experience. For the past twenty years or so, I've had the good fortune to practice this way of doing things in the Diocese of Limoges, in France's Creuse department, and more recently also in the rural part of the Haute-Vienne department. The few priests who work in this area, which I sometimes call the "Amazonian area" due to its relatively remote character (thinking of the Amazon Synod and the exhortation *Querida Amazonia*), meet very regularly (every five weeks) in two separate groups (the two territories being very different) to reflect together—in the form of a "conversation in the Spirit"—upon what God has given us over the previous weeks of pastoral work.

These "returns from mission" raise a number of questions: for example, about the life and "ministry" of pastoral teams and relay teams within the few parishes that have emerged from synodal restructuring (begun in 1985), the missionary presence of communities in this hyper-rural area, Bible groups, sacramental ministry, accompanying people's itineraries, and so on. All these questions require elaboration through debates where, in a friendly climate created by spiritual conversation, different sensibilities and conceptions confront one another and reach the expression of a common pastoral feeling. This "enlightened pragmatism" is supported and inspired by an ever-increasing emphasis on reading the Scriptures. It's not unusual for us to resemble people who, following in Jesus' footsteps, together expel the demon of "pastoral melancholy."

As the years go by, and in view of the current Synod on Synodality, the limits of this experience are becoming apparent. There is no need to enumerate them in this brief excursus, which does not intend to analyze the processes underway in the church of Limoges. Suffice it to mention a fundamental difficulty already mentioned above, that of extending pastoral or missionary synodality to all Christian communities. It's one thing to practice it with priests willing to share their ministry, and quite another to have it practiced by teams and in regular parish assemblies. The difficulties are numerous, whether they are of a practical nature, arising, for example, from geographical distances and the pace of life of the people concerned, or whether they stem from our more or less conscious "clericalisms." I name them here, once again, because they have made me and us understand that the synodalization of the Catholic Church represents a true "cultural revolution." It requires a conversion of mentality that will take time and a great deal of patience on the part of those involved; but it will be able to revitalize in depth a church that is no longer afraid to be a "little flock" (Luke 12:32 and LG 5 and 9).

❖ ❖ ❖

The aim of this chapter was to reflect on the fundamental issues at stake in the current synodal process, as presented in the previous chapter. The desire for the widest possible participation—a desire that corresponds to the vision of a synodal church—necessarily brings into play the *receivers* (or opponents) of Pope Francis's synodal project and *their* diverse, even opposing *expectations*, expectations that reveal their pre-comprehensions. These concern two in-depth dimensions of the synodal process, which we have just examined, one after the other: the difficult articulation between the spiritual experience of conversion and the reform of the ecclesial institution, which are often separated or played off against each other; and taking into account resistance, indifference, or lack of expectations, which are often observed but rarely analyzed in terms of their motivations and integrated into the process.

Now, this second dimension touches on our freedom as baptized Christians and its mysterious nocturnal face, the unheard-of diversity of our charisms and the ideological hardening of our conceptions of faith and the church, discreetly evoked in the central part of the prayer *Adsumus Sancte Spiritus*: "We are weak and sinful; do not let us promote disorder. Do not let ignorance lead us down the wrong path nor partiality influence our actions" (see above, pp. 97–98). Attention to this ambivalent and conflicting dimension of our Christian lives led me to understand the synodal process as a path of reconciliation and creativity, one conditioning the other. This perspective seems so decisive to me. The fact is that when we move away from the face-to-face confrontation between adversaries or the simple juxtaposition of their positions, by agreeing to enter into an exchange of words, we liberate the charisms of each and every one, making them creative and fruitful; in a situation where the church risks becoming sterile if she remains trapped in an architecture where some have the right to speak and others are silent, where some have all the decision-making "power" and others are obliged to follow. In the midst of this crisis, the church is simply called to believe that the Holy Spirit gives the charisms that God's people need to move forward.

The reconciliation of divisions, both within the Catholic Church and in the vast ecumenical world of churches and confessions, and the emergence of a new creativity are therefore, it seems to me, the ultimate goal of an institutional reform that presupposes a genuine conversion and at the same time makes it possible. Given this goal, imposed by changing times and suggested by long post-conciliar maturation, the church can do neither: no conversion without institutional reform, no structural transformation without *metanoia*! It is the spiritual or pneumatological side of the synodal process and of the church as a whole that is at stake here, since the people of God is a "one complex reality," as we have said, that "serve[s] the Spirit of Christ" (LG 8) and "dwells in the church and in the hearts of the faithful" (LG 4, 9, and 17).

It is precisely this first dimension on which the various expectations of Pope Francis's synodal project are divided. The three practices that are both instituted *and* open to conversion—prayer, conversation in the Spirit and debate, and the Eucharist—will, I hope, enable us to move forward together toward reconciliation and release the gift of creativity in all.

Not the least of the resistance to the current synod is expressed in the fear that it will alter the structure of the church and its doctrine, and in the reassuring assertions of the Roman authorities that neither will be touched. In reality, the difficulty that arises here marks the entire synodal process and consists in questioning its relationship to the church's tradition. This difficult but central question lies within or beyond the description of synodality as a path to pacification and creativity, implying a way of proceeding or a "*met-hodos*" made up of the three practices highlighted in this chapter. It touches on the very meaning of Christian tradition and the place of the current synod in the history of the reception of the Second Vatican Council, on the significance of the reflexive formulation of its title "Synod on Synodality" (already mentioned in chapter 2) and, finally, on the new vision of the church as it seems to be emerging at the beginning of a third phase in the two-thousand-year history of Christianity. It would be dishonest not to mention this subplot of the conflicts that are now focusing on the Roman Synod.

I address this point in the last three chapters of this book, first by returning to the assembly of the synod, meeting in Rome during the months of October 2023 and 2024, and then by widening the perspective, allowing us to situate the synodalization of the Catholic Church in human history and society.

# Chapter 5

## The First Session: A Progress Report on an Open Project

Meeting in Rome in October 2023, the assembly of the Synod of Bishops aroused both very high expectations and strong fears, no doubt reinforced by the instructions for discretion given by Pope Francis to the participants. But it was above all the ambition of this synod that provoked unexpected attention, an ambition manifested in its content, summarized by the press with the unofficial description of a "synod on the future of the Church" and in its distinctive process, extensively discussed in the preceding chapters.

Faced with this mingling of expectations, fears, and ambitions, an understanding of what happened must rely in a particular way upon the assembly's Letter to the People of God (October 25, 2023) and its Synthesis Report *A Synodal Church in Mission* (October 28, 2023).[1] We can also add interviews given during and after the assembly by individual members. And I won't hesitate to refer to my own experience as an expert participant, while pointing out from the outset that the participants in the synod experienced this assembly differently and that its historical significance will emerge at a later date when, having had access to other documents and journals (I wrote my own),

[1] These texts can be found on the synod website: https://www.synod.va/en/synodal-process/the-universal-phase/documents.html. (The reader should be aware that this chapter was composed prior to the completion of the final phase of the synodal process and does not take account of documents and other sources produced during or after that time.)

historians will be able to form a panoramic picture of it. This reservation does not prevent me from proposing a provisional interpretation of the documents available and the process underway, without shying away from criticisms likely to stimulate the learning process in which we are all engaged.

With these few preliminary observations in mind, the aim of this chapter is to explain what was at stake in the first session of the 16th Ordinary General Assembly of the Synod of Bishops and in the synodal documents as "milestones" in the immense synodal project opened up by Pope Francis. This is indeed what emerges from the last chapter of the Synthesis Report, entitled "The Synod of Bishops and Ecclesial Assemblies," which, while listing a series of substantive issues to be addressed (20, d to h)[2] and inviting an evaluation of the process (20, i and j), builds on an initial consensus reached, developed in three stages (20, a to c):

a) Even when the experience of "walking together" has been tiring, the Assembly sensed the evangelical joy of being the People of God. The new experiences involved in this stage of the synodal journey were generally welcomed. The most obvious ones include the shift of the celebration of the Synod from an event to a process (as indicated by the apostolic constitution *Episcopalis communio*); the presence of other members, women and men, alongside the bishops; the active presence of fraternal delegates; the spiritual retreat in preparation for the Assembly; the celebration of the Eucharist at St. Peter's; the atmosphere of prayer and the method Conversation in the Spirit; and the very arrangement of the Assembly in the Paul VI Hall.

b) The Assembly of the Synod of Bishops, while preserving its eminently Episcopal character, made tangible on this occasion the intrinsic link between the synodal dimension of the life of the Church (the participation of all), the collegial dimension (the care of the bishops for the whole Church), and the primatial dimension (the service of the Bishop of Rome, guarantor of communion).

[2] I quote from the Synthesis Report, following the chapter number with the paragraph numbers, designated by letters of the alphabet.

c) The synodal process was and is a time of grace which encourages us. God is offering us the opportunity to experience a new culture of synodality, capable of guiding the life and mission of the Church. We recalled, however, that it is not enough to create structures of co-responsibility if personal conversion to a missionary synodality is lacking. Synodal processes do not diminish the personal responsibility of those called to participate in it at every level of the Church by virtue of their ministry and charisms, but rather solicit it all the more.

In what follows, I will first highlight the new image of the church, as manifested by the arrangement of the synod assembly itself. I will then consider the written outcome of the synod's work: namely, the synthesis document. We will then have to tackle a fundamental issue that will determine the future of the process: the place given (or not given) to theology. Having re-examined and prioritized the ecclesiological and theological questions posed by the assembly, it remains for me to consider what we can already foresee for the future.

## The Emergence of a New Synodal Culture

1. Without overlooking the fact that the October 2023 session represented only the beginning of the second phase of the synod which, after the October 2024 assembly, entered a decisive third phase, that of its reception, we can record, with the synthesis document, that a *new synodal culture* has indeed seen the light of day in Rome.

Anyone who approaches the synod solely from a theoretical standpoint, or even a theological one, fails to understand the power of images and the capacity for change and renewal that lies hidden in unprecedented practices. One need only recall the tiered seating arrangement of Vatican II and the first fifteen synods to realize the wordless, peaceful revolution produced by the arrangement of 365 delegates, including 54 women, around 36 tables in the huge Paul VI Audience Hall. Half of the facilitators of the 36 groups were women. This is still too small a percentage, as I pointed out in chapter 3, but, as you'd expect, it had a major impact on the speaking style, favoring inclusive, symmetrical language. The dress code also contributed. With the exception of the first and last General Congregations, bishops and cardinals abandoned their cassocks, and Roman collars gradually disappeared, making way for everyday attire. People moved easily between the tables, and a happy mix of people gathered for long coffee breaks.

Let's not forget that a synod is a very specific liturgy, in which deliberations and, on this occasion, circulation between participants and tables are supported and sustained by times of prayer, the Eucharist, and silence, as well as the enthronement of the Evangeliary, placing the whole assembly under the authority of Christ Jesus (practices which were extensively discussed in the previous chapter). To witness this scene, to be a participant in it, is to enter into a *lived* ecclesiology and to perceive a theology *in action*, in the hope that these will indeed provide an example to be followed and become contagious.

2. As for the deliberations, their progress was punctuated by the four stages of the *Instrumentum Laboris* of 2023, outlined at the end of chapter 3. They began with the question that Paul VI had already posed, sixty years ago, at the start of the second period of the council: "Church, what do you say you are?"[3] Three more specific stages followed, gradually unfolding the implications of a synodal church on mission: How can we live and reform the exchanges—including ecumenical—among all the churches? How can we give more space to the co-responsibility of all in the service of the church's mission? And how, in a synodal church, can we make it possible for everyone to participate in the governance of the church?

Each of these four stages was introduced by the Eucharist and the presentation of the theme to be dealt with, before two half-days of discernment in the *circuli minores*; three half-days of general congregation, during which the assembly listened alternately to feedback and numerous individual interventions; and, finally, a final session, during which each of the thirty-six tables put down in writing the fruit of this long listening in a climate of prayer and discernment. The experts were then given the task of gathering this fruit and preparing the Synthesis Report discussed by the assembly during the fifth and final stage and finally adopted on Saturday, October 28.

[3] See Paul VI, "Discours pour l'ouverture de la deuxième session" (September 29, 1963), in John XXIII and Paul VI, *Discours au Concile: Discours de Terre sainte, de Bombay et à l'ONU, messages au monde* (Centurion, 1966), 107–10.

These five stages were animated from within by the method of "conversation in the Spirit" discussed at length in the previous two chapters. Vatican II presupposed a culture of defensiveness and debate, which could draw on the pedagogy of Catholic Action ("see—judge—act," or "recognize—interpret—choose"), mentioned by the Synthesis Report in 2h. This culture has largely disappeared. The omnipresence of the concept of "action"[4] is giving way to greater attention to listening, empathy, and resonance, particularly at work in conversation, which, it should also be noted, can easily become trivialized.

The practice of this method of discernment leaves room for the unexpected . . . and also for improvisation; the whole synodal itinerary and the experience of October 2023 have amply demonstrated this. Certainly, the ways of proceeding have been repeated throughout the five stages. But this has enabled the assembly to evolve *internally* and even to undergo real "conversions." Historians will be able to analyze and evaluate it on a much broader documentary basis. The subjective choice of three events is only intended to illustrate that such an evolution has indeed taken place, without forgetting that the first assembly had no other purpose than to discern consensus and questions. I want to show that, thanks to the method and layout of the room, and above all to the presence of women, a freedom of speech was gradually established, without fear of publicly addressing a number of taboo issues. This is undoubtedly a *sine qua non* for real reform in Catholicism.

On Monday, October 16, the assembly received the six *circuli minores* summaries and listened to fourteen contributions on module B 2.3: "How can the Church of our time better fulfill its mission by recognizing and promoting the baptismal dignity of women?" Many specific points deserve to be highlighted and commented on, with chapter 9 of the Synthesis Report providing the essential information. Many sufferings were expressed. While provoking a more general reflection on the permanent diaconate (9 k and 11 g to j), women's access to the diaconate was widely praised, with several interventions even speaking of their access to presbyteral ordination; the document simply

[4] See the notion of "pastoral action" (*actio pastoralis*) and "active participation" (*participatio actuosa*) in *Sacrosanctum Concilium* 14, or that of "human activity" (*navitas humana*) in chapter III of *Gaudium et Spes*.

recalls the different positions on the first of these two questions, without revealing any preference (9 j and n). A glass ceiling was broken, if we think of John Paul II's ban on debate on these issues.

On Monday, October 23, the Letter to the People of God was read by the rapporteur and approval by acclamation was proposed to the assembly. The interventions that followed were all critical, to the extent that the synod secretary was obliged to withdraw the text and submit it to an amendment procedure. After incorporating thirty-five amendments, a new version of the letter was proposed to the assembly on Wednesday, October 25, and passed by a very large majority, after the secretary's well-received apology. Having shown signs of great docility, the assembly also demonstrated its freedom.

On the same Wednesday, a first version of the Synthesis Report was submitted to the assembly for discussion. In all, 1,251 amendments were proposed to the Secretariat. A precise comparison between the initial version and the one that was read and voted on in full, paragraph by paragraph, on the afternoon of October 28, would enable us to assess the work accomplished, the criteria for which were not revealed, let alone discussed. The fact remains that the text passed by a wider margin than the two-thirds majority required by synod regulations. Only a few controversial, easily identifiable paragraphs attracted negative votes, and these never exceeded 20 percent. Because of their ambivalent wording, these votes are difficult to interpret (I will come back to this later), and it's regrettable that these internal currents of opinion within the assembly were identified so late.

Notwithstanding these limitations (and others that we don't need to go into here), one of the first results of the October 2023 session was to have put in place the beginnings of a *new synodal culture*, involving a lived ecclesiology and a credible and therefore acceptable way of proceeding, based on the pneumatological dimension of faith.

## Synthesis Report: *A Synodal Church in Mission*

The Synthesis Report of the first session of the synodal assembly, *A Synodal Church in Mission*, is to be interpreted in this perspective. It comprises three parts, framed by an introduction and a conclusion. I reproduce here what the introduction says about this three-part structure:

> The first outlines "the face of the synodal Church," presenting the practice and understanding of synodality and its theological underpinning. Here it is presented first and foremost as a spiritual experience that stems from contemplation of the Trinity and unfolds by articulating unity and variety in the Church. The second part, entitled "All disciples, all missionaries," deals with all those involved in the life and mission of the Church and their relationships with one another. In this part, synodality is mainly presented as a joint journey of the People of God and as a fruitful dialogue between the charisms and ministries at the service of the coming of the Kingdom. The third part bears the title "Weaving bonds, building community." Here, synodality is presented mainly as a set of processes and as a network of bodies enabling exchange between the Churches and dialogue with the world.

Without going into the structural changes that occurred between the first and last versions (the chapter on "People in Poverty, Protagonists of the Church's Journey," which originally closed the first part, eventually became chapter 4), nor observing the internal modifications to the chapters (of which there are many), we must above all emphasize the overall coherence and the multiple internal relationships, which can be identified only on a second or third reading of the text. The first three chapters of the first part (which correspond roughly to the first module [A 1 and 2] of the assembly's *Instrumentum Laboris*) form a unity: placing the experience and understanding of synodality (chap. 1) in a trinitarian and ecclesiological "context" (chap. 2), and the third chapter considers the itinerary of Christian initiation, with its great variety of forms, as the paradigm of every ecclesial journey. Here we find the pastoral orientation of Vatican II (already extensively discussed) integrated into synodality, followed in the next two chapters by a consideration of the place of a "preferential option for the poor" in synodality (chap. 4) and, simultaneously, the church's openness to "every tribe, tongue, people, and nation" (chap. 5). Logically, two final chapters follow on the plurality of Eastern and Latin rites and traditions (chap. 6) and, above all, on Christian unity based on baptismal equality (chap. 7).

Like the first part, the second begins (chap. 8) with the fundamental consideration of identifying the church with its mission,[5] before dealing

[5] This identification goes back to *Ad Gentes* 2.

successively with all disciples-missionaries, women (chap. 9), consecrated life and associations of the faithful (chap. 10), deacons and priests (chap. 11), bishops (chap. 12), and the bishop of Rome within the college of bishops (chap. 13), the "ascending logic" being particularly significant.

Through implicit cross-references, the third part also grafts onto the first, beginning with "A Synodal Approach to Formation" (chap. 14), which links it to Christian initiation (14 g). It is within this overall framework that "open questions" in an inclusive church, touching on sacramental anthropology, ethics, and theology, are listed and subjected to ecclesial discernment, based on Psalm 85—"love and truth shall meet" (chap. 15)—and followed by a long development on a church that listens and accompanies (chap. 16) and that sets out for new lands, namely the digital world (chap. 17). The last three chapters continue the developments at the end of the second part of the text, now tackling questions of structural reform, including "Structures for Participation" (chap. 18), "Groupings of Churches within the Communion of the Whole Church" (chap. 19) and finally, "The Synod of Bishops and Ecclesial Assemblies" (chap. 20, already quoted in the introduction to this chapter).

On numerous occasions, the Synthesis Report calls on theology, whose uncertain place in the synodal process remains to be clarified, and the theological questions raised in its twenty chapters need to be prioritized.

## The Problematic Place of Theology

In the second part of each of these chapters (but not only under this heading), the Synthesis Report raises no fewer than seventy-five "Matters of Consideration," many of which are referred to commissions. At the same time, it has to be said that, although the twenty-seven theologians were very much present in the auditorium, they were separated from the rest of the assembly, seated around three separate tables. They were assigned the task of synthesizing the contributions of the *circuli minores* and individuals and thus preparing the Final Document, virtually depriving them of any opportunity to intervene. It's hardly surprising, then, that in the final assessment, many of the synod fathers and mothers regretted their "absence."

This ambivalent stance on the part of theology is indeed the expression of a persistent malaise. When theologians asked to be included in the *circuli minores*, the Secretariat replied that they risked influencing the emergence of the "sense of the faith of the faithful" (*sensus fidei fidelium*) within the assembly. This (perhaps legitimate) fear reflects the post-conciliar difficulty of articulating the status of theology and its ecclesial roots, a difficulty that is reinforced at a time when a former theology professor, then prefect of the Congregation for the Doctrine of the Faith, ascended to the papacy as Benedict XVI. This is not the place to address this question. Suffice it to recall the care with which Vatican II clarified the place of theology, both at the university level and within the ecclesial institutions of formation, maintaining the distinction of these disciplines while insisting on the necessary intrinsic link between them and on their unity, approached from the pastoral nature already evoked on several occasions.[6]

1. As far as the first session of the synodal assembly is concerned, the Synthesis Report reveals that a certain common theological basis, more or less diversified, was present in the assembly; it is precisely in relation to this that the "Matters for Consideration" emerged, to which I shall return.

But there are several elements to be noted. The first is the virtual absence of any specific references to Scripture or magisterial documents, including the Second Vatican Council. It is also highly significant that the categories of contents to be included in the Synthesis Report eventually became considerably scaled down from what was initially discussed. On the eve of the first session, for example, one proposed approach included all of the following categories: (1) emerging theme(s); (2) convergences and divergences; (3) presuppositions and theological, canonical, and pastoral implications; (4) new aspects (possible "steps forward"); (5) possible bottlenecks (in thinking and/or practice); (6) problems insufficiently or inadequately perceived; (7) possible additions from Scripture, church tradition, *sensus fidei*, magisterium, theology, other theological sources (*signa temporis*, history . . .); (8) varia (personal reflections) plus possible quotation(s) from authors. In the end, only three categories survived the pressures

[6] See *Sacrosanctum Concilium* 16, *Optatam Totius* 16, *Dei Verbum* 21–24, *Gaudium et Spes* 62, and *Ad Gentes* 16.

of time to be included in the published Synthesis Report: "Convergences," "Matters for Consideration," and "Proposals" for each theme addressed.

The main consequence of this reflexive absence of theology is the assembly's difficulty, if not inability, to achieve a collective awareness of its own historical situation within the Christian tradition. Yet this awareness, mainly nurtured and promoted by theology, is the *sine qua non* for identifying what is new today and submitting it to a discernment which, of course, is the responsibility of the whole assembly. This discernment then requires a capacity for argumentation within a controversial debate in which the assembly has not engaged.

The Synthesis Report at least partially acknowledges this difficulty. It appears in the margin of chapter 12 on "The Bishop in Ecclesial Communion": "Some bishops express discomfort when they are asked to speak on matters of faith and morals where full agreement within the Episcopate is lacking. Further reflection is needed on the relationship between episcopal collegiality and diversity of theological and pastoral views" (12 h). The beginning of chapter 15 expresses the same unease in another way: "The experience of Conversation in the Spirit was enriching for all who took part. . . . *It avoided us moving too quickly to a debate based on the reiteration of our own positions without listening first to the reasoning that supports the position of others*" (15 a; emphasis mine). The final chapter formulates this directly and in the form of a *desideratum*: "The contribution to the Assembly's work and the synodal Church's processes, made by experts from different disciplines, particularly theologians and canonists, also has something to offer" (20 g).

2. Given these major limitations of the synodal process, one might well ask whether it could have been done differently. We can't be sure. But the cleavage within the emerging synodal culture, illustrated by the segregation of the three tables of expert theologians, should provoke awareness and inaugurate a new learning process.

This requires a conversion and reform of theology itself, if it is to emerge from the sacred status of that which, within the church, both frightens and fascinates (*tremendum et fascinosum*, according to Rudolf Otto's definition of "sacred"). While maintaining their academic posture, theologians must remember that the people of God—all the baptized—is the *primary "subject"* of Christian theology, for it participates in the prophetic mission (*munus propheticum*) of Christ Jesus, according to the decisive statement of *Lumen Gentium* 12. Along these lines, the Working Document for the Continental Stage of the Synod, *"Enlarge the Space of Your Tent" (Is 54:2)*, evokes in number 8 "the exquisitely theological treasure contained in the experience of listening to the voice of the Spirit enacted by the People of God, allowing its *sensus fidei* to emerge."[7] This first conversion, which requires theologians to "decentralize," a process that was effectively implemented during the October 2023 assembly, leads to a second reform, which concerns the type of intelligibility of faith in theology, involving the latter's style or capacity to develop a collective understanding and a "synodal rationality" (in analogy with "political rationality"). Finally, another question concerns the effects of ecclesial synodality on the *structure of the discipline of theology*, and in particular its relationship with the human and social sciences, which are repeatedly called upon in the Synthesis Report and as early as chapter 2 (2 h).[8]

But not everything depends on the theologians' capacity for self-reform and their academic posture. The divisions within the church between a more historical and differentiated conception of Christian tradition on the one hand, and a more deductive and unitive, even intra-ecclesial, way of understanding its theology on the other, are obviously reflected within theology itself and, let's be clear, in the more or less polemical instrumentalization of this tension by institutional leaders. The aforementioned unease about "the relationship between episcopal collegiality and diversity of theological and pastoral views" (12 h) is an expression of this fundamental difficulty. Pope Francis repeatedly intervened on the reform of theology, as far back as *Evangelii Gaudium* 40 (2013), in his apostolic constitution *Veritatis Gaudium* (2017),[9] and three days after the end of the first session of the synod in *motu proprio* letter *Ad Theologiam Promovendam* (November 1, 2023).

[7] The text can be found at https://www.synod.va/en/synodal-process/the-continental-stage/resources-and-tools/documents.html.

[8] 2 h: "It is important to clarify how conversation in the Spirit can integrate the contributions of theological thought and the humanities and social sciences alongside other models of ecclesial discernment, such as the 'see, judge, act' approach or the steps of 'recognize, interpret, choose.'"

[9] Text available at https://www.vatican.va/content/francesco/en/apost_constitutions/documents/papa-francesco_costituzione-ap_20171208_veritatis-gaudium.html.

I quote the key passage of this text, which clearly orients theology toward a new way of situating itself in human history (which I have repeatedly referred to as "enlightened pragmatism"):

> 4. Theological reflection is therefore called to a turning point, a paradigm shift, a "bold cultural revolution" (Encyclical Letter *Laudato Si'* 114) that commits it, above all, to being a fundamentally contextual theology, capable of reading and interpreting the Gospel in the conditions in which men and women live their daily lives, in different geographical, social and cultural environments, and having as its archetype the Incarnation of the eternal Logos, its entry into the culture, worldview and religious tradition of a people. From there, theology can only develop into a culture of dialogue and encounter between different traditions and different knowledges, between different Christian confessions and different religions, openly confronting all, believers and non-believers alike. The need for dialogue is intrinsic to human beings and to the whole of creation, and it is the particular task of theology to discover the ways in which dialogue is possible to discover "the Trinitarian imprint that makes the cosmos in which we live a 'network of relations' in which 'it is proper to every living being to tend towards other things' " (*Veritatis Gaudium*, Foreword 4a).[10]

It is therefore entirely possible to situate this conception of theology within the "conversation in the Spirit" itself by modifying somewhat the third stage of discernment, which consists of gathering the consensus reached by the group (and then by the assembly), the dissensions that remain, the questions that need to be addressed in the future, and the proposals. It is precisely at this point that more precise information can be provided and, above all, theological argumentation can be put into practice. A fourth step would then consist in synodally weighing the arguments and thus moving toward a consensus that is historically, theologically, and pastorally well founded, in the knowledge that it must be confirmed through its future reception by the whole of God's people (thus relaunching the process).

[10] Text at https://www.vatican.va/content/francesco/en/apost_letters.index.1.html.

## Questions of Substance

Taking seriously this limited yet necessary responsibility of theology in the processes of a synodal church, we can finally attempt to organize and prioritize the many "matters for consideration" in the Synthesis Report, taking into account the internal links and ramifications of the text. I have grouped them here under five interrelated chapter headings.

1. The first question concerns the relationship between the synodal process and the Scriptures, as discussed at length in the first chapter of this book. In the October session, the Scriptures were tangibly present through their liturgical enthronement at the synod. But in the Synthesis Report, they occupy a relatively marginalized position. It is only in chapter 18 that it is forcefully affirmed: "The authority par excellence is that of the Word of God, which must inspire every meeting of participatory bodies, every consultation, and every decision-making process. For this to happen, it is necessary that, at every level, the gathering draws meaning and strength from the Eucharist and takes place in the light of the Word heard and shared in prayer" (18 c). Chapter 2 had already noted, "The contribution that *Lectio Divina* and different spiritual traditions, ancient and recent, can offer to the practice of discernment should be developed" (2 i).

Yet the complexity of the problems involved in interpreting the Scriptures in our more or less secularized cultural contexts is ignored. The third chapter of the Preparatory Document proposed a very specific and innovative way of situating synodality in the life stories of Jesus and the nascent church; I have noted this on several occasions. At strategic points in the Synthesis Report, there is a clear desire to refer to the life of Jesus (within a balance between the Christological and pneumatological aspects of the Christian mystery). These references, introduced in the final version of the text, can be found in particular in chapter 4 on "People in Poverty, Protagonists of the Church's Journey," affirming that "[t]he preferential option for the poor is implicit in Christological faith" (4 b); in chapter 9 on "Women in the Life and Mission of the Church" (9 a); in chapter 11 on "Deacons and Priests in a Synodal Church," who are asked "to reconsider the exercise of authority, modelling it upon Jesus" (11 b); to the decisive one on "Ecclesial Discernment and Open Questions," which should be inspired by the pages of the Gospel that show Jesus' encounters with "people in the uniqueness of their personal story and situation" (15 e; cf. d, g, and h); chapter 16 "Towards a Listening and Accompanying Church" (16 c, d, and l); and, finally, in the conclusion which, highlighting Jesus' way of speaking in parables, compares the Synthesis Report to "a small seed, but full of future," as the introduction had already done, applying this metaphor to the Second Vatican Council. These ultimately coherent Christological shifts were not submitted to the assembly for discernment. They will have to take place in a future reflection on the evolution of biblical hermeneutics since Vatican II's *Dei Verbum* and its reception, an evolution scarcely present in the pastoral and missionary consciousness of either the synod or the church.

2. As far as this "missionary pastoral approach" is concerned, the synthesis document makes a rich contribution. Its only flaw is the lack of articulation between its different approaches. Taking Christian initiation as "the paradigm for every ecclesial experience of walking together," chapter 3 lays the foundations for this "pastoral approach," which is taken up again in several chapters (e.g., 5 c and l), then in 8 b, and above all in the development on "A Synodal Approach to Formation" (chap. 14, remarkably reworked), then in chapters 15 and 16 on "Open Questions" and "a Listening and Accompanying Church." If we link all these contributions together, "pastoral action" (a concept used by Vatican II) moves toward encounter and an effective "presence" to others in their singularity, a "presence" made fruitful through listening and a way of speaking, inspired by Scripture and supported by formation. The genetic or catechumenal form ("graduality") of this pastoral and missionary action, so decisive at Vatican II (see, e.g., *Sacrosanctum Concilium* 9–13 and *Ad Gentes*, chap. 2), is certainly present in the Synthesis Report (3 a to f) but overtaken by another logic that begins with the Eucharist (3 k to m). Tensions between different ways of understanding evangelization are mentioned (5 j), but not really analyzed, even though they greatly handicap the church's pastoral and missionary action.

3. A fundamental aspect of the pneumatological element of this action and of the "presence" of a synodal church in society is attention to the "charisms" of the faithful. This term is omnipresent in the Synthesis Report (twenty-two occurrences), almost always linked to those of "vocation" and "ministry." There are very few passages in

which we can discern an interest in the discernment of a particular "charism," either before or after it is taken up in ministry (2 l and 3 i in connection with the sacrament of confirmation). Chapter 10, originally entitled "The Charismatic Dimension of the Church" and dealing almost exclusively with religious life, now bears the more aptly titled "Consecrated Life and Lay Associations and Movements: A Charismatic Sign." The charismatic dimension is recalled as a mere backdrop, making it possible to talk about consecrated life, even though around a quarter of the synod fathers and mothers were religious.

Indeed, the post-conciliar church, including the current synodal process, finds it hard to grasp the pastoral stakes lurking in *Lumen Gentium* 12 (analyzed in detail in the second chapter of this book) on the participation of "the holy people of God" in "Christ's prophetic office," participation based on respect for and discernment of the Spirit-led and almost infinite variety of charisms (§2) and simultaneously on the *sensus* and *consensus fidelium* (§2) achieved through synodality, whose "constitutive" status[11] results from these two aspects of Christian existence.

4. The cultural and societal roots of Christian life are discussed in chapter 5 of the Synthesis Report on "a Church 'of every tribe, tongue, people and nation.'" Not unrelated to its charismatic dimension, this rootedness has, or should have, an impact on its architecture. In the document, this is approached from a double perspective: on the one hand, from the angle of a theology of local churches and intermediate structures, national and continental, envisaged in the last three chapters of the document but also already in chapters 12 and 13, which deal with bishops and the Petrine ministry; and, on the other hand, from the angle of "the diverse expressions of being Church": "This requires a search for a dynamic balance between the dimension of the Church as a whole and its local rootedness, between respect for the bond of Church unity and the risk of homogenization that stifles variety. Meanings and priorities vary among different contexts, and this requires identifying and fostering forms of decentralization (5 g)."

[11] See Pope Francis, Address Commemorating the Fiftieth Anniversary of the Institution of the Synod of Bishops.

On this second side, we find the distinction between Eastern and Latin traditions within the Catholic Church (chap. 6) and the path toward the unity of all Christians (chap. 7), but also the question of the "hierarchy of truths."[12] Unfortunately, no mention is made of this principle, even though it is hidden behind what the quoted text says about the variation of "meanings and priorities" according to context. If we look closely, most of the contentious issues, already present in the *Instrumentum Laboris*, are strongly marked by this contextuality. They require differentiated treatment at local, national, and continental levels of the church.

A twofold problem needs to be examined in greater depth here: the question of the "hierarchy of truths," which can be fruitfully approached in a dialogical, even "synodal" way in terms of its implementation at the various levels mentioned just now, and, as a result, the question of the "distribution" of discernment and decision-making competences for their resolution (according to the principle of subsidiarity, mentioned several times during the synod).

5. These open questions, which are part of both moral and sacramental theology, form a final field of work. They have been at the forefront of the ecclesial and social scene for two or even three previous pontificates. The synod proposes *a new way of approaching them*, based on the life and ministry of Jesus and anthropological reflection, taking account of "the complexity of the elements emerging from experience or knowledge in the sciences and require greater precision and further study" (15 g). This new approach, outlined in chapter 15, remains fragile because it does not contextualize its novelty in relation to post-conciliar moral and sacramental theology.

These few soundings in the Synthesis Report *A Synodal Church in Mission* were intended to draw attention to the *systemic nature* of the contentious issues raised by the synod, of course, to be resituated within a renewed messianic vision of God's holy people on our changing planet. They were also intended to show that, for the reasons indicated above, which stem from a theological deficit, the synod had difficulty in achieving a sufficiently clear awareness of its precise position in the history of Christian tradition, which perhaps explains certain defensive, even incantatory discourses on the presence of the

[12] Decree on Ecumenism *Unitatis Redintegratio* 11.

Holy Spirit. Indecision still hangs over the whole process, which remains divided between a more historical and genetic approach, undoubtedly influenced by Latin American theology, and a more deductive and intra-ecclesial one.

## How Should We Proceed?[13]

How will the work progress at the construction site left open by the first session of the assembly in October 2023, pending the second session? That's the question on the minds of many faithful followers and observers.

In *Ad Theologiam Promovendam*, Pope Francis addressed the form and function of theology; I quoted the most important passage above. Two other texts are worth mentioning, as they address the "open questions" recognized by the synod, particularly in chapter 15 of the Synthesis Report: first, the "Answers to several questions from His Excellency Msgr. José Negri (Brazil) concerning the participation of transgender and homosexual persons in the sacraments of baptism and marriage (October 31, 2023)"[14] and then the declaration *Fiducia Supplicans* of the Dicastery for the Doctrine of the Faith on the pastoral significance of blessings, with a chapter on "Blessing of irregular and same-sex couples" (chap. III).[15] The second, in particular, might have had greater impact if Rome had waited to publish it until after the deliberations of the second session of the synod.

On December 11, 2023, the synod secretariat published a road map entitled "Towards October 2024," which presents a number of orientations approved by the Ordinary Council.[16] The text is complex.

[13] This part of the text was composed (and published in this book's original French edition) as the synod process was still ongoing. Chapter 7 below was written after the synod concluded and from that point of view.

[14] The document can be found on the website of the Dicastery for the Doctrine of the Faith: Complete List of Documents, https://www.vatican.va/roman_curia/congregations/cfaith/doc_doc_index.htm.

[15] Dicastery for the Doctrine of the Faith: Complete List of Documents. It is regrettable that the text does not use the significant expression of chapter VIII, which speaks of "discernment of 'irregular' situations."

[16] This text, together with a questionnaire and chronological diagram, can be found at https://www.synod.va/en/synodal-process/the-universal-phase/towards-the-2024-assembly.html.

Nevertheless, we can identify two main instructions, inspired by a guiding question: How can we be a synodal church on mission? First, the invitation to the local churches, considered to be the first subjects of the synodal process, to share their "good practices which represent the seeds of concrete synodality" in a new consultation (the results of which are to be collected by the bishops' conferences). Here we find attention to the emergence of a synodal culture, through conversation in the Spirit or other ways of discerning the missionary path to be taken together, in connection with some chapters of the second[17] and third part[18] of the Synthesis Report. It is the collection of these contributions by the bishops' conferences and Eastern hierarchical structures that eventually formed the basis of the *Instrumentum Laboris* of the second session.

The other instruction relates directly to the content of the report's twenty chapters; it is more open and is addressed both to local churches and to the synodal bodies of the church as a whole. Local churches are invited to peruse the report, collect the requests that best correspond to their specific situation, and return them to the General Secretariat. When shared with synod members, they form the broader framework for the assembly's work without entering into the *Instrumentum Laboris* of the 2024 session. As for *all the* many questions in the Synthesis Report, they were summarized as follows:

> These are matters of great importance [says the Secretariat], *some of which need to be considered at the level of the whole Church and in collaboration with the Dicasteries of the Roman Curia*. These matters include, for example, the preliminary study in view of the updating of the CIC and the CCEO (Synthesis Report, ch. 1 lett. r), of the *Ratio fundamentalis* on the formation of ordained ministers (chap. 11 lett. j), of the document *Mutuae relationes* (chap. 10 lett. g); or the deepening of theological and pastoral research on the diaconate and, more specifically, on women's admission to the diaconate (chap. 9 lett. n), etc. *A list of these topics will be submitted to the Holy Father* as the fruit of the Synod Assembly. Groups of experts from all continents together with the relevant Dicasteries of the Roman Curia and coordinated by the General Secretariat of the Synod will be asked to work in a synodal way on the topics

[17] "All Disciples, All Missionaries."

[18] "Weaving Bonds, Building Communities."

indicated by the Holy Father. A report on the progress of this work will be presented at the Second Session in October 2024.[19]

The complexity of these various proposals is, to a large extent, due to the very structure of the synodal process, which seeks to create a genuine circulation among the local churches as the first subjects of synodality, the groups of churches on a national and continental level, and the worldwide church to initiate a way of proceeding and to address the major questions of the Synthesis Report. Different competences are thus involved in this global ecclesial dynamism, within which the synod Secretariat tried to keep a firm grip. The complicated style of this road map is perhaps the trace of conflicts of competence, which, all things considered, are normal, given that we are just beginning to emerge from an acquired distribution of decision-making "powers," mainly concentrated in the hands of the Roman Curia.

Admittedly, the document calls on theological and canonical expertise, as well as the human and social sciences, both locally and church-wide. But the integration of theologians as co-responsible partners in the way we proceed and the reform on all sides that this implies have not really begun, as the document as a whole remains formal on this point, without raising any historical awareness.

❖ ❖ ❖

I cannot end this progress report without reiterating my conviction that the process initiated by Pope Francis in October 2021 is a historic event that, because of its ambition, is on a par with the Second Vatican Council. It will hardly be possible to turn back the clock, given the frankness (*parrhesia*) with which, for the first time, all or almost all contentious issues are being put—literally—on the table to be discerned and led toward solutions that correspond to what the churches and the church hear the Spirit saying today (see Rev 2:7). The Roman Catholic Church has begun a cultural change. Only time will tell whether the new way of proceeding, as practiced by the synod, will have truly taken root in the people of God and effectively created a new synodal culture.

[19] Text at https://www.synod.va/content/dam/synod/news/2023-12-12_towards-2024/ENG_Document_TOWARDS-OCTOBER-2024_XVI_II-Session.pdf.

As for the doctrinal and theological content of the Synthesis Report, one chapter, recalling the Second Vatican Council, says more than all the others about the historical stakes of the first session of the sixteenth synodal assembly: chapter 7, "On the Road Towards Christian Unity." This chapter is the only one to use the biblical vocabulary of "*kairos*," speaking of an "ecumenical *kairos*." Referring to the "Together" prayer vigil, which saw the presence alongside Pope Francis of many other leaders and representatives of different Christian communions, the text states:

> b) Baptism, which is at the root of the principle of synodality, also constitutes the foundation of ecumenism. Through it, all Christians participate in the *sensus fidei* and for this reason they should be listened to carefully, regardless of their tradition, as the Synod Assembly did in its discernment process. There can be no synodality without an ecumenical dimension.

This paragraph creates a link, hitherto little perceived, between number 12 of *Lumen Gentium* on the prophetic mission of Christ Jesus, shared within the people of God—a text I commented on in chapter 2 of this book—and the ecumenical progress made since the Decree on Ecumenism of the Second Vatican Council. The text places particular emphasis on the ecumenism of everyday life and includes ecumenical concerns among the "Matters of Consideration," such as the ways various Christian confessions understand the synodal configuration of the church (7 g), the relationship between synodality, collegiality, and primacy, particularly as understood by the Orthodox Church (7 h), and the question of eucharistic hospitality. Among the five propositions (which I quote here in full), three are particularly noteworthy (7 k, l, and n), as they take up with the beginning of conciliar history and the first doctrinal and liturgical questionings of nascent Christianity, and at the same time with its present situation in the epochal turning point we are currently experiencing:

> The year 2025 marks the anniversary of the Council of Nicaea (325) at which the symbol of the faith that unites all Christians was elaborated. A common commemoration of this event will help us to better understand how in the past controversial questions were discussed and resolved together in Council.

> In the same year, 2025, providentially, the date of the solemnity of Easter will coincide for all Churches and Christian communities. The Assembly expressed a keen desire to come to a common date for the feast of Easter so that we can celebrate the Resurrection of the Lord, our life and our salvation, on the same day.
>
> There is also a desire to continue to involve Christians of other Churches and ecclesial traditions in Catholic synodal processes at all levels and to invite more fraternal delegates to the next session of the Assembly in 2024.
>
> A proposal has been put forward by some to convene an ecumenical Synod on common mission in the contemporary world.
>
> It was also proposed that we might devise an ecumenical martyrology.

These proposals paint a very broad ecumenical picture. In the next chapter, we will see how the second session of the synod approached it.

# Chapter 6

# The Second Session: Final Work and the Beginning of the Reception

Between October 2 and 27, 2024, for its second session, the assembly of the Synod of Bishops took place in a rather different climate from the session of the previous year. Public opinion, which had been highly mobilized in 2023, was no longer enthusiastic about the event, and far fewer journalists came to Rome. In some parts of the world, expectations were focused on a few crucial anthropological questions concerning ecclesial governance: the integration into our communities of people grouped under the acronym LGBTQ+; the place and responsibility of women in the church, including their access to diaconal ordination; the problem of the drastic decline in presbyteral vocations in Europe and the ordination of *viri probati*; and the increasingly contested clericalist attitudes of some priests and bishops, including but not only in the context of the 2021 independent commission report on sexual violence in the church in France and equivalents in other European countries.

But the entrustment of these questions to study groups outside the synod, as well as two high-profile comments by Pope Francis in which he rejected the possibility of diaconal ordination of women (in an American television interview in May and to students at the Catholic University of Leuven in September) just before the 2024 assembly opened on September 28, all served to reinforce a latent skepticism about the reformability of Catholicism by those who considered these issues to be urgent. This was also true in the opposite direction for another type of Catholics and some priests, who feared that the synod would tamper with what they consider to be the substance of the faith. Still virulent in certain extreme groups, their resistance has become generally quieter or more passive, perhaps because they are counting on the synodal movement running out of steam and, ultimately, on a change of pontificate. In any case, *the constitutional importance* of reworking the objectives of the second session of the assembly seems not to have been understood by public opinion. On the contrary, a misunderstanding of its purpose has gradually set in.

Although the assembly was marked by this global climate and by the decreased interest of Catholic media around the world, it took place in a more relaxed atmosphere than the previous year: the joy of reunion was palpable, the participants were already familiar with the way things were done (though some of them had changed, in particular the group of fraternal delegates, which was expanded to include representatives of sixteen other Christian traditions), and the deep experience of the catholicity of a truly global church was shared by all.

This climate must be taken into account when interpreting the synod's second phase, which ended on October 27, 2024, with the closing Eucharist in Saint Peter's Square. Reiterating the methodological precautions of the previous chapter, I refer mainly to the *Instrumentum Laboris* for the second session and to the Final Document, entitled *For a Synodal Church: Communion, Participation, Mission* (= FD).[1] The latter is preceded by an important "Accompanying Note by the Holy Father Francis," and its publication was followed by his inaugural address of October 2 and his final address of October 26, 2024. In what follows I will consider these as well as some interventions by synodal fathers and mothers, and will rely, as in my review of the first session, on my own experience as a participating expert.

While the 2023 synod session consisted of a "progress report" on the immense synodal project initiated by Pope Francis, the 2024 session marked, in a sense, the "end of the project," which now needs to be *received*—that is, to be implemented—by all the local churches

[1] Text available at https://www.synod.va/content/dam/synod/news/2024-10-26_final-document/ENG---Documento-finale.pdf.

and the church as a whole. This is clearly expressed in the introduction to the Final Document, which summarizes all the progress made since 2021:

> The synodal process does not conclude with the end of the current Assembly of the Synod of Bishops but also includes the implementation phase. As members of the Assembly and as synodal missionaries within the communities from which we come, we feel it is our responsibility to promote this process. The local Churches are asked to continue their daily journey with a synodal methodology of consultation and discernment, identifying concrete ways and formation pathways to bring about a tangible synodal conversion in the various ecclesial contexts (parishes, Institutes of consecrated life and Societies of apostolic life, movements of the faithful, dioceses, Episcopal Conferences, groupings of Churches, etc.). Planning for an evaluation of the progress made in terms of synodality and the participation of all the Baptised in the life of the Church should also occur. (FD 9)

I will return to the canonical status of the Final Document and attempt to interpret the state of consensus reached at the end of the second phase of the synod. But first, it is necessary to consider the intersessional period and the composition of the second *Instrumentum Laboris*, before being able to retrace the itinerary of the second session, return to the thorny question of the place of theologians in the process, and consider the Final Document and the assets it offers to work toward a true reform of world Catholicism.

## Intersession

1. In the previous chapter, I already began to reflect on the follow-up given by the Secretariat of the Synod to the work of the first session. It should be noted that the twenty chapters of the Synthesis Report, voted on at the end of the first session, left the church with eighty "questions," preceded by the observation of a significant number of "convergences" and followed by a series of "proposals."

How, in concrete terms, can such an impressive range of issues be addressed, covering both topics already addressed by the Second Vatican Council and other, newer ones? It is understandable that the unprecedented freedom with which all these topics were put on the table, without excluding any, may have caused some dizziness or even a wave of panic. For this reason, in December 2023, the Secretariat of the Synod issued a roadmap, entitled "Towards October 2024," which included some guidelines that it then clarified on the following March 14 in two documents: *How to Be a Synodal Church on Mission?* (not to be confused with the *Instrumentum Laboris* for the second session, published just four months later with the title *How to Be a Missionary Synodal Church*), which offered "five perspectives for theological exploration" by the synod's second session, and *Study Groups for Questions Raised in the First Session of the XVI Ordinary General Assembly of the Synod of Bishops to Be Explored in Collaboration with the Dicasteries of the Roman Curia.*[2] A strategy emerges from these that will have to be assessed in the light of the ecclesial climate mentioned at the beginning of this chapter and the fundamental problems raised by the first session. The way forward, chosen by Pope Francis and the secretariat, was to approach these issues in *two series*.

The five perspectives offered in the first of the two documents are intrinsically linked to the central theme of the process and oriented toward the guiding question of the second session: *How* to be a synodal church? These perspectives focus first on the "missionary architecture" of the church as a whole, considering its three levels: local (in section I), national/continental (II), and universal (III). The other two perspectives are cross-cutting and concern the synodal method (IV), a decisive issue that accompanied the synod from its convocation, and the issue of "territory" or "place" (V) at a time when mobility is profoundly transforming our relationship to the dimension of space.

While during the first session theologians acted as simple secretaries, preparing the Synthesis Report, they were then more involved in the preparation of the new Working Document, thanks to five working groups, each focusing on one of the five perspectives.

In a second document, *all other questions* formulated during the October 2023 session were entrusted to ten study groups, made up of experts from all over the world and members of the various dicasteries of the Roman Curia, under the direction of the Secretariat of the

[2] Texts available at www.synod.va.

Synod, which was responsible for ensuring their "authentically synodal treatment." The ten themes to be considered from a synodal and missionary perspective are: (1) the relationship between the Eastern Catholic Churches and the Latin Church, (2) listening to the poor, (3) the digital environment, (4) the revision of the norms for the training of priests, (5) ministerial roles, including access of women to the diaconate, (6) the relationship between the episcopate, consecrated life, and associations of the faithful, (7) the ministry of the bishop, (8) the role of papal nuncios, (9) controversial doctrinal, pastoral, and ethical questions, and finally, (10) the fruits of the ecumenical journey.

Clearly, dealing with this second series of topics requires specific theological, anthropological, pastoral, and canonical skills, and it changes the pace of progress for the "synodal caravan." How, then, can the link between these ten working groups and the synodal assembly be maintained? This is the question answered by these two documents, which insist that this link is primarily institutional but also procedural. It is institutional because the ten study groups will have to report on the start of their work to the assembly in October 2024 and complete it, if possible, before the end of June 2025. As for the way forward, the challenge is to "listen together to the voice of the Spirit, the true master of harmony and communion, who overturns our plans and our expectations to create something new,"[3] according to the secretariat's March 14, 2024, policy document, which also calls for the involvement of the Roman Curia, referring to the synodal method, which I will come back to.

Let us add that the boundary between the work of the ten study groups and the specific objective of the October 2024 assembly remains porous. The *Instrumentum Laboris* for the second session, which I will come back to, makes explicit reference to the questions put to each of these groups, even quoting some of them twice, and establishes strong links between these themes and the synodal future of the missionary church. It thus reopens the process of discernment by announcing from the outset that the assembly will not provide answers to all the questions and that it can be expected that other questions will emerge on the path of conversion and reform that the

[3] See *Study Groups for Questions Raised*, 2.

second session will invite the whole church to undertake.[4] However, it promises "concrete changes that can be seen quickly," especially concerning the synodal functioning of ecclesiastical councils and the procedures for evaluating people in positions of authority.[5]

When publishing the *Instrumentum Laboris* for the second session, on July 9, 2024, the Secretariat of the Synod announced the composition of all the working groups, except for Group 5 (on specific forms of ministry, including the access of women to the diaconate), adding the laconic remark: "The Dicastery [for the Doctrine of the Faith] has begun its study according to the procedures established in its own Regulations, with a view to the publication of a specific Document."[6] This is in stark contrast to what the *Instrumentum Laboris* states about the necessary transparency of ecclesial decisions. This was not without consequence, as we shall see, throughout the second session of the Synod.

2. The titles and styles of the *Instrumentum Labori* of the first and second sessions are very different: while the title of the first simply expresses the overall orientation of the synod—*For a Synodal Church: Communion, Participation, Mission*—and, based on the feedback from the first phase, the text brings together three series of worksheets, consisting of questions to be addressed by the assembly, the second is entitled *How to Be a Missionary Synodal Church* and takes the form of a composed and skillfully structured text. We thus move from a kind of major ecclesial brainstorming to the question of a concrete implementation. The second *Instrumentum Laboris* begins with an introduction that summarizes the progress made over the past three years, followed by twenty-one paragraphs that set out the theological "foundations of the vision of a missionary synodal Church." This emphasis on the "vision" is particularly important in a situation in which public opinion is focused on a particular issue, deemed urgent, and pastoral care largely operates in silos. Let us note the programmatic remark that makes the secretariat's strategy clear: "Responding to the question 'How to be a synodal Church in mission?' requires a

[4] See the *Instrumentum Laboris* for the second session, *How to Be a Missionary Synodal Church*, July 9, 2024 (= IL2), Introduction, X.

[5] See IL2 1.

[6] See the list of members of the study groups at www.synod.va.

horizon within which to place pastoral and theological reflections and proposals, helping to orient us on a path of conversion and reform. In turn, the concrete measures implemented by the Church will allow the horizon to be brought into sharper focus and a deeper understanding of foundations to be gained in generative reciprocity between theological reflection and pastoral practice that marks the entire history of the Church" (IL2, introduction to Foundations).

As for this vision, which incorporates some elements of the ecclesiology of the Second Vatican Council and, notably, introduces a development of the common meaning of synodality and of "unity as harmony of differences" (in the spirit of the pneumatology of St. Basil), the text holds a surprise for readers. Among the "foundations," it deals with the place of women in the church under the heading "Sisters and Brothers in Christ: A Renewed Reciprocity" (IL2 13–18; thus abandoning the classical language of "complementarity"). These paragraphs already make clear the secretariat's "strategy," which I will come back to later: the text begins by basing equality between women and men in the church on baptism, then promotes a change in mentality, lists all the existing (and often underutilized) possibilities for women's participation, encourages the exploration of new ministerial and pastoral forms, and reports a series of concrete requests from local churches (for example, the participation of men and women in preaching, including during the Eucharist). "While some local Churches call for women to be admitted to the diaconal ministry, others reiterate their opposition. On this issue, which will not be the subject of the work of the Second Session, it is good that theological reflection should continue, on an appropriate timescale and in the appropriate ways," the *Instrumentum Laboris* (17) reports, then refers immediately to the work of study group 5.

The core of the document is made up of three parts, entitled respectively "Relations," "Pathways," and "Places." These titles are very simple, as is the concrete and accessible language of the entire text.

The first part begins by referring to the "web of relationships" that constitutes human existence and which, for Christians, is rooted in the journey of initiation; from the first session, this pathway (*synhodos*), indeed, this genetic conception of Christian life and the church, determined this synod's particular synodal, missionary style. The rest of the text gradually brings out the concrete implications, starting with the "charisms" of each baptized person, so little considered in our ordinary pastoral care, and the different types of ministries, old or new, to arrive at the questions currently raised by the exercise of the ordained ministry "at the service of harmony." The text summarizes the classical theology of the priestly and episcopal ministry, while introducing nuances, insisting, for example, on the traditional link between the episcopal function and the presidency of a local church. "Re-establishing the traditional link between being a bishop and presiding over a local Church is important, restoring the correspondence between the communion of bishops (*communio episcoporum*) and the communion of Churches (*communio Ecclesiarum*)" (IL2 41). This part ends with a long development on synodality as an "exchange of gifts" in the local church and between churches, an exchange that is particularly difficult but significant in neocolonialist or violent contexts.

The second part, "Pathways," addresses the processes that contribute to nurturing and developing the relationships discussed in the first part. Four "distinct but profoundly intertwined areas" within the church's life are analyzed: the integral and shared formation of all pastoral ministers, ecclesial discernment for mission, decision-making processes (including a call for the correction of current language in canon law that risks diminishing the value of consultation of the faithful by leaders), and the transparency of the church's processes, requiring accountability. At the heart of this methodological journey is a brief phenomenology of the experience of listening that, together with spiritual conversation, is perhaps the main achievement of the synodal process thus far, touching on both the pneumatological constitution of the church and the way of living it out in concrete terms. The aim is to listen to God, who has spoken and continues to speak to his people today. It is a listening that I call "stereophonic," because it passes simultaneously through different "channels," a plurality of voices: Scripture and the life of the Church, the "voices" of others, of the earth, and ultimately of each person's own conscience, a space where all these other voices are heard and where our decisions are formed (IL2 61).

Finally, the third part deals with "Places," that is, the contexts and cultures in which the church lives its life. The perspective is innovative because it consists of analyzing the mobility, both physical and digital, that is so easily available to people today:

> Without forgetting that life always takes place in physical contexts and concrete cultures, it is necessary to move away from a purely spatial interpretation of place: places, even and especially those of the Church, are not just spaces but environments and networks in which relationships can develop, offering people rootedness and a basis for mission, which they will carry out wherever their lives unfold. The synodal conversion of minds and hearts must be accompanied by a synodal reform of ecclesial realities, called to be roads on which to journey together. However, this does not mean consigning pastoral action to elective affiliations. The aim is to encounter every man and woman. (IL2 86)

On this basis, the document reviews the structure of the church, starting from the local church, the parish (with a long development on councils at various levels, their accountability, the appointment of their members, their composition, etc.), and then moving on to the other ecclesial levels (and their councils, for example, the bishops' conferences, whose authority, including doctrinal, should be clarified), including the continental assemblies, and finally the service of the unity of the bishop of Rome (IL2 100–108).[7]

The conclusion of the document returns to the vision discussed in the presentation of the theological "foundations" of a synodal, missionary church, taking up and completing the messianic "utopia" of the prophet Isaiah (Isa 25:4-8) already cited in the epigraph of the text.

On the basis of this document, the seven "continental" churches organized assemblies to prepare for the October session. A significant number of European delegates and theologians met for two days in August 2024 at the Faculty of Theology in Linz (Austria) under the aegis of the Council of European Bishops' Conferences. The question,

[7] See also the important study document, Dicastery for Promoting Christian Unity, *The Bishop of Rome: Primacy and Synodality in Ecumenical Dialogues and Responses to the Encyclical* Ut Unum Sint, June 13, 2024, https://www.christianunity.va/content/unitacristiani/en/documenti/altri-testi/the-bishop-of-rome.html.

asked by delegates from other continents, about the place of the churches of Europe in the *Communio Ecclesiarum* was heard for the first time, and the desire was expressed to get to know each other better, going beyond the images that the churches have of each other.

## The Synodal Itinerary of the Second Session

1. As in the previous year, the second session began with a two-day retreat for all the members of the assembly. It was preached by Fr. Timothy Radcliffe, OP, who created an atmosphere of contemplation and listening and subtly challenged the assembly with his British humor. He commented on the apparitions of the risen Christ in John 20–21; this text subsequently provided the biblical framework for the synod's Final Document. Two further periods of prayer helped to support the assembly's discernment, at the beginning of the last week (October 21), when it received the first version of the Final Document, and on Saturday, October 26, to prepare for the afternoon voting session. In the previous chapter, I already drew attention to the fact that a synod is a liturgy that places the assembly under the authority of Jesus Christ and in a position to listen to "what the Spirit is saying to the Churches." In addition to the prayer services at the beginning of each morning's general congregation, often accompanied by a brief commentary on the day's biblical text, each of the four modules and the final week of recapitulation culminated in a eucharistic celebration.

Two other celebrations, in particular, marked the spiritual journey of the assembly. The first was the penitential vigil that closed the retreat, centering the synod on the God of *mercy*, so central in the thinking of Pope Francis and his predecessors:[8]

> We cannot deny that we have faced fatigue, resistance to change and the temptation to let our own ideas prevail over listening to the Gospel and the practice of discernment. Yet, the mercy of God, our most loving Father, purifies our hearts, thus enabling us to continue along this journey. Acknowledging this, we began

[8] See esp. Pope Francis, *Misericordiae Vultus: Bull of Indiction of the Extraordinary Jubilee of Mercy*, April 11, 2015, https://www.vatican.va/content/francesco/en/bulls/documents/papa-francesco_bolla_20150411_misericordiae-vultus.html.

> the Second Session of the Assembly with a penitential vigil, through which, feeling our shame, we asked forgiveness for our sins, and we lifted up our prayers for the victims of the evils of the world. We identified our sins: against peace, against Creation, against indigenous peoples, migrants, children, women, and those who are poor, in our failure to listen and to seek communion. We were brought to a renewed understanding, namely, that synodality requires repentance and conversion. (FD 6)

The other celebration took place on October 11 in the historic Piazza dei Protomartiri Romani ("square of the Protomartyrs of Rome") between St. Peter's Basilica and the Domus Sanctae Marthae. It was an ecumenical vigil led by fraternal delegates in memory of the opening of the Second Vatican Council (October 11, 1962) and the promulgation of the Constitution on the Church, *Lumen Gentium*, and the Decree of Ecumenism, *Unitatis Redintegratio*. There is no better way of emphasizing that there are places in Rome and in the heart of the Vatican that are not the "property" of Catholicism but belong to all Christians who refer to the origins of the Christian tradition. The ecumenical prayer vigil in St. Peter's Square at the opening of the first session of the synod was of a similar nature. Celebrated with many leaders of other churches and representatives of other Christian traditions alongside Pope Francis, with all the members of the synod and with many young people from Taizé, this vigil presented a vision of the unity of all Christians in which the Petrine ministry can play an ethical and theological role—perhaps the only truly global one on our planet—recognized by all Christians without their having to embrace the Latin and Roman model of the church's catholicity. Before considering the Final Document, it is worth looking at the deliberative side of the synod.

2. As in the first session, the debates of the second session were guided by the four parts of its *Instrumentum Laboris*. The synod dealt successively with the theological "foundations" of missionary synodality, "relations" within the church and between churches, methodological "pathways" to be taken, and the "places" of embodiment of the church. Each of these four modules was organized in more or less the same way. After a presentation of the theme by the rapporteur, two sessions in *circuli minores* initiated discernment according to the method of spiritual conversation already explained, resulting in a

two-page text. This initial deliberation was then followed by three sessions (two for the first module) in general congregation in which the assembly heard individual voices.

A new system was put in place to organize these debates. At the end of the first small-group work, one delegate from each table participated with her or his language-group peers in a meeting to discuss, in the presence of one of the theological experts, the themes to be addressed in the general congregation.

The results of these five "language tables" were then summarized by the secretariat and communicated to the members of the synod. Unfortunately, the very general formulation of these themes meant that the interventions in the aula were somewhat scattered and there was a lack of real debate among the participants. A second mechanism was undoubtedly more effective. Four forums of almost two hours each were intended to help participants address the theological issues of the synod. The synod fathers and mothers could reflect, in the first series (October 9), alternately on "the people of God as the subject of mission" or "the role and authority of the bishop in a synodal Church," and in a second series (October 16) on "the mutual relations between the local Church and the universal Church" or "the exercise of the primacy and the synod of bishops." A theologian, a canon lawyer, and a bishop first presented the subject and then answered questions and reactions from the audience.

However, the individual interventions during two or three general congregations for each of the four modules did not have the final say. They were followed by a final meeting in *circuli minores*, in which the two pages written at the end of the first two meetings were reread and, if necessary, corrected and/or completed according to the discernment after everything that had been heard previously. All these pages from the thirty-six tables and the individual interventions were then sent back to the secretariat to be "synthesized" by the theologians and included in the first draft of the Final Document.

This was submitted to the assembly at the beginning of the last synodal week, on Monday, October 21, in the spiritual atmosphere of a third day of retreat, before being discussed in the *circuli minores* and in the general congregation, giving rise to 1,135 amendments. These were organized by the theologians and then integrated or rejected by the elected members of the commission for the drafting of the Final Document. On Saturday, October 26, the assembly received the final version of the Final Document, which was put to the vote on the afternoon of the same day. With at least two-thirds support for each paragraph, the text was adopted. Pope Francis's final greeting and the singing of the *Te Deum* brought this very last general congregation to a close.

3. This initial description of the proceedings of the second session is an inadequate account of what actually happened. For the time being, only the participants can testify to it, pending a much broader documentary account by historians. Several facts, events, and themes profoundly marked the *inner* development of this second session.

We have already mentioned the more relaxed and almost "family-like" *atmosphere* that prevailed in the assembly. It might have made us forget the presence of representatives of local churches from 116 nations across the planet, from fifteen Eastern Catholic Churches, from religious orders and congregations, and from sixteen non-Catholic churches and traditions. With each intervention in the general congregation, a new window opened for a few moments, briefly revealing a different kind of Christian and ecclesial life, sometimes in a corner of the world that many of us did not know. While most of the contributions focused on one of the themes on the synodal agenda, it often happened that at the end of a module, those who had not yet spoken used their speaking time to provide a glimpse of some aspect of the life of their church. Thus, on October 17, at the eleventh general congregation, toward the end of the debate on the *Instrumentum Laboris,* we heard about much suffering: wars, migrations, persecutions, political imprisonments, and so on, in Bolivia, Sudan, Eritrea, Lebanon, the West Bank, and elsewhere. But hope is never far away, as in the brief account by a Marist brother about the rebuilding of a school in Haiti.

The warm atmosphere could also have made people forget the obvious asymmetry between the continental churches. It is clear that the churches of Latin America, North America, Africa, and Europe exercised a certain leadership; the churches of Asia and Oceania and the Eastern Catholic Churches had the status of dispersed minorities, which colored their experience of synodality, not to mention the diversity of their positions within their societies and among other religions.

Within the synod hall, a dizzying experience of catholicity gradually emerged: a catholicity *in depth*, given the diversity of the churches; a catholicity *in the process of becoming ecumenical*, given the fraternal delegates who gathered around the tables, enjoying the same rights as the Catholics (except the right to vote); and finally, a catholicity as social *"prophecy,"* given the contrast in the way differences and conflicts within the assembly were managed and the divisions that mark our societies.

As for the *events and themes* that marked the second session of the synod, we must first mention a certain failure of the pope's visit to the University of Louvain (in contrast to his highly publicized visit to Indonesia, Papua New Guinea, East Timor, and Singapore). This failure was reinforced by the lack of transparency in the work of study group 5 on questions concerning specific ministerial forms (with theological and pastoral research on the ordination of women to the diaconate). These setbacks weighed heavily on the assembly throughout its journey.

At the first general congregation, on the afternoon of October 2, the ten study groups, the commission of the episcopal conferences of Africa and Madagascar on polygamy, and the canonical commission each reported on the beginning of their work and presented their members. The exception to this was study group 5, whose president, the cardinal prefect of the Dicastery for the Doctrine of the Faith, Víctor Manuel Fernández, hid behind a mandate from the pope, received *prior to* the establishment of the ten study groups, to refuse to give the names of the members of his commission (in accordance with the rules of his dicastery) and provided only basic information on the group's work. At the same time, the members of the synod were informed that it would be possible to meet with these groups and commissions on Friday, October 18, during the assembly's break. When the time came, Cardinal Fernández did not attend, sending two priests from the dicastery to answer the participants' questions. This was perceived by many members of the synod as a sign of contempt, a feeling that a press release published late in the evening and a subsequent attempt at an explanation—without an apology (!)—failed to dispel. Finally, the cardinal proposed a new meeting, which took place two days before the end of the synod, on Thursday, October 24. The exchange did not change anything: faced with the objections of a few theologians, the prefect defended the lack of representation within the study group (largely Roman and Italian-speaking) for practical reasons, pointed out the lack of clarity regarding the identity of the permanent diaconate, insisted on the lack of consensus regarding women's access to this ministry, and reiterated classic arguments (such as the feminine nature of the church), while recalling the numerous still-unused possibilities for women's leadership at all levels of the church.

In the meantime, a few women delegates, facilitators, and theologians, with great boldness and quiet confidence, requested an audience with the pope, which was granted. No doubt this unexpected meeting, which took place the day after the unfortunate meeting of October 18 without Fernández, somewhat changed the climate and the situation, even if many believed that Pope Francis's opinion was fixed. In any case, it should be noted that no other study group has generated as much interest as the one on the place of women in the church, perhaps because public opinion, which had lost interest in the process, had put the spotlight on this decisive issue.

A second theme, which was prominent during the first session, emerged more discreetly in the dual context of the rejection of *Fiducia Supplicans* by many African bishops and the African commission on the pastoral care of persons living in polygamous marriages: both of these ethical questions were entrusted to study group 9. When Kinshasa's Cardinal Fridolin Ambongo, president of the polygamy commission, called for patient pastoral accompaniment of polygamous Catholics, Fr. James Martin, SJ, supporter of the LGBTQ+ community in the United States, appealed for similar treatment for the people he serves.

Other issues aroused a certain amount of interest, in particular the integral formation of Christians and pastoral ministers (module 3), episcopal conferences and their doctrinal authority (module 4; a question that the pope had already addressed in the apostolic exhortation *Evangelii Gaudium*), and small communities as a place of an authentically evangelical life, the topic of a whole series of interventions by participants from several different continents. The vast majority of synod fathers and mothers felt significantly more at ease in dealing with pastoral issues than with doctrinal, ecclesiological, or even canonical matters.

Quite quickly, a feeling of stagnation set in at the general congregations, due to a certain repetitiveness and generality of many interventions and the fact that the synod is not conceived as a decision-making body. With time and fatigue, the atmosphere even became somewhat depressive—the conversations during the breaks showed this. But this did not prevent the assembly from pulling itself together and finding interest in dealing with the subjects mentioned above. Also, the times of prayer and celebration carried it, especially during times of desolation. The uncertainty regarding the outcome of the second session and the nagging desire to return to the local churches with tangible and realistic results—commensurate with the enormous investment—weighed heavily until the end, with some (including myself) arguing in favor of a third session to receive the work of the study groups in a synodal manner, while others saw little point in it.

## The Place of Theologians

In addition to the canonical status of the synod, to which I will return, the relatively limited place occupied by theology also had something to do with the spiritual climate of the assembly (I must acknowledge here the personal character of my observations on this subject). In the previous chapter, I offered a detailed analysis of the role played by women and men theologians during the synod. This time, there were thirty-one of them. Their task, carried out with the same care during the second session, consisted mainly of synthesizing the contributions of the *circuli minores* and the individual interventions during the general congregations and also of preparing the Final Document, written by four of them, two Italian-speaking and two English-speaking. For this work, they divided into four language groups: Italian, English, Spanish, and French. The latter immediately began working together and gradually introduced the desiderata of the assembly and its requests for corrections into the second *Instrumentum Laboris*, the result of collective intelligence that was praised by the Secretariat of the Synod.

The integration of theologians into the overall synodal process was considerably strengthened after the first session. They participated in the preparation of the themes of the second *Instrumentum Laboris* in five theological commissions dealing with the structure of the church (with its three levels: local, national or continental, and universal), method (*met-hodos*), and the "places" where the churches take root. They were present in the linguistic groups that, at the beginning of each module, determined the topics to be discussed in the general congregations. And finally, they were involved in the four "theological forums." On two occasions, they were called upon at short notice: during the discussions on the doctrinal authority of the episcopal conferences and to help the participants understand the canonical status of the Eastern Catholic Churches, also known as churches *sui iuris*.

This is undoubtedly the maximum that could be implemented under the current conditions of the synodal institution. In addition to the limits of time and the rules of the game, already expanded by Pope Francis in his apostolic constitution on the Synod of Bishops, *Episcopalis Communio*, an important cultural issue came into play. While the Second Vatican Council was able to rely on a culture of debate and argumentation—as I have emphasized several times in previous chapters—the Synod on Synodality operated within a *culture of conversation* (or palaver in Africa) that thrived on each other's experiences and their narration. Both cultures have their strengths and weaknesses: the first runs the risk of abstraction or of distancing itself from concrete cultural realities, while the second is threatened with becoming locked into a particular experience or local situation and encountering difficulties when it comes to problematizing and universalizing the subject; the first thrives on the confrontation of arguments and ideas but can also degenerate into an ideological battle between opinions and trends, while the second is more irenic but sometimes hides a fear of conflict, thus risking anemia.

As for the Synod on Synodality of the church, the culture of conversation favored a rather synchronic approach to ecclesial reality, without referring extensively to the history of the Christian tradition. Admittedly, the Final Document understands the synod as an "act of reception of the Council," using the biblical parable of the sower to explain the fecundity of the council, and of course it quotes extensively from its main texts:

> Rooted in the Tradition of the Church, the entire synodal journey took place in the light of the conciliar Magisterium. The Second Vatican Council was indeed like a seed thrown onto the field of

> the world and the Church. The daily life of believers, the experience of the Churches in every people and culture, the many testimonies of holiness, and the reflection of theologians represented the soil upon which it has taken root and grown. The Synod 2021-2024 continues to draw upon the energy of that seed and develop its potential, putting into practice what the Council taught about the Church as Mystery and Church as People of God, called to holiness through a continual conversion that comes from listening to the Gospel. In this sense, the synodal journey constitutes a further act of reception of the Council, thus deepening its inspiration and reinvigorating its prophetic force for today's world. (FD 5)

This reference is relatively general and risks not only obscuring the complexity of the council's reception process and, by extension, the fundamental issues at stake in the current synodal process, but also underestimating, at a time when we are experiencing a "change of era,"[9] the need to draw on the history of Latin and global Christianity in order to become collectively aware of our unprecedented situation within a tradition that is two millennia old. It could have been the role of theology to introduce this perspective into the spiritual conversation and missionary discernment of the synod. But perhaps it should be humbly recognized that this very (too?) demanding aim would have exceeded the culture and the possibilities of the assembly.

It therefore draws a future scenario, inviting the churches to engage with theologians to work toward an articulation of the culture of conversation and the culture of argumentation. The Final Document recognizes the specific service of the "charism of theology." It calls "theologians to do theology in a synodal way" and considers as "urgent" the need for "dialogue between Pastors and those engaged in theological research according to appropriate institutional forms" (FD 67). In this vein, two symposia, one prior to the synod (April 27–29, 2023) and another following it (October 28–30, 2024), organized by the Secretariat of the Synod and the Gregorian University, laid the foundations for such a cultural and institutional articulation, which were then taken up by a large gathering of representatives from all the faculties of theology, led by the Dicastery for Culture and Edu-

[9] Pope Francis, "Meeting with the Participants in the Fifth Convention of the Italian Church," November 10, 2015.

cation, on "The Future of Theology: Legacy and Imagination" (December 9–10, 2024).

These few notes on the progress of the second session and on the cultural conditions of the drafting work, which was entrusted to the theologians, now allow us to read the Final Document itself, to evaluate its coherence and relevance, to present the tools it offers for its reception, and to consider the degree of support it ultimately found in the assembly.

## The Final Document and Its Prophetic Thrust

1. Let us first recall the Final Document's title: *For a Synodal Church* (which risks being reduced to the abstract term *synodality*). This echoes the title of the Preparatory Document (2021), abandoning the "how" of the second *Instrumentum Laboris*. It therefore indicates an aim, ultimately messianic, that requires a path of conversion. The subtitle, *Communion, Participation, Mission*, has not changed since the beginning of the process; it is made up of three key words, the middle one of which points to the *novelty* of this synod.[10] Of course, it had a prominent place in Vatican II's Constitution on the Sacred Liturgy *Sacrosanctum Concilium* (1964) in the call for "fully conscious and active participation" in the liturgical action, situated on the *path* that starts from the proclamation of the faith and *passes through* Christian initiation *toward* the eucharistic liturgy as the "summit and source" of *all* the missionary activity of the church (see nos. 9–11). Today, *participation* in the church is therefore expressed through synodality, which, based on baptism, is in a way inserted between the hearing of the word of God and the eucharistic celebration (see FD 27) and becomes—and this is the *new* development—"the specific *modus vivendi et operandi* of the Church, the People of God, which reveals and gives substance to her being as communion [the first of the three key words] when all her members journey together, gather in assembly and take an active part in her evangelising mission [third key word]" (FD 31).[11]

[10] See Pope Francis, Address on the Occasion of the Moment of Reflection for the Beginning of the Synodal Journey, October 9, 2021; see above, p. 22.

[11] See above, pp. 128–35.

The structure of the Final Document (which follows that of the second *Instrumentum Laboris*, with a few significant changes) is the following:

| | |
|---|---|
| Introduction | |
| Part I | The Heart of Synodality:<br>Called by the Holy Spirit to Conversion |
| Part II | On the Boat, Together:<br>The Conversion of Relationships |
| Part III | "Cast the Net": The Conversion of Processes |
| Part IV | An Abundant Catch: The Conversion of Bonds |
| Part V | "So I Send You":<br>Forming a People for Missionary Discipleship |
| Conclusion | A Feast for All Peoples |

Let's start with a few preliminary remarks, before going into more detail.

First, the retreat preached at the beginning of the second session by Timothy Radcliffe focused on the accounts of the resurrection in the Gospel of John, chapters 20 and 21. These same accounts also form the biblical framework of the Final Document's text: each section opens with a paragraph of figurative exegesis that creates a link between characters of the Gospel story and believers today. A similar approach was employed at the heart of the Preparatory Document and in the second chapter of the Working Document for the Continental Stage which, like the conclusion of the Final Document, refers to the prophet Isaiah.[12]

Second, the key word of the five parts—indeed, the main issue of the synodal process—is *conversion*, which appears in the titles of four of the five parts. This conversion is a process that is at once individual and fraternal, inseparably spiritual and institutional (thus also implying a reform of the institutions[13]). The penitential vigil that ended the

[12] See above, pp. 11–14 and 69–70.

[13] See above, pp. 101–3.

inaugural retreat of the synod is an expression of this desire for conversion. Published to everyone's surprise during the last week of the synod, on October 24, Pope Francis's encyclical *Dilexit Nos*, on the human and divine love of the heart of Jesus Christ, seemingly has no connection with the synodal process. However, it designates the central "place" of conversion, the human heart, repeatedly pointed out in the Final Document.[14]

Third, the Final Document retains the broad structure of the second *Instrumentum Laboris*, with one difference: the latter's Part II, "Pathways," deals successively with "integral and shared formation," and the three practices of discernment, decision-making, and accountability, whereas the Final Document separates them into two parts, the third ("The Conversion of Processes") and the fifth ("Forming a People of Missionary Disciples").

Addressed separately in the Working Document, in the form of a quasi-introduction, the "Theological Foundations" of synodality now constitute the first part ("The Heart of Synodality: Called by the Holy Spirit to Conversion") of the Final Document.

2. On this basis, we can now look more closely at each of the five parts.

Part I sets out the theological and spiritual foundations of synodality. Compared to the second *Instrumentum Laboris*, a few significant changes are worth noting.[15]

Initially appearing at the very beginning of the Part I of the latter ("Relations"), the reflections on Christian initiation (so decisive throughout of the synodal process) were introduced in the first part—the theological part—of the Final Document, immediately after the first section on "The Church as the People of God, a Sacrament of Unity," now forming a beautiful unity with it. The theological and pastoral effect of this change is considerable. It confirms the council's choice to deal with the baptismal equality of all Christians within the one people of God before considering the "hierarchical" distinctions

[14] See FD 43 on synodal spirituality; FD 51 (with a quote from *Dilexit Nos* 17) on our relationships; FD 110 on the heart, the primary "place" where all our relationships resonate, rooted in each person's personal relationship with Jesus Christ and his church; and FD 154 (conclusion), which recalls FD 51.

[15] See above, pp. 143–47.

within it.[16] It also takes the sacramentality of the church (see LG 1, 9, and 48) out of a certain abstraction by reconnecting it to the sacramental *roots* of the people of God: baptism, confirmation, the Eucharist. This is a paradigmatic *path* of initiation in a church becoming catechumenal.[17] It is particularly fortunate that this same section ends by recalling the close link between *synaxis* and *synodos*, between the eucharistic assembly and the synodal assembly (FD 27). It is only in the third section ("Meaning and Dimensions of Synodality") that the sacramentality of the church appears for the first time, but now from a dynamic or missionary, even eschatological, perspective:

> By being close to all without distinction of persons, preaching and teaching, baptising, and celebrating the Eucharist and the Sacrament of Reconciliation, all the local Churches and the whole Church respond concretely to the Lord's command to proclaim the Gospel to all nations (cf. Mt 28:19-20; Mk 16:15-16). By appreciating all charisms and ministries, synodality enables the People of God to proclaim and witness to the Gospel to women and men of every place and time, making itself a "visible sacrament" (LG 9) of the fellowship and unity in Christ willed by God. Synodality and mission are intimately linked: mission illuminates synodality and synodality spurs to mission. (FD 32)

It should also be noted that the "subjects" of this path, which is simultaneously missionary (or initiatory) and synodal, are the *local churches*. From the very first section of this part, the Final Document effectively incorporates ecclesiological knowledge that was barely present at Vatican II, which, for the most part, still had a universalist and uniform conception of the church:

> In the holy People of God, which is the Church, the communion of the faithful (*communio fidelium*) is at the same time the communion of the Churches (*communio Ecclesiarum*), which is manifested in the communion of Bishops (*communio Episcoporum*) by reason of the very ancient principle that "the Church is in the Bishop and the Bishop is in the Church" (St. Cyprian, Epistle 66,

[16] See above, chap. 2, pp. 21–26.
[17] See above, p. 130.

> 8). The Lord placed the Apostle Peter (cf. Mt 16:18) and his successors at the service of this manifold communion. By virtue of the Petrine ministry, the Bishop of Rome is "the perpetual and visible principle and foundation" (LG 23) of the Church's unity. (FD 18)

It is unsurprising to find in this first section "a special place for the poor" (FD 19), a concept already advocated during the council by the group known as Jesus Christ and the Church of the Poor (see LG 8),[18] and, subsequently, a brief review—more cross-disciplinary than in the second *Instrumentum Laboris*—of the ecclesiology of Vatican II, based on what this number 20 calls a "crisis of participation."

A second new feature of this first part is found in the section on *synodal spirituality*. It is the direct result of the call to conversion, the key word (as already mentioned) of the entire Final Document. The four paragraphs devoted to it introduce the decisive point of the synod, namely, "hear[ing] what the Spirit says to the churches" (Rev 2:7, etc.), the personal dispositions that this listening requires (FD 43), its community aspect (FD 44), the tool of conversation in the Spirit (FD 45), and, perhaps above all, the healing and reconciliation that synodality necessitates, given the urgency of rebuilding trust everywhere (FD 45).

Third, we note in passing that the section on the place of women in the church, called "Sisters and Brothers in Christ: A Renewed Reciprocity" and included among the "Foundations" in the second *Instrumentum Laboris* (13–18), was introduced in Part II of the Final Document, on "The Conversion of Relationships." Some participants regretted this, mindful of the sensitivities of many of our contemporaries. However, this displacement corresponds to the overall logic of the text.

Fourth, entitled "Synodality as Prophetic in Today's World," the last section of Part I develops an insight from the second *Instrumentum Laboris* concerning the "important perspectives for humanity offered by the synodal style of the Church." The two paragraphs of this text

[18] See Luis Martinez Saavedra and Pierre Sauvage, *Le pacte des catacombes: Une Église pauvre pour les pauvres: Un événement méconnu de Vatican II et ses conséquences* (Lessius, 2019).

are indeed decisive for a better understanding of the missionary aspect of synodality.

Part II of the Final Document effectively develops the anthropological basis of the relational aspect of synodality. This concept is presented in Part I of the second *Instrumentum Laboris* only in an intra-ecclesial way; the Final Document does it from the perspective of conversion of the heart and reform of our relationships and structures.

The first two sections are entirely new. They deal first with the "desire for more real and meaningful relationships" (FD 50) within our humanity, the church's ability to nourish them, and their renewal and their conversion through the Gospel by adopting Jesus' practices of hospitality and gratuitousness (with a quote from the encyclical *Dilexit Nos*), thus joining the revelation of God the Father in him and in the Spirit: "When our relationships, even in their fragility, allow the grace of Christ, the love of the Father, and the communion of the Spirit to shine through, we confess *with our lives* our faith in God the Trinity" (FD 50; emphasis added). It is in this context that the text deals for the first time with the relationships of equal dignity and reciprocity between men and women (citing Gen 1:27 and Gal 3:27-28), without ignoring the recurring expressions of pain and suffering of women from all regions and all continents (FD 52).

This relational game is, then, situated *in a plurality of contexts*, with the text then referring to "distorted relationships that are not in keeping with the Gospel," not only in society but also within the church (FD 53–55). This emphasis on the interweaving of good with evil—the church being, according to St. Augustine, a "mixed body" (*corpus permixtum*), so clear in the wake of the abuse crisis—led the synod to reconsider its "sacramentality" (LG 1) as a work in progress (see FD 56). But such interweaving within the church and societies is not only negative but also positive: "At the same time, being open to the world allows one to discover that the Spirit has sown the seeds of the Gospel in every corner of the globe, in every culture and in every human group. These seeds bear fruit in the ability to live healthy relationships, cultivate mutual trust and forgiveness and overcome fear of diversity. They also give life to welcoming communities, promote an economy respectful of people and the planet and bring about reconciliation after conflict" (FD 56).

Continuing its inductive approach of "deepening" our relationships, the second part then essentially takes up the section of the first part of the *Instrumentum Laboris*, which deals with charisms and ministries. The novelty of the Final Document consists in first broadening, following the first two sections, the charismatic structure of all baptismal life to the presence of Christians not only and primarily in the church but also and above all in ordinary life, thus once again specifying the challenges of mission and the necessity of discernment and ecclesial accompaniment:

> Each Baptised person responds to missionary needs in the contexts in which they live and work, according to their dispositions and abilities. This demonstrates the freedom of the Spirit in bestowing God's gifts. Owing to this dynamism in the Spirit, the People of God, listening to the reality in which they live, discover new forms of commitment and new ways to fulfil their mission. Christians, each according to their diverse roles—within the family and other states of life; in the workplace and in their professions; engaged civilly, politically, socially or ecologically; in the development of a culture inspired by the Gospel, including the evangelisation of the digital environment—walk the paths of the world and proclaim the Gospel where they live, sustained by the gifts of the Spirit. (FD 58)

The text then goes through these different life situations, starting with that of women in society and in the church (FD 60), a text that continues the anthropological reflection begun in FD 52, then speaking of children (FD 61), young people (FD 62), people with disabilities (FD 63), spouses (FD 64), and the various expressions of consecrated life (FD 65), before dealing with the configuration of certain charisms as "ministries" (FD 66) and the "specific service" of the "charism of theology" (FD 67).

The next section, which deals with ordained ministry "at the service of harmony," takes up the developments of the second *Instrumentum Laboris* (35–41) but focuses them more directly on the ministry of bishops, priests, and deacons (FD 68–73), reserving an entire section to "Collaboration between Ordained Ministers within a Synodal Church" (FD 74).

A final section, entitled "Together for Mission," continues the reflection on the ministerial nature of certain charisms. Having been interrupted by the paragraphs on the ordained ministry, this topic is now taken up again from a creative perspective that, following two texts by Pope Francis on the ministries of lector, acolyte, and catechist, described as "sacramental" (FD 75), consists of opening up a whole field—ministerial or otherwise—of participation *by women and men* "in response to the pastoral needs of our time in a spirit of collaboration and differentiated co-responsibility" (FD 75–78).

Part III of the Final Document (which partially incorporates Part II of the second *Instrumentum Laboris*, on "Pathways") builds on this broadening of the church's charismatic and ministerial terrain, showing that it is doomed to failure if it is not supported by a *conversion of processes*. Since this part focuses on working toward a cultural change in Catholicism, I will deal with it in the next section of this chapter on the reception of the synod. I have also opted for this order of presentation because Part IV of the Final Document actually continues the reflections of Part II. Like Part II, it is situated on an anthropological and ecclesiological level, but now on a higher scale, both planetary and at the level of the communion of the churches (*communio ecclesiarum*), guaranteed by the college of bishops (*communio episcoporum*) and the Petrine ministry of the bishop of Rome.

Part IV, corresponding to the section entitled "Places" in the second *Instrumentum Laboris*, now places greater emphasis on the "bonds" between geographical and cultural spaces and their evangelical conversion,[19] addressed on a human level and on an ecclesial level, in accordance with the orientation of the entire Final Document: "This is the synodal Church in action—it is founded on bonds of communion that unite us and with space for all peoples and all cultures. In a time when there is great change occurring in the way we conceive of the places where the Church is rooted and on pilgrimage, we need to cultivate new forms of the exchange of gifts and the network of bonds that unite us. In this, we are sustained by the ministry of the Bishops in communion amongst themselves and with the Bishop of Rome" (FD 109).

[19] With an implicit reference to the encyclical *Dilexit Nos* in FD 110; see above, note 14.

The first two sections of the text, on the tension between our local and cultural *roots* in the world and our status as nomads or *pilgrims*, as well as on the evangelical principle of the *exchange of gifts*, offer a rapid but precise diagnosis of the situation of human beings on our planet at a time of increasingly massive urbanization, a redefinition of rural areas, increased mobility, intercultural communities, and the spread of digital culture (see FD 110–13). "These social and cultural developments challenge the Church to reconsider the meaning of 'local' in its life and to review its organisational structures so that they can better serve its mission. It is essential to understand 'place' as the real and actual setting in which we come to experience our humanity, without denying that there is a geographical and cultural dimension to this as well. Here, where the web of relationships is established, the Church is called to express its sacramentality (cf. LG 1) and to carry out its mission" (FD 114).

It is worth noting in passing that this paragraph offers us a third mention of the sacramentality of the church, calling for the concept to be rooted again in the sacraments of initiation (FD 32), understood in a dynamic and evolving way, without concealing the failings of the church (FD 56), and expressed in its deep-rooted relational networks (FD 114). The text then goes through these different expressions in the church as a "house" (FD 115), as a local church (FD 116), and as a parish (FD 117), followed by some general remarks on the transversal action of consecrated life (FD 118) and on the " 'intermediate' spaces" between the local church and the universal church (FD 119).

As for the evangelical principle of the *exchange of gifts* that gives life to the interrelations between all these ecclesial "spaces," chapter 2 of *Lumen Gentium*, on the people of God, had already fully explained it (see LG 13 and FD 120). This brings to mind the institution of "*Fidei Donum* priests," who, in the twentieth century, were sent from their home dioceses in Western nations to mission territories of Africa; today it is African priests who largely keep the ministerial structures of the churches of Europe alive. Some sensitive debates in the synod assembly on the sending of priests from churches with many clergy to those with few and on economic aid to poorer churches from richer ones, including acknowledgment of the history of colonization and the problem of the lack of cultural awareness, are reflected in just a few general remarks of the Final Document (see FD 121). The document also mentions three *supranational and intercultural geographical areas* that are particularly significant for this exchange of gifts—the Amazon, the Congo River basin, and the Mediterranean Sea—and the more traditional areas of ecumenism (FD 122) and interreligious dialogue (FD 123).

It is in this evangelical context of exchange of gifts that the text addresses, in its last two sections, the role of episcopal conferences and ecclesial assemblies, which are intended to strengthen the unity formed by bonds, as well as the service of the bishop of Rome. On all these points, the Final Document adopts a rather programmatic, general style, anticipating subsequent canonical determinations and more detailed clarifications. From the outset, it sets out a principle to guide the reforms: "A synodal style allows local Churches to move at different paces. *Differences in pace* can be valued as an expression of legitimate diversity and as an opportunity for sharing gifts and mutual enrichment. This common horizon requires discerning, identifying and promoting concrete practices which allow us to be a synodal Church on mission" (FD 124; emphasis mine).

The Final Document remains hesitant regarding the relationship between the different ecclesial "levels" and their respective competencies. This is the case when it comes to the need for a greater understanding of the doctrinal authority of the episcopal conferences, which Vatican II (in *Ad Gentes* 22) already called for in order to facilitate inculturation of the faith. This is also the case for "specifying that decisions made by an Episcopal Conference impose an ecclesial obligation on each Bishop who participated in the decision in relation to his own diocese" (FD 125), a delicate situation in highly divided national episcopates. A fortiori, the same difficulties are manifest at the level of continental, regional, and national ecclesial assemblies (see FD 126 and 127). The unclear distinction between "purely pastoral or disciplinary questions" and "issues of faith, morals, or sacramental discipline" (FD 129) shows that the fundamental problem of the "pastorality of doctrine" and the "hierarchy of truths" (UR 11) in a context of inculturation is not really perceived and even less addressed.

As for the service of the bishop of Rome, the Final Document reiterates the classical definition of the Petrine ministry, as found in the First Vatican Council and taken up by the Second Vatican Council in its constitution *Lumen Gentium* (no. 23). But it significantly complements this approach from the perspective of synodality as a "constitutive dimension of the Church" (FD 28):

> We can, therefore, understand the extent of the Council's affirmation that "within the ecclesiastical communion, there are lawfully particular Churches which enjoy their own proper traditions, while the primacy of the see of Peter remains intact, which presides over the universal communion of charity and safeguards legitimate differences while taking care that what is particular not only does no harm to unity but rather is conducive to it" (LG 13). The Bishop of Rome, who is the foundation of the Church's unity (cf. LG 23), is the guarantor of synodality: he is the one who convokes the Church in Synod and presides over it, confirming its results. As the Successor of Peter, he has a unique role in safeguarding the deposit of faith and of morals, ensuring that synodal processes are geared towards unity and witness. Together with the Bishop of Rome, the College of Bishops has an irreplaceable role in shepherding the whole Church (cf. LG 22–23) and in promoting synodality in all the local Churches. (FD 131)

In view of this synodal approach, the final section of the Final Document clarifies the relationship between the Latin Church and the Eastern Catholic Churches and refers to the three most recent texts of the magisterium on the exercise of the Petrine ministry: the apostolic constitution *Praedicate Evangelium*, on the Roman Curia and its Service to the Church in the World (March 19, 2022; see FD 134–35); the apostolic constitution *Episcopalis Communio*, on the Synod of Bishops (September 15, 2018; see FD 136); and the text of the Dicastery for Promoting Christian Unity on *The Bishop of Rome: Primacy and Synodality in Ecumenical Dialogues and Responses to the Encyclical* Ut Unum Sint (2024; see FD 137).[20]

Part V, entitled "'So I Send You': Forming a People for Missionary Discipleship," is of decisive importance in the reception phase of the synod. I will therefore deal with it in the next section of this chapter, in connection with "the conversion of processes." In Part II of the second *Instrumentum Laboris*, the discussion on integral and shared formation had introduced the topic of ways of proceeding.

[20] These texts are available at vatican.va.

The Final Document's very beautiful conclusion articulates its Johannine framework, opening with the scene of the disciples' lunch with the Lord by the lake (John 21:9, 12, 13); the text also quotes Acts 10:41 and Isaiah's messianic vision of the banquet for all peoples (Isa 25:6-8), the latter of which had already been used to introduce the second *Instrumentum Laboris*, thus proposing a new (and ancient) way of approaching the nagging question of "salvation":

> Living through the synodal process, we have renewed our awareness that the salvation to be received and proclaimed is inherently relational. We live it and witness to it together. History reveals itself to us tragically marked by war, rivalry for power and thousands of injustices and abuses. We know, however, that the Spirit has placed the desire for authentic relationships and true bonds in the heart of every human being. Creation itself speaks of unity and sharing, of diversity and of variously interconnected forms of life. Everything stems from and tends towards harmony, even while being devastated by evil. The ultimate meaning of synodality is the witness that the Church is called to give to God, Father, Son and Holy Spirit, the harmony of love that pours Himself out, to give Himself to the world. We can live the communion that saves by walking in a synodal way, in the intertwining of our vocations, charisms and ministries, by going forth to meet everyone in order to bring the joy of the Gospel: communion with God, with the entire humanity and all of creation. In this way, thanks to this sharing, we have already begun to experience the banquet of life that God offers to all peoples. (FD 154)

The last paragraph of the conclusion is dedicated to Mary, recalling her Constantinian title of *Hodegetria*, "she who shows the way and guides."

3. Before considering what the Final Document says about its own reception, it is worth taking an initial look at what is clearly its *distinct and new theological focus*. As already noted, the text is understood as an act of reception of the Second Vatican Council, "deepening its inspiration and reinvigorating its prophetic force for today's world" (FD 5). It is particularly inspired by the fundamental decision taken by the council, in its drafting of *Lumen Gentium*, to precede the two chapters on the hierarchy (chap. 3) and the laity (chap. 4) with a

chapter on the people of God.[21] The novelty of the synod can be understood as *a new reading of this chapter*, because, contrary to what one might have expected, the Final Document bases the synodality of the church not on the *priestly* function of this people and the *common priesthood of the faithful* (not once does it quote LG 10, which introduces the distinction between the common priesthood and the ministerial priesthood[22]) but on the *prophetic* ministry of Jesus Christ, *shared by the "holy people of God" and every baptized person*, a function that is extensively discussed in *Lumen Gentium* 12.

Without going back over the more technical elements, which are covered in detail in chapter 2 of this book, I would like to emphasize this point because it represents *the focus of the Final Document*.[23] This closely links the church's prophetic way of achieving its own unity through conversion and the prophetic function of this way of proceeding for today's world; this is why the document considers synodality to be "social prophecy" (FD 153):

> Practised with humility, the synodal style enables the Church to be a prophetic voice in today's world. "A synodal Church is like a standard lifted up among the nations (cf. Is 11:12)" (Francis, *Address for the Commemoration of the 50th Anniversary of the Institution of the Synod of Bishops*, 17 October 2015). We live in an age marked by ever-increasing inequalities; growing disillusionment with traditional models of governance, disenchantment with the functioning of democracy, increasing autocratic and dictatorial tendencies and the predominance of the market model without regard for the vulnerability of people and of creation. The temptation can be to resolve conflicts by force rather than by dialogue. Authentic practices of synodality enable Christians to be a critical and prophetic voice over against the prevailing culture. In this way, we can offer a distinctive contribution to the search for answers to many challenges faced by our contemporary societies in building the common good. (FD 47)

[21] See chapter 2 above, esp. pp. 21–32.

[22] See above, pp. 24–25.

[23] There are seventeen occurrences of prophetic vocabulary (use of words like *prophecy, prophetic, prophecies*): FD 4, 5, 11, 20 (which include one reference to LG 12), 22 (two references to LG 12), 47 (three references), 65 (two references), 78 (one reference), 81 (one reference), 113, 121, 146, and 153 (two references), to which we must add a fifth reference to LG 12 in FD 57.

This *prophetic focus* of the text is based on four theological emphases that have concrete pastoral consequences.

First, at the forefront of the church's prophetic ministry is *the relational "flavor" of the Christian tradition* (see FD 17), affirmed for the first time with such force: relationships and bonds, especially with the poorest and most excluded, always rooted in specific "places." The whole challenge of the Final Document is the *conversion of these relationships and bonds*. "Thus, synodal conversion calls each person to enlarge the space of their heart, the heart being the first place where all our relationships resonate, grounded in each believer's personal relationship with Jesus Christ and His Church" (FD 110). This missionary outreach, therefore, has its source in the human heart but aims at the unity of the whole world. From now on, it consists of working toward the communion of the faithful as a communion of churches (*communio ecclesiarum*) on a path of differentiation *and* unification, thanks to the communion of bishops (their collegiality) and the Petrine ministry of the bishop of Rome. In a prophetic or messianic way, it is simultaneously *directed toward* the kingdom of God, the banquet of the risen Lord, announced by the prophet Isaiah.

Second, this relational flavor, specific to the prophetic ministry of the church, is expressed today more particularly in an acute and necessarily critical sensitivity to the *equality of all the faithful*, whoever they may be (see chapter 2 of this book). Little present at Vatican II, which was more interested in freedom—freedom of conscience and religious freedom—it was, however, clearly affirmed in *Lumen Gentium* 31 and 32. But the synod identified *baptismal equality* as "single root of synodality," which also and at the same time establishes ecumenism: there is no synodality without ecumenism and no ecumenism without synodality (FD 23).

Third, with the emergence of this sensitivity—more or less new—the sense of *differences within the church* is also reinforced. These are both charismatic (see LG 12) and cultural, but also dependent on our different Christian traditions, as shown, for example, by the Eastern Catholic Churches, known as churches *sui iuris*, or "of their own right." This is the first time that a synod has dealt with this almost infinite, admirable charismatic diversity, given by the Holy Spirit, which must be constantly reoriented, precisely through the prophetic path of synodality, toward a consensus of unity understood as harmony of differences, with pastors having a constitutive place in the service of this harmony. The exchange of gifts (see LG 13 and FD 120–23) is the evangelical way par excellence of recognizing that these differences (and what they convey in terms of benefits and possible distortions) are not primarily a threat but a gift and an invitation to go beyond, on a political level, "conflicts of human beings, from the well-known *homo homini lupus* of Thomas Hobbes."[24]

Fourth, due to abuses of all kinds, the prophetic ministry entrusted by Jesus Christ to the people of God has largely lost its credibility. The challenge of the synod is to restore it, knowing that it is difficult to discern what, in the ministerial constitution of the church, is constitutive or constitutional and what is related to historical and cultural conditions, which are variable and reformable. The question of the equal place of women, including in this ministerial structure, has become a crucial indicator of a credible "social prophecy." The Final Document recognizes this, particularly in paragraphs 52, 60, and 77. The strategy consists of reopening the laboratory of "specific ministries, distinct from ordained ministries" and a set of responsibilities to be exercised in a spirit of collaboration and differentiated coresponsibility, equally accessible to women and men. Whether this is sufficient to honor the prophetic character of the synod will be seen in the ongoing synodal discernment of the whole church going forward.

Perhaps the reader will now want to object that the Final Document is full of words that are immediately contradicted by the "reality" of our churches. I would like to honor this objection by reflecting on a possible reception of the synod on the ground.

## A Way of Proceeding: The Beginnings of a New Catholic Culture

After the Second Vatican Council, Fr. Karl Rahner was credited with a significant quip: "In the Catholic Church, it is easier to interpret dogmas than to change pews in a church." The synod is in fact just the beginning of the beginning of *a new Catholic culture*; I will come back to this in the last chapter of this book. However, a cultural

[24] Pope Francis, Address to the Fifth Convention of the Italian Church.

change of this dimension—Catholicism is a global reality on our planet—cannot be imposed from above. The only way forward is indeed to change the pews (or tables, as was done for the first time for this synod in the Paul VI Hall) and to propose *a new way of proceeding*. Parts III and V of the Final Document provide us with this new way of living and working ("*modus vivendi et operandi,*" FD 31).

1. To better understand the decisive issue of this *modus*, it is worth looking back at its history and more particularly at its roots in the Second Vatican Council. It should be recalled that the historic gesture of the council was to situate the churches and the church as a "messianic people" (LG 9) within the "ecumenical" network of Judaism, Islam, other religions, and all the spiritual components of humanity. It was then necessary to reflect on *how to relate to them and to all the others*.

It is particularly significant that this reflection originated in the conciliar bodies that were in direct contact with these *others*, above all in the Secretariat for Christian Unity but also in the mixed commission that drafted the pastoral constitution *Gaudium et Spes*. In the Decree on Ecumenism *Unitatis Redintegratio* and in the Declaration on Religious Freedom *Dignitatis Humanae*, as well as in *Gaudium et Spes* and other texts, the distinction emerges between what these documents propose to the faithful, on the one hand, and a *discourse on method*, on the other—a "metadiscourse," one might say, that shows *how* and *by what means* the theoretical and practical content of these texts has been generated and can continue to be generated, with due regard for the interpretative competence of all those involved in the search for truth (see DH 3).

This "metareflection" in contact with the other emerges in a dispersed manner in the textual corpus of the council. However, two main issues can be identified. First, the Decree on Ecumenism reflects on dialogue (already addressed by Paul VI in his encyclical *Ecclesiam Suam*) and emphasizes the equality of the partners (UR 9) and the attitudes that the exchange presupposes (UR 11). Then the Declaration on Religious Freedom recognizes the "search for truth" without constraint and according to the modalities of the social nature of the human being to be a fundamental right (DH 3), followed by the indications of *Gaudium et Spes*, which integrates these reflections on human dignity into the broader framework of discerning the "signs of the times" (GS 4 and 11). While the first methodological focus is based on *dialogue between* people, the second is based on the three stages of Catholic Action pedagogy: see, judge, act.

By conducting an intense reflection on its methodology, the current synodal process has brought these *metadiscursive indications* of the council out of their dispersion and initiated their unification. The novelty of the synod consists in bringing to the fore the "conversation in the Spirit" in the context of the two central practices of the Christian tradition: listening to the word of God and the celebration of the Eucharist (this was discussed at length in chapter 4 of this work). Of course, the *synodal method* is not limited to this type of conversation, which is *one way* of realizing it. But *this way* reveals the *heart of the synodal method* insofar as it realizes and manifests the very center of the Christian tradition, namely, the experience of listening, of the resonance in each person of what is heard and of the word that responds freely to it, with *parrhesia*. The ultimate aim of the method is to hear God himself speaking to us or even to hear what his Spirit is saying to the churches today (see Rev 2:7, etc.). This is only possible if we experience silence, if our ears become more refined and learn to enter into what can be called "stereophonic listening" (see FD 79 and 82–83).[25]

Part III of the Final Document places this "conversation in the Spirit" within a methodological process in three "closely intertwined" practices (FD 79–80).

While the second *Instrumentum Laboris* sets out these three practices, the Final Document emphasizes their harmonious sequence: we move from (first) ecclesial discernment for mission to (second) a new articulation of decision-making processes, all of which is experienced in a climate of transparency, requiring the ability of those involved to (third) report back to others. It goes without saying that this *modus procedendi*, which could usher in a new Catholic culture, can only become a *habitus* through the comprehensive training of all pastoral ministers and, of course, the faithful, in accordance with the recommendations of the final chapter of the Final Document.

[25] This concept has been explained above, at p. 34 and pp. 39–41.

Regarding discernment, the Final Document mainly addresses the attitudes that this "spiritual practice grounded in a living faith" (FD 82) entails. It insists on the complexity of the experience of stereophonic listening to the voice of the Spirit (FD 83) and draws attention to the elements that ought be included in this process of ecclesial discernment:

a) clearly setting out the object of discernment and disseminating information and the means for adequately understanding it;

b) giving sufficient time for prayerful preparation, for listening to the Word of God and for reflection on the question;

c) an inner disposition of freedom regarding one's own interests, both personal and as a group, and a commitment to the pursuit of the common good;

d) listening attentively and respectfully to each person's voice;

e) searching for the widest possible consensus which will emerge when our hearts burn within us (cf. Lk 24:32), without hiding conflicts or searching for the lowest common denominator;

f) the leaders of the process formulate the consensus in such a way that allows the participants to say whether they recognise themselves in it or not. (FD 84)

Let us add that the text also brings in, albeit on the sidelines and characterized as "appropriate means," the contributions of the various theological disciplines and the human, historical, social, and administrative sciences to discernment (FD 85, following FD 67).[26]

The intermediate stage of the *modus synodalis*, which deals with decision-making processes, is particularly important. The Final Document first recalls a rule dating back to Christian antiquity: "The Fathers of the Church reflect on the communal nature of the mission of the People of God with a triple 'nothing without': 'nothing without the Bishop' (St. Ignatius of Antioch, Letter to the Trallians 2,2) and 'nothing without your advice [of Presbyters and Deacons] and the consent of the People' (St. Cyprian of Carthage, Letter to the Brothers Presbyters and Deacons, 14,4). When this logic of 'nothing without'

[26] See above, p. 127.

is disregarded, the identity of the Church is obscured, and its mission is hindered" (FD 88).

It then criticizes the unfortunate use of the distinction between "deliberation" and "consultation" (which in canon law has become "the vote *is only* consultative"; see FD 92), which has removed all confidence in our clerical institutions that consult a lot but then make decisions in which those who have been consulted no longer recognize their proposals. It is precisely this way of proceeding that the Final Document corrects, without diluting the specific responsibilities of each person but by clarifying them (FD 92 and 93). We will recall all the ways of overcoming possible conflicts by distinguishing between *decision-making* and *decision-taking*, while linking them:

> It is appropriate to reflect on decision-making processes to ensure their effective functionality. These processes typically involve a period of elaboration and preparation "through a joint exercise of discernment, consultation and co-operation" (ITC 69), which informs and underpins the subsequent taking of a decision by the competent authority. There is no competition or conflict between the two elements of the process; rather, they both contribute to ensuring that the decisions taken are the fruit of the obedience of all to what God wants for His Church. For this reason, it is necessary to encourage procedures that make reciprocity between the assembly and the person presiding effective in an atmosphere of openness to the Spirit and mutual trust in search of a consensus that could, possibly, be unanimous. Once the decision has been reached, it requires a process of implementation and evaluation in which the various participants are once again involved, yet in new ways. (FD 90)

Hence the need for transparency and the ability to account for decisions made in order to restore trust, the key word of the second and third practices of the *modus synodalis*. The Final Document makes a series of recommendations for developing existing "accountability" bodies, evaluation and control mechanisms at all levels of the church (FD 99–102). At the same time, it insists on the change in attitudes that these practices require:

> Decision-making does not conclude the discernment process. It must be accompanied and followed by practices of accountability and evaluation undertaken in a spirit of transparency inspired

> by evangelical criteria. Accountability to the community for one's ministry belongs to our oldest tradition: to the Apostolic Church itself. Chapter Eleven of the Acts of the Apostles offers us the example of Peter's being held to account upon his return to Jerusalem for baptising Cornelius, a Gentile, when "the circumcised believers criticised him, saying, 'Why did you go to uncircumcised men and eat with them?'" (Acts 11:2-3). Peter responded by setting out the reasons for his decision. (FD 95–98)

2. It is consistent with the practical orientation of this part of the Final Document that after the three practices of the *modus synodalis*, it immediately deals (and not, as in the second *Instrumentum Laboris*, in the following part) with a key "place" in which this synodal way of working has become radically uncertain, namely, the organs of participation at various levels of the church known as councils, which have often fallen into disuse or become chambers for the recording of decisions taken elsewhere: "In the Latin Church these are: Diocesan Synod (cf. CIC, can. 466), Presbyteral Council (cf. CIC, can. 500, § 2), Diocesan Pastoral Council (cf. CIC, can. 514, § 1), Parish Pastoral Council (cf. CIC, can. 536), Diocesan and Parish Finance Council (cf. CIC, cann. 493 e 537)" (FD 103).

Being unable to legislate (a point to which I will return), the synod makes strong recommendations regarding the mandatory nature of these bodies (FD 104), their synodal methodology (FD 105) and their composition (FD 106), the creation of new bodies of "ecclesial assemblies at all levels" (FD 107), and the regularity of diocesan synods (FD 108). One may regret the absence of clear and unambiguous legislation. But it should also be noted that it does correspond to a way of reforming the church based on "best practices" invented at the grassroots and in the local churches (FD 107), without immediately freezing their diversity; this in no way excludes the definition of a certain number of basic rules and obligations, to be prepared by the synod's canonical commission (FD 8).

I therefore think that the very first steps in a conversion and reform of the church consist of "changing the pews or the tables," of inaugurating a new way of proceeding and of training ourselves to discern together, to articulate the resulting decisions, and to reexamine them in the light of their confirmation or rejection "on the ground," all in a fraternal climate of transparency.

3. It is clear that these *early stages* of a new "Catholic culture," already alive here and there, must be accompanied by "focused formation processes" (FD 141).

In Part V, the Final Document first returns, fittingly, to Christian initiation, which was discussed from the beginning of its theological section ("The Sacramental Roots of the People of God"; see FD 21–27) by situating the formation of missionary disciples in the personal history of each one and in the encounters made possible by the catechumenate (FD 142). But this formation cannot end with initiation; it lasts a lifetime, with the Sunday Eucharist being, for many Christians, the only place where it continues.

On this basis, the text then offers general comments on synodal formation (FD 143), before adding more specific remarks on the classical "places" of formation, such as family, catechesis, and academic institutions (FD 144–46), the formation necessary for ministries and different forms of life (FD 147), the training of candidates for ordained ministry in a synodal style (FD 148, with a reference to study group 4), and finally a few particular areas, such as the digital environment (FD 149), the culture of protection (FD 150), and the decisive themes of the social doctrine of the church (FD 151).

This relatively comprehensive description of the scope of synodal training, necessary if the synodal transformation of Catholicism is to succeed, is ultimately inspired by a declaration of intent of the synod, destined to become the soul of its realization on the ground:

> One of the requests that emerged most strongly and from all contexts during the synodal process is that the formation provided by the Christian community be integral, ongoing and shared. Such formation must aim not only at acquiring theoretical knowledge but also at promoting the capacity for openness and encounter, sharing and collaboration, reflection and discernment in common. Formation must consequently engage all the dimensions of the human person (intellectual, affective, relational and spiritual) and include concrete experiences that are appropriately accompanied. There was also a marked insistence throughout the synodal process upon the need for a common and shared formation, in which men and women, laity, consecrated persons, ordained ministers and candidates for ordained ministry participate together, thus enabling them to grow together in knowledge and mutual esteem and in the ability to

> collaborate. This requires the presence of suitable and competent formators, capable of demonstrating with their lives what they transmit with their words. Only in this way will formation be truly generative and transformative. Nor should we overlook the contribution that the pedagogical disciplines can make to providing well-focused formation, adult learning and teaching methods and the accompaniment of individuals and communities. We, therefore, need to invest in the formation of formators. (FD 143)

## The Final Surprise

1. After the presentation and reading of the Final Document on the morning of Saturday, October 26, in an atmosphere of contemplation and silence, the assembly proceeded in the afternoon to the electronic vote on each of the 155 paragraphs of the text (with each participant casting a negative or positive vote for each paragraph), a process that lasted about three hours, after which the results were posted and announced. All the paragraphs obtained the necessary two-thirds of the 355 voters to be adopted. Only then could a somewhat accurate picture of the movements of opinion within the assembly be formed. Even if individual interventions in the general congregations made it possible to anticipate the outcome of the vote, the precise number of opposition votes in certain well-defined areas was a surprise.

2. But we should point out straight away that it is very difficult to interpret these negative votes. A brief survey allows us to offer a few hypotheses that may help us understand the difficulties and limitations of the synod.

First, the clearest case is seen in paragraph 60, on the place of women in the church. As we have seen, this question had already been addressed in the second *Instrumentum Laboris* and by study group 5, led by the Dicastery for the Doctrine of the Faith. Be that as it may, the preliminary draft of the Final Document, prepared before the meeting between Pope Francis and the women of the synod on Saturday, October 19, and submitted to the assembly for amendment on Monday, October 21, contained (in no. 58) a version that fell well short of the proposals of the second *Instrumentum Laboris* and the speeches on the topic made in the general congregations.

Section 60 of the Final Document, on the other hand, reestablishes the principle of equality and, in particular, reintroduces the possibility for women to exercise leadership roles in the churches and reopens the question of women's access to the diaconate, contrary to what Pope Francis had previously said in one of his interviews and in Belgium. "What comes from the Holy Spirit cannot be stopped," affirms the Final Document:

> By virtue of Baptism, women and men have equal dignity as members of the People of God. However, women continue to encounter obstacles in obtaining a fuller recognition of their charisms, vocation and place in all the various areas of the Church's life. This is to the detriment of serving the Church's shared mission. Scripture attests to the prominent role of many women in the history of salvation. One woman, Mary Magdalene, was entrusted with the first proclamation of the Resurrection. On the day of Pentecost, Mary, the Mother of God, was present, accompanied by many other women who had followed the Lord. It is important that the Scripture passages that relate these stories find adequate space inside liturgical lectionaries. Crucial turning points in Church history confirm the essential contribution of women moved by the Spirit. Women make up the majority of churchgoers and are often the first witnesses to the faith in families. They are active in the life of small Christian communities and parishes. They run schools, hospitals and shelters. They lead initiatives for reconciliation and promoting human dignity and social justice. Women contribute to theological research and are present in positions of responsibility in Church institutions, in diocesan curia and the Roman Curia. There are women who hold positions of authority and are leaders of their communities. This Assembly asks for full implementation of all the opportunities already provided for in Canon Law with regard to the role of women, particularly in those places where they remain underutilised. There is no reason or impediment that should prevent women from carrying out leadership roles in the Church: what comes from the Holy Spirit cannot be stopped. Additionally, the question of women's access to diaconal ministry remains open. This discernment needs to continue. The Assembly also asks that more attention be given to the language and images used in preaching, teaching, catechesis, and the drafting of official Church documents, giving more space

> to the contributions of female saints, theologians and mystics. (FD 60)

This new version was certainly a surprise, but it should not be forgotten that this paragraph received ninety-seven negative votes, which was about 27 percent of the assembly.

Second, other cases are much less clear, with "no" votes of around 10 percent. They primarily concern ordained ministry, particularly the role of the bishop and expressions of collegiality, but also the training of ordained ministers. For example:

- no. 70, on the selection of bishops and a bishop's constitutive link with the local church (which does not appear to be the case for titular bishops) received twenty-five negative votes;
- no. 92, on the decision-making power of the bishop, received thirty-nine negative votes;
- no. 125, on the role of episcopal conferences, received forty-five negative votes;
- nos. 126, 127, and 129, on continental and ecclesial assemblies and on decentralization, received thirty-two, twenty-six, and thirty-eight negative votes, respectively;
- no. 136, on the participation of non-bishops in the Synod of Bishops, received thirty-seven negative votes; and
- no. 148, on the formation of candidates for ordained ministry in a synodal style, received forty negative votes.

A third area of opposition or difficulty is even more diffuse but is generally ecclesiological in nature. It concerns, for example:

- the meaning of the *sensus fidei* (FD 22, with twenty-two negative votes) and the participation of all Christians in it by baptism (FD 23, with nineteen negative votes);
- the description of cultural and religious diversity with reference to the Basilean conception of "unity as a harmony of differences" (FD 42, with twenty-one negative votes);
- the progress of the churches at different rates (FD 124, with thirty-two negative votes); and

- the proposal "to establish a Council of Patriarchs, Major Archbishops and Metropolitans of the Eastern Catholic Churches presided over by the Pope, which would be an expression of synodality and an instrument for promoting communion [and] would also serve as a means of sharing liturgical, theological, canonical and spiritual patrimony" (FD 133, with thirty-seven negative votes).

Are these negative votes indicative of the difficulty of a minority to accept a vision of the church based on baptismal equality, its internal differentiation, and its synodality (without touching on the constitutive dimension of the ordained ministry)? Is it the manifestation of the fear—expressed, for example, on Monday, October 14, by Cardinal Müller—of a drift of Catholicism toward an Anglican model of the church, doomed, according to him, to failure?

Fourth, we should ask the reason for opposition to the link between *synaxis* and *synodos* (FD 27, with forty-three negative votes). Is it because this link affects the style of our liturgical celebrations, making them more synodal? Other resistance may still come as a surprise—for example, to the call for dialogue between pastors and theologians (FD 67, which received fifteen negative votes) or to the establishment of "a ministry of listening and accompaniment" (FD 78, with thirty-three negative votes).

Fifth, it should also be noted that some are opposed to the Final Document being too prescriptive, for example, by proposing that reference to "merely consultative" votes be deleted from the Code of Canon Law (FD 92, with thirty-nine negative votes) or that participatory councils at various levels of governance be made mandatory (FD 102, with twenty-five negative votes, and FD 104, with twenty-six negative votes).

For the moment, it is impossible to go any further in identifying and interpreting the votes cast by the synod fathers and mothers. But what has just been explained reveals a limitation of the synodal institution. One could legitimately hope that the final vote would be preceded by one or more indicative votes, making it possible to identify agreements and disagreements more clearly, to then initiate a well-informed argumentative debate on the points of contention and to engage in a spiritual weighing of the positions.

3. What is the canonical status of the Final Document, and what is its precise scope? Everyone was surprised by the pope's final declaration: "I do not intend to publish an 'Apostolic Exhortation': what we have approved is enough. The Document already contains very substantial indications which can guide the mission of the Churches, on different continents, and *in particular contexts*: hence I am making it available to everyone straight away; hence *I have asked* for it to be published. *In this way, I want to acknowledge the value of the synodal journey which has been made, and which, by means of this Document, I entrust to the holy faithful People of God.*"[27] To a certain extent, Pope Francis returned to the approach followed by Pope Paul VI after the 1971 Ordinary General Assembly of the Synod of Bishops (only the second such gathering after the establishment of the synod following Vatican II; the first assembly, in 1967, produced no document at all). After meeting on the dual topics of the ministerial priesthood and social justice, the 1971 synod published its own summary document, *Justice in the World*. It was only after the third ordinary assembly, in 1974, on the topic of evangelization, that the synod handed over its work to the pope, and Paul VI published the first post-synodal exhortation, *Evangelii Nuntiandi*. In the case of the Synod on Synodality, the synod handed over the summary of its work to the pope, and he immediately placed it in the hands of the people of God, thus declaring by an act of his "ordinary magisterium" that the "synodal path completed" is and must become that of the whole people of God.

What about the ten "study groups"? I am thinking in particular of group 5 on "specific ministerial forms" (dealing in particular with women's access to the diaconate) or group 9 on controversial pastoral, ethical, and doctrinal issues (for example, the presence of LGBTQ+ people in our communities)? Some (including myself) would have liked a third session to receive the work of these study groups synodally. Let us remember that between the two sessions, the pope had, in fact, identified synodality "as a constitutive dimension of the Church"—a question of "fundamental ecclesiology," according to an expression of the theologians—and the Secretariat of the Synod had

[27] Pope Francis, "17th General Congregation, Final Greeting," published in the Final Document's Appendix (emphases mine).

enumerated a whole series of particular questions, including those I have just mentioned.

Here is what Pope Francis had to say about it in his final statement:

> Time is needed in order to arrive at decisions and choices that involve the whole Church on some aspects of the life of the Church to which the Document draws attention, and on the themes entrusted to the ten "Study Groups," which need to work freely in order to offer me proposals. I shall, therefore, continue to listen to the Bishops and the Churches entrusted to them.
>
> *This is not the classic way of putting decisions off for ever.* [!] It is what corresponds to the synodal style with which the Petrine ministry, too, is to be exercised: listen, convene, discern, decide and evaluate.[28]

*This final declaration quite simply calls for trust.*

❖ ❖ ❖

Since the second session also closed the second phase of the synod, inaugurating the reception phase, I want to go beyond a detailed presentation and initial theological interpretation of the Final Document and analyze its complex genesis in the synodal assembly, going back to the turning points during the intersession period. It is, after all, the *synodal process* as such, as experienced by the Roman assembly, that Pope Francis proposed for reception by the people of God. At the end of this journey, it can indeed be said that the result corresponds, in the current circumstances of the churches and of the church as a whole, to what it has been possible to achieve by listening to what the Spirit is saying to them today. The assembly was able to record its synodal experience in a good Final Document that, in the very apt words of Pope Francis, "already contains very substantial indications which can guide the mission of the Churches, on different continents, and in particular contexts."[29]

This generally positive assessment does not ignore the limitations of the process and the Final Document or the pending results of the

[28] Pope Francis, "17th General Congregation, Final Greeting" (emphasis mine).
[29] Pope Francis, "17th General Congregation, Final Greeting."

ten study groups, the canonical commission, or the discernment by the Symposium of Episcopal Conferences of Africa and Madagascar on the pastoral care of people living in polygamous marriages. One of the pedagogical challenges of the reception will be to dispel the misunderstanding aroused in public opinion and in the church by the necessary distinction between the constitutional question of synodality, dealt with by the synod, and the other questions entrusted to commissions.

Other limitations may then be recognized, not without recalling the "fundamental issues" already discussed at the end of the previous chapter.

First, the reference to the Holy Scriptures as the basis of synodality and the life of the church and of the churches is not ensured by the simple quotations of John 20 and 21 at the beginning of each part of the text, however fruitful this intuition may be. Certainly, as never before, the synod became aware of the distinction between reading the Scriptures and the current ("stereophonic") listening to the Word or the very Voice of God and his Spirit.

But the hermeneutic problem posed by the historical distance between the nascent church and its contemporary figures is hardly perceived. However, since the Second Vatican Council, this question remains unresolved, particularly when it comes to working toward an inculturated proclamation of the Gospel of the kingdom of God and understanding what meaning to give to mission—an omnipresent term in the Final Document but one that was ultimately given little thought by the synod—today.

Second, on several occasions I have addressed the *limits of the synodal institution*, which has nevertheless been greatly expanded by Pope Francis in its composition and its powers.[30] The Final Document certainly acknowledges the distinction between ecclesial assemblies, especially continental ones, and the synod as an episcopal body but also notes that it is subject to future theological clarification (FD 126–27). In addition to this, the absence of a genuine culture of debate and

[30] See the apostolic constitution *Episcopalis Communio*; FD 136; and Pope Francis, "1st General Congregation, Inaugural Address," published in the Final Document's Appendix.

the late vote on the text mean that opposition and disagreement, while freely expressed, could not be subject to reasoned discernment.

Third, as a result, the two questions, already raised at the end of the previous chapter, of the "hierarchy of truths," allowing a *differentiated inculturation* of the Catholic faith as always, and of the transfer of competences that are also interpretative on a doctrinal level (according to the principle of subsidiarity) to continental, national, and local bodies, remain unanswered.

Fourth, the ecumenical progress made by the synod is substantial, thanks to the "synodalization" of the Catholic Church and the clarifications provided by the recent document of the Dicastery for Promoting Christian Unity on *The Bishop of Rome*. How can we take advantage of these clarifications to develop, with our separated sisters and brothers from other churches and Christian traditions, models of communion, acceptable to all?

Fifth, to the disappointment of several (mainly European) episcopates, prominent *pastoral issues* such as the ordination of *viri probati* and priestly celibacy, which have been under discussion since the beginning of the process, have disappeared from the Final Document. These questions will resurface, challenging the churches not only to rethink and fully realize the differentiated equality between men and women (and other questions of an anthropological nature) but also to continue to confront the problems of ministerial governance of our communities, especially in Europe in a situation of priest shortage.

To mention these limitations is not to disparage the synod that has just ended or its considerable achievements, but to bear in mind that it represents only a moment, undoubtedly historic and inaugural, but limited in a much longer process of cultural change. This will be discussed in the last chapter of this book.

# Chapter 7

# A Synod on the Holy Spirit: A New Vision of the Church in History and Society Takes Shape

In this final chapter, I'd like to widen the angle of view and address the synod's relationship to Christian tradition. The question concerns both these terms, and first of all the very meaning of tradition, which is often called upon to legitimize or reject a given position (e.g., access to Communion for divorced and remarried people, ordination of women deacons, etc.). A first fork in the road presents itself here, confronting us with the difficult question of the function of the "doctrine of faith" in Catholicism's fidelity to the risen Jesus and the nascent church. This is where John XXIII introduced the pastoral nature of doctrine, emphasizing the church's relationship with the culturally situated recipients of God's Gospel, thus sparking debates that have continued unabated to this day. A second fork in the road appears here. Depending on the meaning we give to tradition, and on the type of relationship—"pastoral" or otherwise—we enter into with doctrine, the current synodalization of the Catholic Church is given a different place within the history of the people of God: either it is accepted, to put it briefly, as a *concession*, within the hierarchical structure of the church, which dominates the second millennium of its history, or it becomes the basis of a new vision of Christian and Catholic ecclesiology, adjusted to our context.

We can also approach this second fork in the road by asking ourselves *why*, at this point in the history of the church and of our human societies on our planet, *synodality is suddenly arousing such interest*, to the point of becoming, in the words of Pope Francis, the "path" that "God expects of the Church in the third millennium."[1] There are also societal reasons for this, such as the questions our democracies are asking about their future, stemming from the epochal change we are experiencing. This change inevitably affects the church's perception of its own missionary identity and its ecumenical way of relating to the apostolic tradition and proclaiming the Gospel. We are then led back to the first fork in the road.

This approach appears right from the start of the Second Vatican Council and remains present throughout the history of its reception. The "hermeneutic of continuity" advocated by Pope Benedict XVI is just *one* way of relating to the council and the church's tradition. One might think that the other way of referring to it would be a "hermeneutic of rupture," the specter of which provokes much fear among those who are attached to the "timeless" Catholic identity.

However, those who fear the sterilizing effect of the "hermeneutic of continuity"—often summed up by the phrase "all the Council, nothing but the Council"—do not deny the necessary continuity of Christian tradition but understand it as the acquisition of a discernment that must be constantly renewed, especially when the people of God is confronted with cultural change and becomes aware of the fractures and discontinuities in human history that it has had to go through.

Here we can see the novelty of the synod in relation to the Second Vatican Council. I hypothesize that this synod is the very first of the Latin Church on the Holy Spirit, who is omnipresent in the Final Document, in the interventions of Pope Francis, and perhaps also—I hope—in the synodal process itself. The Nicene-Constantinopolitan Creed confesses of the Holy Spirit that "he has spoken through the prophets," and the synod recognizes that he still speaks today through the prophetic ministry of the church, received from Christ Jesus (see Luke 10:23-24 and Acts 2:14-36). However, the issue at the synod was not to discuss the *subject* of the Holy Spirit but to consider how to *hear together what he is saying here and now to the* churches (see Rev 2:7,

[1] Pope Francis, Address Commemorating the Fiftieth Anniversary of the Institution of the Synod of Bishops.

etc.). The theological and even doctrinal novelty of the synod consists in having asked this "constitutional" question and having answered it *by practicing and proposing* to the whole church a synodal way of discerning what has been heard and of making decisions accordingly, in a transparent manner.

First, therefore, I shall return to this conflict of interpretation of the Second Vatican Council, which lies at the heart of our current debates on the synodal church. This has already been discussed in the second chapter of this book, but without addressing the neuralgic point of controversy that is the relationship with tradition and Catholic doctrine. I shall therefore attempt to clarify this link between the church's reception of tradition and synodality as a constitutive element of the church, hoping in this way to contribute to the pacification of the conflict of interpretation of the council and to answer the question: why is the church's synodality taking on such importance today? Of course, we have to bear in mind that theological reasoning cannot resolve conflicts rooted in what others "see" or "don't see," as cultural mutations or paradigm shifts inevitably confound our assumptions and intuitions. It is by becoming aware of this phenomenon—which, in the history of humanity and of the church, presents itself as a spiritual struggle—that the call of the Holy Spirit and of the prophetic ministry of the church, heard through the synodal discernment of the baptized, finds its full meaning. It is indeed through this new spiritual way of proceeding, to be explained by theologians, and by exercising it effectively, that a new vision of the church—a prophetic or messianic vision within humanity—can take shape.

## Vatican II: Just the Beginning of the Beginning?

Only a few days after the Second Vatican Council, which ended on December 8, 1965, the German Jesuit theologian Karl Rahner drew up an initial balance sheet, urging modesty: "The Council marked the decisive beginning of the *aggiornamento*, it established the renewal, it called us to the ever-necessary repentance and return; in other words, it was only the beginning of the beginning."[2] In 1979, a year

[2] Karl Rahner, "Le concile—un nouveau commencement," in Rahner, *Le deuxième concile du Vatican: Contributions au Concile et à son interprétation, Œuvres* 21

after the election of John Paul II, he proposed a global reading of the council based on the long history of Christianity, distinguishing three major periods: (1) the brief period of Judeo-Christianity; (2) that of the church in a specific culture, Hellenism and European civilization; and (3) the present phase in which the ecclesial space is from the outset the whole world. These three eras are precisely characterized by three fundamentally different situations in terms of the proclamation of the Gospel and the church's place in society, eras that may be marked by other profound caesuras, as in the case of the second period, which encompasses the transition from antiquity to the Middle Ages and the threshold of colonialism and the European Enlightenment. But the tripartition is necessary, according to Rahner, if we take into account the fact that the transition from one historical and theological situation to another, substantially new one has so far taken place only once, thanks to the mission of the apostle Paul, and is now taking place a second time, thanks to the birth of a worldwide Christianity.

Yet these two transformations represent not just cultural mutations but events that touch on revelation itself. This is self-evident in the case of the Pauline writings and (let us add) the discernment of the Jerusalem assembly (see Acts 15:1-29). Rahner's thesis is to give the Second Vatican Council a similar status and to understand it as the first council of a globalizing church. Given the radical difference between Western culture and the cultures of Africa and Asia, and despite the levelling veneer of global civilization created by Europe and the United States, the inculturation of Christianity involves a true re-creation (*Neuschöpfung*).

Here Rahner touches on the most delicate problem of the reception of the apostolic tradition, that of "creativity":

> It's an open question whether and to what extent the Church of the post-apostolic era still has the creative potential and powers it possessed at the time of its first becoming, in apostolic times, and which it claimed in fundamental and irreversible or seemingly irreversible decisions, constituting first of all concretely its

(Éditions du Cerf, 2015), 766. English version: Rahner, "The Church after the Council," *U.S. Catholic*, September 13, 2012 (November 1966 issue), https://uscatholic.org/articles/201209/the-church-after-the-council/.

> essence, beyond what reaches it in an immediate actuality of Jesus, the Risen One. The question therefore arises as to whether, at times of transition such as the second (towards a global Christianity), the Church can legitimately exercise possibilities that it never actualized during its second "great epoch," because to do so would have been absurd and therefore illegitimate.[3]

Indeed, this is the central question that the reception of the Second Vatican Council has had to address, and still has to address, with the Synod on Synodality providing one element of the answer.

More recently, the French Benedictine theologian Ghislain Lafont has put forward a similar interpretation of the council. In his book *Le Catholicisme autrement?* (2020),[4] he also distinguishes three periods of Christianity. The Second Vatican Council represents the turning point toward a new type of Christianity and a new type of church: "the Church, period III," as he puts it. "My conviction," he writes, "is that Vatican II is *not a new reform, but a new stage in the history of the Church that has begun.*"[5]

This remark is very enlightening, as it makes us aware that the notion of "reform," analyzed in the central chapter of this book,[6] can be understood in very different ways. Here, Lafont introduces an important distinction between a series of *reforms* in response to abuses in the church and the *form itself* of a certain type of Catholicism—based on the idea of a "hierarchy" of a world order that descends from above, and on that of the "sacred"—a *form* that has lost all plausibility today. Vatican II was widely seen as a "reform" in the former sense of the term, rather than a "refoundation" in the sense of a new "beginning" that opened a new stage in the history of Christianity, marked by a new "form" of Catholicism: "The Church, Period III."

This goes to the heart of the possible misunderstanding of the nature of the current synodal process, as shown, for example, by the distinction, introduced by the Polish synthesis, between changes in "doctrine" or "ecclesial structure," identified with the "German way,"

[3] Karl Rahner, "Interprétation théologique fondamentale du deuxième concile du Vatican," in Rahner, *Le deuxième concile du Vatican*, 1005.

[4] Ghislain Lafont, *Le Catholicisme autrement?* (Éditions du Cerf, 2020).

[5] Lafont, *Le Catholicisme autrement?*, 158.

[6] See above, pp. 94–96.

and developments in "functioning" that can be associated with "reforms" in the first sense of the term. Benedict XVI's "hermeneutics of continuity," which he transformed into "hermeneutics of reform" in his famous speech of December 22, 2005, also remains close to the first meaning of the term, even if he attempts to make allowances for the contingencies of history and to introduce a distinction between apparent discontinuities and fundamental continuity: "It is precisely in this combination of continuity and discontinuity at different levels that the very nature of true reform consists."[7] Lafont is right to introduce a remark on the liturgy as a "sensitive barometer of the Church" and to delicately criticize Benedict XVI's opposition to Paul VI's liturgical reform, an opposition relayed by an increasingly widespread discourse on "the reform of the reform." The "hermeneutic of continuity" can be seen as the generalization of this liturgical posture.

The difference between this approach to church "reform" and that advocated by Rahner and Lafont lies in the place given to the history of our human societies and the epochal change we are currently experiencing: Yes or no: does our fundamentally different situation compared to the 1960s—the arrival of hyper- or post-modernity, globalization, and cultural and convictional pluralism, the new insistence on equality for all, whatever their "gender," as well as the digitization of all our circuits and the entry into the age of the Anthropocene—reflect on the proclamation of the Gospel and on the shape that the church should take within our societies?

If this is the case, this mutation, with the interpretive work it imposes on the church, inaugurally accomplished by Vatican II—"the beginning of a beginning"—must take place according to a logic of "refoundation" or "reform" of Catholicism in the second sense of a resumption of its "form" in its systemic wholeness. In my own rereading of the Second Vatican Council and its reception, I introduced the terminology of a "paradigm shift,"[8] to which I will return later. What was plausible for Rahner in 1979 has become much clearer

[7] Text available at https://www.vatican.va/content/benedict-xvi/en/speeches/2005/december/documents/hf_ben_xvi_spe_20051222_roman-curia.html.

[8] Christoph Theobald, *La réception du concile Vatican II: I. Accéder à la source*, Unam sanctam—Nouvelle série 1 (Éditions du Cerf, 2009, new ed. 2023), 683–93.

today, with Pope Francis having spoken of a "change of era" and the church's crisis in Europe at least partly due to its failure to adjust to this new situation. As for the consequences of this for the interpretation of the Gospel and the image to be given to the church, the terms of the conflict have not changed, causing Christians and their communities to oscillate between two different conceptions of a "reform," perceived as necessary by many.

However, there is no doubt that Catholicism must remain faithful to the risen Jesus and the nascent church. The differences of opinion concern the way in which this is to be done and above all the place to be given to the doctrinal development of the first and second millennia, a development clarified at the time of the Second Vatican Council by the principle of "pastorality." I shall now take up the explanation of this principle where I left off in the third chapter, showing how it determines both the conception of tradition and the meaning that should consequently be given to synodality.

## Tradition and Synodality

1. Tradition is often identified with the liturgical, doctrinal, and canonical heritage of Catholicism, without realizing the historical evolution it has undergone and the breaks in tradition, oversights, and revivals it has faced. Pope Francis's principle of "pastorality," received from the Second Vatican Council, introduces a new parameter—namely, the recipients of the proclamation of the Gospel. By distinguishing herself from the world and from a now-global society, the world to which God's Gospel is addressed, and the world in which the church is situated, *the church becomes aware of itself* as the universal sacrament of salvation (LG 1), decentralized both in relation to Christ Jesus and to those to whom the Gospel is sent in his name. So there are three parameters that must now be held together in a relationship in which none of the three can be isolated from the other two: the Gospel of God (or God as Gospel), those who proclaim it—Christ Jesus, the One, in the first instance, and the church—and the recipients of this proclamation.

In the background of this structure of tradition, newly emphasized by Vatican II, is of course the emancipation of Western society from Christianity, sometimes referred to as "secularization." But the church and society are not completely distinct from one another, for Christian communities are situated *within human society*, with the Holy Spirit present in it and throughout the universe. And insofar as they truly decentralize themselves, opening themselves up to the trinitarian design of all creation (LG 2–4), they come up against the experience of God's inevitability but also discover the task of discerning the presence of his Spirit in the midst of human beings, on our planet, and in the universe (GS 4, 11). Let's face it, this discernment of "signs of God's presence and purpose in the events, the needs, and the desires" (GS 11) of humanity is a difficult undertaking in societies that are questioning the beginning and end of life, opening up their relational game to LGBTQ+ people, and, above all, relying on nano- and biotechnologies with a view to a profound transformation of the human being.

But a church which, in the name of its faith, does not renounce this discernment of the "signs of the times" becomes a *church that learns* to hear what the Spirit is saying to it. At the same time, it discovers that it must "adjust" its proclamation of the Gospel to what it perceives of the Spirit's work in the recipients of the proclamation and "adjust" its own ecclesial form to this mission. This is what the council records at the very end of its last period in an important passage of *Gaudium et Spes*, taken up again in another form in *Ad Gentes*. Let's take a moment to read these two texts. The first is an important development on "the help the Church receives from today's world":

> The church learned early in its history to express the christian message in the concepts and languages of different peoples and tried to clarify it in the light of the wisdom of their philosophers: it was an attempt to adapt the Gospel to the understanding of all and the requirements of the learned, insofar as this could be done. Indeed, this kind of adaptation and preaching [*accommodata praedicatio*] of the revealed word must ever be the law of all evangelization [*lex omnis evangelisationis*]. In this way it is possible to create in every country the possibility of expressing the message of Christ in suitable terms and to foster vital contact and exchange between the church and different cultures. . . . *With the help of the holy Spirit, it is the task of the whole people of God*, particularly of its pastors and theologians, *to listen to and distinguish the many voices of our times and to interpret them in the light of God's*

> *word, in order that the revealed truth may be more deeply penetrated, better understood, and more suitably presented.* (GS 44 §1; emphasis mine)

The same law of accommodation applies to the structure of the church:

> The church has a visible social structure, which is a sign of its unity in Christ; as such it can be enriched . . . by the evolution of social life, not as if something were missing in the constitution which Christ gave the church, but in order to understand this constitution more deeply, express it better, *and adapt it more successfully to our times.* (GS 44 §2; emphasis mine)

Written at the same time, the following passage from the Decree on the Church's Missionary Activity underlines the earth's cultural diversity and, in this missionary context, reformulates the same demand for an "accommodated evangelization" and an ecclesial form "adjusted" to each culture, requiring "a new examination" of revelation:

> To achieve this [goal], it is necessary that in each of the great socio-cultural regions, . . . theological investigation should be encouraged and the facts and words revealed by God, contained in sacred scripture, and explained by the fathers and magisterium of the church, submitted to a new examination in the light of the tradition of the universal church. In this way it will be more clearly understood by what means the faith can be explained in terms of the philosophy and wisdom of the people, and how their customs, attitude to life and social structures can be reconciled with the standard proposed by divine revelation. Thus a way will be opened for a more profound adaptation in the whole sphere of christian life. This manner of acting will avoid every appearance of syncretism and of false exclusiveness; the christian life will be adapted to the mentality and character of each culture, and local traditions together with the special qualities of each national family, illumined by the light of the gospel, will be taken up into a Catholic unity. So new particular churches, each with its own traditions, have their place in the community of the church, the primacy of Peter which presides over this universal assembly of charity. (*Ad Gentes* 22 §2)

Only if we take into consideration the intrinsic or "systemic" link among the three nuclei mentioned above—the Gospel of God, those who live it and proclaim it, and the recipients of this proclamation—and the "feedback" of what disciples-missionaries and churches learn from these receivers, while staying indifferent to the shaping of the church and the expression of faith, can we reasonably hope to overcome the conflicting interpretations of the council and the Synod on Synodality. By entering for the first time into this never-definitively-stabilized, back-and-forth movement between the Gospel and its historically and culturally situated recipients, the most recent council did not leave us without landmarks or criteria for discernment. In the face of an ahistorical globalization of the concept of "tradition," the council introduced important distinctions between the apostolic tradition of the nascent church, entrusted to the inspired and inspiring Scriptures, and the complex body of dogmatic or doctrinal discourse (found, for example, in the *Catechism of the Catholic Church*) pertaining to the history of the church and the interpretation of the Gospel over the centuries.

Referring to the apostle Paul (1 Cor 11:23 and 15:1-15), to St. Irenaeus, and to several previous councils, Vatican II maintains that apostolic tradition is a *relational process* that links the apostolic and ecclesial act of "receiving" the Gospel of God and the paschal *kerygma with* the act of "delivering" or "transmitting" what is received to recipients. In this sense, it *is essentially* "pastoral" and "missionary," as the third chapter affirms. Not only does it seek to reach and transform those it is addressed to, but it also allows itself to be worked from within by what it learns from those it speaks to—an aspect particularly emphasized by the council, as we have just seen.

As for Catholic doctrine (with its liturgical, ethical, and other aspects), and even dogma, this is the result of all the historical expressions of the Gospel: a precious "treasure trove" of multiple discernments made by Christians and the church of the generations that have gone before us, within the same uninterrupted relational interplay between the reception of the Gospel and its delivery to new recipients, and thanks to the learning that these acts imply. With this "treasure" of experience and discernment—which, like the treasure ("deposit"= *depositum fidei*) of Jesus' parable (see Matt 13:44) is hidden in the field of the churches—we are bequeathed the task of drawing out what binds us and is normative, not only in itself but also above all in relation to today's recipients.

This is an immense task, especially when the church is faced with a change of era, having renounced—since John XXIII and the council—the literary means or genre of the "dogmatic definition" and the condemnation—"anathema"—that accompanies it![9]

2. This brief development of the concept of "tradition" enables us not only to situate the present Synod on Synodality within the controversial process of reception of the Second Vatican Council, of which it inaugurates a new stage, but also and above all to place it within the tripolar structure of apostolic tradition. It focuses on those who proclaim the Gospel, on "missionary disciples," and on the church, and is essentially concerned with the "figure" of the church. By clarifying this positioning, we can immediately understand the limits of the synod and its objectives in relation to the problems identified from the beginning of this book. It did not address questions of the interpretation of the Gospel of God for our time and in the different cultures of our planet, nor Christological and sacramental pastoral questions that arise today in connection with evangelization (first pole). Nor did it deal with all the anthropological questions that arise when one sets about discerning the signs of the times (third pole).

But this synod lays new foundations for tackling all these problems. It is not content to expect their solution from the pastoral and magisterial authority of the church and the specific competence of theologians—two bodies which, in the past, have often been in conflict—but it places its trust in all the baptized. As I showed in the second chapter, the synodal church is in fact founded on their equality. Their charismatic diversity, frequently distorted by conflicts of all kinds, requires a way of coming to agreement and reaching a fraternal/sororal "consent," a synodal way of proceeding that the Final Document was able to clarify, attempting to transform it into the daily practice of the churches. The fundamental challenge is to

[9] For further information and bibliographical references, I refer once again to Christoph Theobald, "La 'pastoralité' de l'enseignement du concile Vatican II: Bilan d'une réception controversée," in Theobald, *Le courage de penser l'avenir: Études œcuméniques de théologie fondamentale et ecclésiologique*, Cogitatio fidei 311 (Éditions du Cerf, 2021), 35–58.

learn to listen—the stereophonic listening that has been mentioned several times, enabling us to hear God speak to us and to hear what his Spirit is saying to the churches. Only when this practice is acquired can the synodal church tackle other problems. That the pastoral authority of the ordained minister and the competence of the theologian retain a *constitutive function* in this experience of listening was also established in the second chapter. That they must, however, be subjected to a reform that does not consist in correcting this or that defect or abuse, such as a certain academic isolation or lack of critical spirit but concerns their self-understanding within a church that has become synodal, as the synod has started to clarify.

Indeed, it is to be hoped that this path of reconciliation and creativity, as I called it in chapter 4, will also enable us to move away from the sterilizing oscillation between the two conceptions of "reform" we distinguished above and the two controversial interpretations of the event and the textual corpus of the Second Vatican Council, on which these ways of looking at church reform depend. Entrusting them to the "sense of faith" of *all* the faithful and to their discernment in search of a "universal consent" frees them from possible isolation, always threatened by a false abstraction, and roots them in the daily life of the churches and their communities. The self-reform of pastoral ministry and the exercise of theological ministry is an inescapable condition for this, both difficult to achieve and indispensable for a creative overcoming of the current crisis. The ecumenical openness of this shift toward the baptismal equality of all Christians and the reframing of the church's structure, giving a more substantial place to the particular and continental churches, is unexpected; it is still necessary, in the future, to transform it into a path toward the unity of all Christians.

All these new intra-Catholic and ecumenical possibilities make us aware of the mysterious nature of Pope Francis's unexpected choice to consider synodality as the "path" that "God expects of the Church in the third millennium" (address, October 17, 2015). We could compare it to the surprise that John XXIII created on January 25, 1959, when he convoked a new council; a convocation that, in his diary, he attributed to a "sudden inspiration." However, such a prophetic experience in no way prevents what is manifested at a very precise moment from being preceded and prepared by history, still awaiting its realization.

3. Why, then, at this point in the history of the church and of our human societies on this planet, has synodality aroused so much interest, even if it cooled down during the second session? This is the question I asked at the start of this chapter. The first reason, internal to Christian tradition, has just been explained: to put it briefly, is the fundamental controversy over our understanding of it, a controversy that began at the time of the council and has continued to the present day. This controversy must be overcome by taking seriously the call to listen to what the Spirit is saying to the churches today. The other reason lies precisely in this learning process, which has been mentioned several times as a constitutive part of the apostolic and Christian tradition, and its ability to situate itself within the history of human societies.

This learning process cannot ignore the fact that the church evolves very much within our democratic societies. At the opening of the synod on October 9, 2021, Pope Francis stated: "I want to say again that the Synod is not a parliament or an opinion poll."[10] And in its motivation for the appointment of non-bishops, the secretariat reminds us that they are not elected by a *demos* or *coetus* whose representation they would assume. These negative formulations, perfectly correct in their order, do not, however, suffice to positively clarify the difference between the synodal functioning of the church and that of our parliamentary democracies.

These clarifications are all the more important as there is a certain sharing of values between Christian communities and democratic society, with liberty, equality, and fraternity being a "secularized" heritage of Christianity that the Catholic Church has struggled to reintegrate and realize within itself: Vatican II finally emphasized the values of freedom of conscience and religious freedom, while the church of Pope Francis insists on equality and the path that leads from equality to fraternity, never acquired once and for all. It is also significant that the nascent Christian communities were not inspired by the religious or sacred vocabulary of their time but adopted terms that were already present in their societal environment, such as "assembly" (*ekklesia*), "elder" (*presbyteros*), "watchman" (*episkopos*), and so on.

[10] Text at https://www.vatican.va/content/francesco/en/speeches/2021/october/documents/20211009-apertura-camminosinodale.html.

Whereas our democracies are founded on the social contracts of their citizens, parliamentary representation, the transfer of legitimate violence to the state, and the separation of powers, *the church originates*, as its name indicates, in its "convocation" by the word of God and its ever-present intimate relationship with Christ Jesus and its obedient listening to the Spirit—the same Spirit that dwells in every human being and is also manifest in the responsible freedom of citizens, their respect for the equality of all, especially the least, and their desire to overcome human conflict through sister- and brotherhood. Within this "humanist" underpinning of our democracies and the baptismal equality of all Christians, the theological difference of the church is signified and manifested by a communal care and attention to the charismatic uniqueness of each and every person, and by the search for a unity founded on a "common feeling" in the faith, a "*conspiratio*" (as *Dei Verbum* puts it) stronger than the ever-recurring divisions, as well as by an ordained ministry that, in this synodal church, publicly symbolizes the difference between the self-constitution of human societies and the divine convocation of ecclesial communities. We can dream, as Pope Francis does at the end of his address of October 17, 2015, drawing on the quote from the prophet Isaiah, applied by the First Vatican Council to the church as a "standard lifted up among the nations (cf. *Is* 11:12)," that this difference will not lead her into defensive isolation but "help civil society to be built up in justice and fraternity, and thus bring about a more beautiful and humane world for coming generations."[11]

This learning by the church of what she is by situating herself rigorously "in today's world" and more particularly within our parliamentary democracies—the second reason for her synodalization—clearly shows that "adapt[ing] [the figure of the church] more successfully to our times," already recognized as necessary by the council (GS 44 §2), in no way minimizes her theological difference but, on the contrary, consists in placing it at the service of humanity. This is precisely what the Final Document calls "social prophecy" (FD 4, 5, 47, 48, and 153).

[11] Text at https://www.vatican.va/content/francesco/en/speeches/2015/october/documents/papa-francesco_20151017_50-anniversario-sinodo.html.

## To See or Not to See What We See

Having set out these two reasons, intra-ecclesial and contextual, for the current interest in synodality, I cannot fail to return once again to the resistances to change, regularly referred to by Pope Francis in the form of "risks" or "temptations." In the previous two chapters, I tried to differentiate between them; in this chapter, I situate them in the perspective of apostolic tradition, as clarified at the Second Vatican Council, using the theory of "paradigm shift" and "reframing," already mentioned several times in connection with the cultural mutations we are currently experiencing.[12]

1. To explain what's at stake, we need only turn to the Scriptures, and in particular to Jesus' parables. These "metaphorical" stories—like the metaphors mentioned in the first chapter—present situations of human existence in the world, not according to the logic of the "old world" but in a strangely altered way, with implausible features, transformed by the unpredictable irruption of a "new world," the reign of God: huge debts are forgiven (Luke 7:36-50); wages are paid equally, even to those who have not worked like the others (Matt 20:1-16); the feast is organized not for the son who works but for the one who has gone astray (Luke 15:11-32), and so on. The horizon of expectation of the world as it is remains present. But the story makes the listener perceive it differently, "reframing" it. Without being able to force the listener to listen or substitute itself for his or her freedom, it aims to convince him or her that this new perspective on the world, a perspective that is properly divine, is not only possible and plausible, but also essential for human existence. It is therefore situated within a "pastoral" relationship, as we might say with Vatican II, between Jesus and his listeners, a relationship projected into the text itself. It is the very form of the parable as metaphor, or the free "transfer" of the speaker and listener to another scene, that speaks to its *core*, namely the mystery of the very communication of a Word that "reframes" ordinary existence; an *event* which, when it actually takes place, is called the "reign of God."

[12] For further information, see Theobald, *La réception du concile Vatican II*, 683–93.

However, as it encounters the freedom of the receiver, this Word also comes up against the deafness and blindness of some of its recipients. The evangelists have recorded this with a quotation from the prophet Isaiah: "Then his disciples asked him what this parable [of the sower] meant. He said, 'To you it has been given to know the secrets of the kingdom of God; but to others I speak in parables, so that "looking they may not perceive, and listening they may not understand"'" (Luke 8:9-10; cf. Acts 28:26-27). The miracle-worker Jesus also spent a significant part of his ministry healing the deaf and blind. Indeed, seeing and hearing are primarily individual acts. But when the risen Jesus appears to his disciples on the road, it is a collective "seeing" of faith that is aroused—"With that their eyes were opened and they recognized him, but he vanished from their sight" (Luke 24:31)—and in Revelation, this same "seeing" is shared between the visionary and the seven churches of Asia Minor. Note that the synodal process—like all conciliar celebrations—is designed to make such collective "seeing" and "hearing" possible once again.

The Jewish and Christian Scriptures' acknowledgment of blindness and deafness has left important traces in certain contemporary conceptions of human rationality. The deafness and blindness of entire societies have always existed, and history provides us with a multitude of examples. Current "negations"—for example, the denial of the ecological crisis, or attempts to leave its management to future generations—are of this order. The representatives of the Frankfurt School, Max Horkheimer and Theodor Adorno, and Ivan Illich, were well aware of this: reason itself can become ideological, or even insane, when it is reduced to a way of managing strategic processes without questioning their meaning or nonsense; it can also be lucid, as in the perception of the ecological threat, without our being able to believe what is happening, and therefore to muster our energies to anticipate it and react. It's not an increase in reason that overcomes our collective deafness or blindness. Hearing what we hear without hearing it, and seeing what we see without seeing it, is more a matter of healing or pedagogical work, making conversions and reforms possible.

2. When mutations of all kinds occur, especially cultural ones, the process of theological "reframing" of the world that has become different must begin again, without starting from scratch, the foundation

being laid forever by the apostolic tradition, namely the original and constitutive relationship between Christ Jesus and the church, as inscribed in the New Testament that "reframes" the Old, while maintaining it to the end. If the term "reframing" originally refers to Jesus' way of introducing the eschatological dimension of God's reign into the world of his interlocutors, we can use it analogously to describe the relationship that, in a new cultural situation, the church has with an earlier way of "reframing" a given worldview: from a new point of view, it rereads and understands differently its earlier way of expressing the same paradox of faith.

There are two possible scenarios here. The "reframing" may take place within the same cultural ensemble and, through dissent, tend toward a finer and fairer balancing of the terms of the paradox. It can also take place, in completely different dimensions, when we change cultural cycles; here we find the distinctions made by Rahner and Lafont among the three cultural phases of Christianity. We reserve the term "paradigm shift" for the second case. It is more radical and more difficult to manage, because it affects not only the interpretation of faith but also and above all the rules of discernment and the instances that enable us to reach the end of the problems of interpretation that arise at these thresholds. This was the case at the Second Vatican Council, when a minority of the council fathers occasionally challenged or circumvented the "rules of the game" set down by John XXIII and amended by Paul VI. Historians of science see this type of contestation by a section of the scientific community as a sign that a "paradigm shift" (Thomas Kuhn) is taking place, the contestation of Gödel's theorem or the transition from classical physics to Einstein's theory of relativity being well-known examples. We can apply this type of analysis to the ecclesial community, obviously taking into account the differences between the two.

While any new "beginning," especially when changing cultural cycles, inevitably produces conflict and even division within the universal church, it is important to agree on the rules of the conciliar or synodal game—the "*met-hodos*," explained in Part III of the Final Document—and on their purpose. Here we find again the desire for "consensus" but also the ability to be content at times with "compromise," both of which are characteristics of the Catholic community. What is at stake in doctrinal compromises is precisely the supreme good of unity and consensus. This good obliges the various parties to "relativize" persistent divergences, whether or not they can be precisely designated—a task made all the more difficult when the various parties determine differently what appears to them to be the foundation of unity and what can be left to future debate. The formulations resulting from these compromises, whether substantive or dilatory, are frequently the product of a negative theology: failing to state what is true, they indicate what it is not, or even the "limits" within which it lies. The most famous example is the Christological definition of the Council of Chalcedon (451). When it tackles the mystery of the incarnation using the words available at the time, thus approaching the "*un*speakable" uniqueness of the "person" of Jesus by relating his entirely human "nature" to his entirely divine "nature," it recognizes that in him, they relate to each other "*without* confusion, *without* change, *without* division, *without* separation."

These habitual ways of proceeding, faithfully applied by the Second Vatican Council and similarly in the synod that has just ended, must nevertheless reckon with persistent "blindness" and "deafness" that limit the desire for an "inclusive" church, the history of the churches being indeed strewn with a multitude of dissidences. Blindness can be found on all sides. The caricatured use, for example, of otherwise essential statistics and political schemas or their interpretations to understand the divisions between older Catholics and younger Catholics is part of this type of hardening and risks reinforcing tensions. Remembering this is a modest way of acknowledging that we all live in the provisionality of history and participate in its ambiguities, and that *only* the holiness of Christ Jesus and that of the countless saints, anonymous or recognized, can finally affirm the continuity of the Catholic faith and the permanent presence of the same universal church, even in its inevitable "compromises" and damaging "blindnesses."

## Synodality within a Messianic Worldview

Synodality as a way of "reframing" the Catholic faith and, above all, of "reshaping" the universal church when times change, is therefore part of a worldview that lucidly recognizes that "truth" makes its way through what humans see without seeing and hear without hearing, sometimes stubbornly. It is the hallmark of biblical messianism to pay attention to this, and now, at the end of our journey, I'd like to return to this vision, a few basic outlines of which I sketched out in the first chapter.

1. Biblical messianism situates the "today" and the "here" between the beginning of the world and its end and draws from the origin of creation—in God—the energy to anticipate justice, peace, and reconciliation among people and within creation. Because it is convinced of God's radical and unconditional goodness, which guides all creation toward a Sabbath rest—its own and that of humanity—it is also, by contrast, very sensitive to the presence of evil lurking at the door of our common home: murderous violence, blindness and deafness, the ever-present hardening of our hearts, but also the fall of human societies and the earth that carries them into chaos. Consider, for example, the episode of the flood at the beginning of the first book of the Bible (Gen 6–8). In the book of Exodus, we find other figures of de-creation, such as the famous "plagues of Egypt": here, the environment and human bodies, closely linked to society, are affected and shaken (Exod 7:8–10:29). The last book of the Bible, Revelation, takes up these phenomena, universalizing them, adding others, and mixing them with a whole dreamlike imagination (Rev 8:6–9:21). Chapters 16 to 18 culminate in the political and economic downfall of the symbolic city of Babylon, dominated by the figures of the "dragon" and the "two beasts," idolatrous (or totalitarian) power and its false prophets (or propagandists spreading *fake news*).

Christian tradition is part of this biblical messianism, a variant of which emerged with the figure of the Jewish Jesus of Nazareth *and* the church at the beginning of our era. Grafting itself onto the articulation of the figure of the "messiah" *and* the coming of the "messianic times," specifying it on the basis of the Nazarene's itinerary and his crucifixion as a criminal, his disciples at Antioch (Acts 11:26) accepted the name of "Christians" (*christianoi*), which translates as "messianic" or "followers of the messiah." These established a new type of human relationship based on social mixing—"There is neither Jew nor Greek, there is neither slave nor free person, there is not male and female" (Gal 3:28); baptism in the death and resurrection of the Messiah Jesus and the "Lord's Supper" form the basis of a new messianic rituality, the aim of which is to communicate to the faithful the very holiness of the Messiah, who has given it a very specific form—radically hospitable, always singular and eminently concrete, and, as such, universalizable.

2. One of the most remarkable features of the Second Vatican Council was its updating of this messianic vision. In the second chapter, I recalled the decision taken by the council during its second period (1963) to introduce a new chapter on the people of God (chap. 2). Yet it is at the beginning of this chapter (see LG 9) that the church is twice referred to as the "messianic people," a designation that characterizes this people in its link to Christ—the Messiah—in its eschatological orientation toward the reign of God and in its appearance as a "little flock" (Luke 12:32). If we read the Constitution on the Church from this chapter, as Pope Francis does in his apostolic exhortation *Evangelii Gaudium*,[13] this people is part of a universalist vision of history that has its origins in God's "Trinitarian economy," and is on a pilgrimage toward its destiny in God; it occupies a decentralized position "between" Christ Jesus and the peoples of the earth (LG 1), having heard—in the wake of Christ Jesus and in intimate relationship with him—the call to holiness (which is the messianic mystery of the world); this has been discussed. Within this universal vision of humanity's spiritual history, *Ad Gentes* clarifies the Spirit-driven or communicational aspect of Christian messianism.

Today, we have to acknowledge that this global vision has largely been lost in the shifting sands of the council's reception, to the benefit of countless controversies over questions of detail and structure. The texts of the council themselves, and above all the "compromises" they represent, are largely responsible for this, even if they remain the *best possible* expression *at the time* of the desire for unity of all or almost all. In the second chapter, I showed that the decision to under-

[13] See, for example, the summary of the first three chapters of the Constitution on the Church offered in the apostolic exhortation *Evangelii Gaudium* 111: "Evangelization is the task of the Church. The Church, as the agent of evangelization, is more than an organic and hierarchical institution [chap. III]; she is first and foremost a people advancing on its pilgrim way towards God [chap. II]. She is certainly a mystery rooted in the Trinity [chap. I], yet she exists concretely in history as a people of pilgrims and evangelizers [chap. II], transcending any institutional expression, however necessary [chap. III]. I would like to dwell briefly on this way of understanding the Church, whose ultimate foundation is in the free and gracious initiative of God" (with the addition of the relevant chapters of *Lumen Gentium*).

stand the church as a messianic people was not implemented consistently and to the end. Thus, in the developments of *Lumen Gentium* on the people of God, the principle of baptismal equality on which the synodality of the church is based, is only *implied*, the distinction between the "sacred power" of clerics and the "secular status" of the laity remaining decisive, not to mention a persistent confusion between the "sacred" and the "holy," the latter being indeed recognized as the messianic vocation of all Christians. A more fundamental limitation of the council's messianic vision stems from the difficulty of fully recognizing the otherness of the other, and of all others; this is notable—and to this day debated—in the field of the relationship of the people of God to other believers, in particular to the Jewish people, but also to non-Christian religions and atheisms. More embarrassing, in the same vein, is the lack of in-depth reflection on human conflict and, above all, the tacit presupposition of transparency in our discourse, a presupposition insensitive to the blindness and deafness and hardening of our hearts, when their humble recognition is so decisive in biblical and Christian messianism. While the post-conciliar magisterium has gone back on this or that point, it is above all Pope Francis who balanced the essential parameters of Christian messianism. In his encyclical *Laudato Si'*, he not only corrected the anthropocentrism of *Gaudium et Spes*, but he also shifted the emphasis from the freedom of faith, emphasized by Vatican II and still essential within a messianic vision of history, to the *path* that, from the equality of all, especially the last, leads through a certain type of crossing of human conflict to brother- and sisterhood. In his encyclical *Fratelli Tutti*, he shows that this path concerns not only the baptized but all human beings, with particular emphasis on the role of politics.

It is remarkable that, from the beginning of the synodal process to the Final Document, this prophetic and messianic vision of the biblical and Christian tradition has remained decisive; I have shown this on several occasions, especially in the chapter on the second session. This perspective not only determines the framework of the Final Document, using the vocabulary of prophecy (see FD 4, 5, and 153) in an Isaian and Johannine perspective. It also marks the body of the text in its five parts, each time it deals with human relationships and their wounds, probed in their contextual depth, at once current, future, and eschatological (see FD 19, 20, 39–42, 56, 106, 123, 151).

3. Finally, there is an intrinsic link to be highlighted—a link actually experienced by the council without being thought of as such by it—between its messianic vision of the world and its way of proceeding. Indeed, his vision is not imposed from outside, but instead it is the fruit of the work of Christ's Spirit, in history and in every human being, and at the same time, the fruit of the church's way of relating to other believers. This always-concrete way of relating to other believers must also concur with that of conceiving the internal relations between the faithful and particular churches, and therefore with the "internal" figure of the church, and vice versa.

It's only in the last two periods (1964 and 1965) that the council is becoming its "path" or its "way of proceeding." As I showed in the previous chapter, the synod succeeded in bringing these methodological elements out of their dispersion in the textual corpus of Vatican II[14] and unifying them in its *modus synodalis* in three stages: ecclesial discernment for mission, which leads to a new articulation of decision-making processes and ends in a responsible rereading of what has been discerned and decided, knowing how to report to others. The intrinsic relationship between this way of proceeding, which must be rigorously respected, and its specifically theological or spiritual aim, listening both individually and as a church to God who speaks here and now and to what his Spirit is saying to the church, cannot be emphasized enough. It is here, when this relationship between the synodal *met-hodos* and its pneumatological implications becomes conscious, that the hypothesis formulated at the beginning of this chapter is verified, namely, that the Synod on Synodality can ultimately be understood as a synod on the Holy Spirit, *who is heard and who speaks through the prophetic ministry of the churches and of the church as a whole within God's creation, oriented toward its messianic fulfillment*.

In his final address to the assembly on October 26, 2024, the pope himself suggested this, referring to St. Basil's *Treatise on the Holy Spirit* (474) to highlight the concept of harmony, identifying it with the Holy Spirit: "Saint Basil has a beautiful theology on this: if you can, read his treatise on the Holy Spirit" (see also FD 42). Now, this treatise played a significant role in the formulation of the third article of the

[14] See above, pp. 171–73.

Creed, which was added by the Council of Constantinople (381) to the Nicene Creed. The addition, which is both pneumatological and ecclesial, not only creates a link between the church's trinitarian confession and the liturgy—"who with the Father and the Son is adored and glorified"—but also with the prophetic economy of all biblical and human history—"who has spoken through the prophets." The Synod on Synodality refocuses the church ("one, holy, catholic, and apostolic"), which, in the Creed, follows immediately from this prophetic economy through its own *prophetic ministry*, always threatened by a lack of credibility, always in need of reform by placing itself under the authority of the Holy Spirit in a synodal manner.

❖ ❖ ❖

In these last chapters, I've set out not only to present the first two phases of the current synodal process (chaps. 3, 5 and 6) but also to reflect on some historical presuppositions and theological implications.

The main challenge of this last chapter was to situate synodality, a constitutive element of the church according to Pope Francis, within the apostolic tradition, a tradition that allows itself to be worked from within by what is happening in human societies and on earth, including by the opposition it encounters or even the human blindness and deafness it has to face, even within its own bosom. I've made a point of clarifying this conception of Christian tradition because it seems to me that the debates accompanying the current reception phase of the synodal process run the risk of reproducing in other terms those that divided the post-conciliar church over the hermeneutics of continuity and discontinuity—debates fanned by traditionalist fundamentalism and the liturgical conflicts already mentioned.

We could get used to this situation, consider these divisions as unbridgeable, and be content with a simple juxtaposition of different "Catholicisms" or "Christianities," secretly despairing of any possible thinking or feeling in common. Yet the synod and the Final Document offer us an unexpected opportunity (a *kairos*) to move away from a sterile repetition of these oppositions. This was discussed in the previous chapters and more specifically in chapter 4, when I spoke of the synod as a pathway to reconciliation and creativity, and its way of proceeding, centered on three practices: prayer to the Holy Spirit, conversation in the Spirit with indispensable moments of debate, and the Eucharist. As we have seen, the spiritual experience of conversion and the reform of the ecclesial institution are inseparable. But individual and institutional "reform," as we have understood in this chapter, are divided by their relationship to apostolic tradition: one is understood as a reaction to dysfunctions, the other affecting its very form. We can only hope that, in the reception phase that has just begun, one fruit of the synod will be to become aware of this difference—that the churches will not avoid it out of fear of the spiritual battle it will give rise to, but instead they will courageously trust their own experience, which is not immune to pleasant surprises, to be attributed to the work of the Holy Spirit.

In the last chapter, I have therefore anticipated to some extent the issues at stake in the current reception phase, which will gradually reveal themselves. The fact remains, however, that the very fact of this synod having been convened, and the preliminary inquiry having been carried out in synodal form at community, diocesan, national, and continental levels, is a unique phenomenon in the history of humanity, and as such it already activates the messianic vision of the world referred to at the end of this chapter: a vision of "messianic times" centered on the "local," whatever that may be on earth (the "Galilee"), and therefore the universal (becoming the "Galilee" of the nations). It is an open vision, based on the specific, messianic vision of missionary disciples and their church, while recognizing the presence of the Holy Spirit in "quiconque" ("whomever"), offering itself to the discernment of each and every one; a vision founded on the equality of all human beings and oriented toward justice and reconciliation, brother- and sisterhood within a social mix, constantly to be sought, activated, and defended in a tireless search for new ways of getting along, with synodality at its heart; a vision rooted in the unfathomable depths of God, whose mysterious intimacy has been made accessible to humanity through Jesus' hospitable way of committing his life to "quiconque," and through the Holy Spirit, who never ceases to work so that people can adjust this style of Jesus to the unforeseen circumstances of the moment and of history.

# Conclusion

## And Now?

With the final greeting of Pope Francis at the last general congregation on Saturday, October 26, 2024, and the closing Eucharist at St. Peter's the following day, the Synod on Synodality has entered its third phase. Many are wondering what will happen now. How will the Final Document be received, and above all, how will the synodal practice that the assembly has implemented and delivered to the whole church be received?

Let's start with a warning: the spiritual battle fought during the first two phases is far from over; the temptations are many. Here and there, we hear that everything set out in the Final Document has already been achieved in the West, with the synod being important for other countries and other continents; it is a subtle way of refusing to learn new things, as befits disciples and missionaries of Jesus Christ.

Others are content to adopt a wait-and-see attitude, expecting everything from their bishop or bishops, who are tempted to look out for signals from Rome. Still others are making their involvement in the third phase conditional on the outcome of the ten study groups on what are, indeed, very urgent issues, finding it hard to believe in the reformability of Catholicism. There is also concern that, in the diversity of national paths, the great novelty of the synod, which is the beginning of a continentalization, will simply be forgotten. The church of Europe, for example, remains very divided, and the churches that make it up live with a number of caricatural images to overcome in a true continental synodality yet to be invented.

The challenge of the reception phase is therefore to involve as many people as possible—small communities and parishes, permanent pastoral workers, priests, and deacons. This is no easy task, as the first two phases have shown. It is, therefore, imperative to develop a *pedagogy of reception*. At least two perfectly accessible entry points can quickly be opened. The first is the Final Document's perspective on Christian initiation (FD 21–27), which could benefit from the joyful vitality of our catechumenates in France, both in learning to listen to the word of God with others and in progressive access to the sacraments of initiation. The second is the establishment of conversation in the Spirit and the three-stage methodological process that such conversation makes possible: discernment, the ability to prepare decisions, and rereading.

Perhaps this somewhat systematic learning process is already making it possible to review the functioning of a number of our participatory bodies, especially at the most basic ecclesial level (communities, relays, parishes, etc.), and to remedy dysfunctions of all kinds that use up a lot of our energy.

But the purpose of this conclusion cannot be to develop an educational program for the reception. A more serious temptation still lies ahead of us: to begin thinking about a next synod, thus relativizing this one, forgetting its particularity in the whole series of Roman synods and finally glossing over the "change of era" constantly recalled by Pope Francis.

It is precisely this temptation that the title of this book aimed to overcome and still aims to overcome. But one could forget the question mark.

Yet the question the title poses was inspired not only by Cardinal Martini's address to the 1999 European synod, mentioned at the beginning of this book, but also and above all by an observation made in the second chapter. The synodal process inaugurated by Pope Francis is indeed ecclesiologically far-reaching. The synod's title is *For a Synodal Church*. This project is bound to reflect on the structure of the Latin Church, as laid down in the councils of Vatican I, which dealt with the Petrine ministry, and Vatican II, which defined episcopal collegiality.

If we compare both the first session's Synthesis Report and the second session's Final Document with the sixteen documents of the council, we discover some significant analogies. This is clearer in the Synthesis Report.[1] Its first part "reframes" the ecclesiological texts

[1] See above, pp. 129–33.

of Vatican II, in particular *Lumen Gentium*; the second part, which opens on the theme introduced by the Decree on the Missionary Activity of the Church—"Church Is Mission"—deals with all those engaged in mission, as understood by *Lumen Gentium* and the conciliar decrees on bishops, priests, lay people, and religious; the third part, particularly chapters 15, 16, and 17, are concerned with the themes of the Pastoral Constitution on the Church in the Modern World. Certain themes, such as the church's relationship with Scripture and revelation, its relations with the Jewish people, which so preoccupied the council, and religious freedom, remain in the background, while others, such as the traditions of the Eastern churches and ecumenism, take center stage, and still others, such as the new anthropological questions, raise many questions.

The relationship of the Final Document to the sixteen documents of Vatican II is less apparent, because in the meantime a new structure, more focused on the synodal constitution of the church and its prophetic ministry, has been developed.[2] But the fundamental axes of the conciliar corpus, with its three poles, remain decisive.[3]

The fact remains that, since Vatican II, it will be hard to find another synodal assembly of the whole church that has been entrusted with such a broad and all-encompassing thematic field as the current Synod on Synodality. The "reframing" that the synod has carried out is, therefore, at the same level as the two councils of the nineteenth and twentieth centuries, *without being conciliar*! We must acknowledge this "limit," while at the same time recognizing the tension between the ambitious content of the deliberation and its canonical form.

I'm therefore making the assumption that the synod is committing what it's possible to commit today, given the constraints we face, and it's in doing so that it represents a great promise for the future!

There are many reasons that a new council of the kind celebrated by the Catholic Church in modern times would be impractical. Two stand out clearly. The first is the Synod of Bishops itself, instituted by Paul VI and recognized by the Second Vatican Council. Pope Francis chose to embrace it, while expanding or "reframing" its canonical structure—some would say "forcing" it. The other, even more important reason is ecumenical. Historians have not only highlighted

[2] See chapter 2 above.

[3] See above, pp. 36–37.

the diversity and complexity of Christianity's conciliar and synodal tradition, but they have also relativized the Roman list of councils considered ecumenical, drawn up by Cardinal Bellarmine after the Council of Trent. From an ecumenical perspective, Vatican I and Vatican II are *general councils* of the Roman Church, not *ecumenical councils* of the undivided church. To celebrate a new ecumenical council today would mean either being content with the status of a general council of the Roman Church or getting the three great traditions—Orthodoxy, Catholicism, and the churches of the Reformation—to agree on a way of committing themselves together to their unity and the meaning they give to it.

In the absence of being able or willing to adopt either solution, the synod must be understood—as the Final Document expressly states—as an act of Catholic reception of the Second Vatican Council, which limits its normative scope without taking away from it. Accepting this limitation does not mean diminishing its importance but rather probing and recognizing its promise for the future. If we stop restricting ourselves to the horizon of one lifetime or two or three generations, as our faith in the resurrection requires us to do, then we must learn to discern *the possibilities that present themselves today*, to realize them courageously *without knowing what their implementation will become tomorrow*, especially at a time when the future has become radically uncertain, and to receive here and now an *inner energy* and *hope* that are nourished by the vision of the "messianic times" that have come since Jesus, the Holy One of God. It is from this perspective that I have presented and analyzed, in this book, the Synod on Synodality of 2021–2024 and reflected on some of its implications.

The individual and collective experience of reception it inaugurates, an experience of inner renewal and institutional reform, is "spiritual" in the pneumatological sense of the term. It certainly confronts us with the vertigo that the range of problems to be solved provokes, but it also takes us out of the dangerous normality in which European Catholicism has settled in recent decades. It both keeps us "worried" about the future, which is critical at both societal and ecclesial levels, and calls for unprecedented ecumenical courage. But it also brings us rest and peace when, having adopted a synodal way of proceeding, we let ourselves be carried along by the assurance that the Holy Spirit never ceases to work in favor of the church and humanity on our planet and to help us discern the next steps to take.

# Index